AROUND ATLANTA WITH CHILDREN

A GUIDE FOR FAMILY ACTIVITIES
Second Edition

DENISE BLACK • JANET SCHWARTZ

Illustrations by Jill Dubin

Published By Sigma Publications Inc.
1431 Woodmont Lane, Suite 101
Atlanta, Georgia 30318
(404) 350-9355

Illustrations by JILL DUBIN

Typography by STAN HIXON

ISBN 0-9628349-0-4

To David and Nathan, my eager explorers, and to Bruce for always supporting me in whatever I do. - D.B.

To Allison, Daniel and Ira, "the best family in the whole-wide world." - J.H.S.

TABLE OF CONTENTS

F amily outings create lots of happy memories. With this special guide, planning those family outings is easy. Decatur Federal, the Family Bank, is pleased to sponsor this book and wishes you and your family many exciting days of discovery.

DECATUR FEDERAL®

The Family Bank

FDIC INSURED

1. Introduction

INTRODUCTION
TO
SECOND EDITION

We are thankful for how well received our first edition of *Around Atlanta With Children* was, selling over 8,000 copies in less than a year! Many of you have come to us with grateful comments communicated in relieved voices and gestures. Some well-organized parents and teachers claim to have planned out the upcoming year's activities on a household calendar with every weekend and each summer month packed with great places to go. Even we haven't done that... yet. Some of you have made helpful suggestions about places we did not know existed, some corrected our inadvertent errors, and yet others have told us what your child's interests are asking if, just maybe, there might be more to do in Atlanta.

Well... encouraged by your enthusiasm, buoyed by the growing demographic heterogeneity of our city, and prodded by our own personalities to be as comprehensive and accurate as possible, we once again set out to explore Atlanta. And yes, we have included over a hundred and fifty new places to go and things to do! Some of our favorite discoveries are:

- the stunning Vines Botanical Gardens in Gwinnett County
- Noah's Ark–a rehabilitation/petting farm for wild and exotic animals
- ice carving demonstrations at Goree's Ice House
- more airplane museums
- an antique fire station museum in Roswell
- cave explorations
- more fun historical hikes and nature trails
- 24-hour-a-day storytelling on the telephone
  ... and by popular demand, a new resource list...
- School and Scout Group Activities

We have painstakingly updated the attractions, exhibits and activities discussed in the First Edition of *Around Atlanta With Children* to keep you abreast of what's new and different and what no longer exists, not to mention the ever-changing phone numbers and admission prices.

Special note: Georgia is getting a new area code–"706"–in May of 1992 which will apply to customers outside the Atlanta metropolitan toll-free calling area. There will be a grace period between May 3 and August 2. The Atlanta metropolitan local calling code remains "404."

INTRODUCTION
TO
FIRST EDITION

If you're like us, you're always looking for new ideas for weekend family outings and creative ways to keep your children busy during the summer months. We discovered there was no guidebook for families on what to see and do in Atlanta, so we knew we would have to do the leg work ourselves. With our eager children by our sides, we began seriously investigating things for tots to teens to do in metropolitan Atlanta. Of course we knew about such fun attractions as Zoo Atlanta and SciTrek, but we discovered so much more–from climbing on a real caboose, to scampering up a hiking trail–from watching children's theater, to participating in a dramatic re-creation of Colonial days. We have visited and explored hundreds of great activities. Parents, grandparents, teachers and tourists will find this guidebook indispensable.

We describe each activitiy and provide information to keep you up-to-date with each listing, to give you an idea of the cost involved if any, and directions on how to get to the attractions and day trips. Phone numbers change, locations of special events may vary and admission costs always go up! So whenever it is possible, we suggest you phone ahead for current information.

Between us, we have traveled in every state of the United States, through Canada, Western and Eastern Europe, Africa and the Far East, and have lived with our families in California, New York, Illinois, Atlanta and Kenya. We are convinced Atlanta is the best place to raise a family!

2. Places to Go

T he listings in this chapter are arranged alphabetically to make it easier for you to locate all of the major attractions, museums, recreational facilities and historical sites in the metropolitan Atlanta area. If you cannot find an attraction that you expected to find, be sure to look in the next chapter, "Tidbits: More Good Things to Do," which contains information about the smaller or more unusual places to visit in this city.

We have placed symbols at the top of each listing to designate the general categories that the attraction fits into. These symbols will help you recognize the essence of each "Place to Go" at a glance.

 NATURE

 SCIENCE

 UNIQUE ATTRACTIONS

 HISTORY AND GOVERNMENT

 PERFORMING ARTS

 FINE ARTS

AMERICAN ADVENTURES

250 North Cobb Parkway • (Next to White Water Park)
Marietta, Georgia 30062 • 424-9283

American Adventures is Atlanta's newest family amusement park. The unique 8.5 million dollar complex is bright, colorful, cheerful, clean and very exciting. Rain or shine, there is plenty to keep a family happily occupied for hours.

The outside portion of the Park has lots of amusement rides. Racing enthusiasts can drive the Formula K racing cars. (If children are not quite tall enough to go it alone, then parents can chauffeur the kids around the track!) Children over 6 can drive the bumper cars solo, and those younger get to co-pilot along with parents. Our 3 and 6 year olds smiled and laughed throughout both of these great rides even though they were only passengers. For the younger crowd, there is Rio Grande Railroad train ride, Timberline Truckers, a convoy truck ride with steering wheels and horns that really beep, the Circus Spin animal ride, and the Barn-stormers airplane ride where children can shoot a noisy gun and steer the plane up and down as it goes around. For the braver crowd, you can try the Balloon Ride which goes higher and faster than the other rides; the Ridgeline Roller Coaster which is a real roller coaster–fast and jerky; American Revolution, spinning tea cups; and, Galleon, a pirate ship that swings to and fro. Finally, there is the Hidden Harbor miniature golf course complete with fun and scary sound effects.

An old-fashioned Carousel Ride and Main Street Miniature Golf in a turn-of-the-century setting top the list of indoor attractions. The Penny Arcade is geared mainly toward school-age children but with a few games for preschoolers (basketball, skee ball and Whack the Mole). Best of all for young children is Professor Plinker's Laboratory. Allow yourselves plenty of time to enjoy this play area because your children will not want to leave. Kids and parents take off their shoes and jump into Playport, a large area about two or three feet deep filled with plastic balls, with connecting slides and climbing rope areas. There is also a floor with lots of Roller Racers, a Widget Wall with stick-on shapes for constructing 3-dimensional art, a Shadow room and a building area.

- Parents are encouraged to participate with their children on all of the rides and to play with their children in the indoor Professor Plinker's Laboratory. Parents may ride free when accompanied by a child.

- Seasonal special events for Halloween, Christmas and Easter are a real hit.

- There is a large, reasonably priced restaurant in the Park.

- Handicapped access is available.

- The women's restroom has a changing table. Water fountains are available.

Hours: The Park is open year-round from 11:00am to late evening.

Admission: There is no General Admission. Tickets are puchased separately for individual activities (costs range from 50¢ to $4.00), or you may buy a combination ticket with White Water for a cost of $16.99 for adults and $11.99 for children (under 4 feet tall) which permits unlimited all day usage. Parking is $2.00 per vehicle.

Directions: Take I-75 to Exit #113, and follow the signs to North Cobb Parkway and the Park; about 8 miles north of Downtown Atlanta.

ATLANTA BOTANICAL GARDEN

1345 Piedmont Road (between 14th Street and Monroe Drive)
P.O. Box 77246 • Atlanta, Georgia 30357
24-hour recorded message: 876-5858
Offices: 876-5859 • Plant Hotline: 875-GROW

The Atlanta Botanical Garden is a great place to go for a hike in the woods, stroll through beautiful gardens, smell spring flowers, experience a tropical environment or commune with some rare and exotic plants.

The map you get upon entering the Garden is helpful in planning your tour route and locating such essential services as drinking fountains and restrooms. Once you orient yourself, you will realize that your family can make a complete overview of the garden area before anyone gets tired. On subsequent visits you may want to focus in on just a few areas, spending more time at each. When your family is in a hiking mood, visit Storza Woods for 15-acres of walking trails through one of five remaining hardwood forests in Atlanta. And for an easier walk visit the Upper Woodlands paved trail - it's great for strollers.

The Dorothy Chapman Fuqua Conservatory deserves a special mention. The Conservatory is a $5.5 million haven for thousands of tropical, desert, Mediterranean and endangered plants from around the world. You will see plants with leaves as big as small children, stunning desert flowers, Cavendish banana trees, a cocoa tree, and a vining orchid (*Vanilla planifolia*) from which we get vanilla bean. On one of our visits we saw the amazing Ant Plants, an ecosystem wherein plant and ants feed off of and nourish each other.

You and your children might also be interested in the twice-yearly Plant Sale, the Super Sunday live musical performances outdoors in the Garden, Spring Moon Strolls, and the many Flower Shows and other special programs offered throughout the year.

Several exciting new additions to the Garden are planned or recently opened on the south side of the Fuqua Conservatory. The **Vegetable Garden** includes numerous Southern crops (cotton, okra and tobacco, among others) and an Urban Family Garden will be a demonstration plot capable of feeding a family of four. The **Children's Vegetable Patch** is part of the Vegetable Garden and is the location for summer gardening classes for children. The **Orchard** has a "Briar Patch" for blueberries, blackberries, raspberries, kiwi fruit, grapes and several dwarf fruit trees, including cherry, peach and plum. Future plans for the Garden also include a living **Maze** of carefully designed and trimmed hedges. Visit the Garden. You won't be disappointed!

- Throughout the year, the Garden offers Saturday morning classes for children age 7-10 years covering many diverse topics relating to nature and science, and an "Environmental Summer Day Camp" program for children age 5-11 years.

15

- Picnicking is not permitted, but Rafeedie's Caterers at Ansley II serves lunch Tuesday-Saturday year-round and Sunday breakfast and lunch during daylight savings hours in the Garden on Lanier Terrace behind Day Hall. Or, combine a picnic in nearby Piedmont Park with your visit to the Garden.

- There is a pleasant gift shop with cards, knick-knacks, garden supplies and lots of books for the serious and casual gardener and for children. There is also a room with healthy, interesting plants, many of which were grown in the Garden's Day Support Green houses.

- Strollers are not permitted in the Conservatory.

- Handicapped access is available for most of the Garden. Call for more information.

- Restrooms and water fountains are available.

Hours: *Garden:* Open Tuesdays through Saturdays from 9:00am-6:00pm and on Sundays from 12:00noon-6:00pm. Longer hours during daylight savings time. Closed on Mondays and on major holidays.

Conservatory: Open Tuesdays through Saturdays from 10:00am- 5:00pm and on Sundays from 12:00noon-6:00pm. Longer hours during daylight savings time. Closed on Mondays and on major holidays.

Admission: Cost is $5.00 for adults; $2.50 for seniors, students and children ages 6-12; children under 6 years are FREE. Free on Thursdays and summer Sunday afternoons. Yearly Family Membership is $50.00 and includes many privileges, including free admission.

Directions: Enter the Garden on Piedmont Road at The

Prado, one block south of Monroe Drive and one block north of 14th Street. By bus, take the #36 North Decatur bus from MARTA's Art Center Station directly to the Garden. On Sunday, take the #31 Lindbergh bus from MARTA's Five Points or Lindbergh Station directly to the Garden.

ATLANTA CELEBRITY WALK

1 CNN Center - South Tower, Suite 1250
Atlanta, Georgia 30303 • 522-7133

The Celebrity Walk, Atlanta's version of the Hollywood Walk of Fame, contains the names of ten famous Georgians in a marble walkway beginning in front of the Chamber of Commerce Building on International Boulevard at Marietta Street. As more inductees are added, the walkway will extend east along International Boulevard to Peachtree Street and Piedmont Avenue, connecting CNN and the Georgia World Congress Center with the Georgia Dome and Peachtree Center. The first ten inductees were author of *Gone With the Wind*, Margaret Mitchell; baseball great, Hank Aaron; former President, Jimmy Carter; civil rights leader, Dr. Martin Luther King, Jr.; musician and singer, Ray Charles; developer and architect, John Portman; former mayor, Andrew Young; anesthesia developer, Crawford W. Long; Girl Scouts founder, Juliette Gordon Lowe; and, Coca-Cola founder and philanthropist, Robert Woodruff. Each marble slab bears a bronze nameplate and a bronze phoenix, the symbol of Atlanta, lying on a marble field sandblasted with the shape of the State of Georgia. About 50 more Georgians are up for nomination and the public is encouraged to send in their nominations to the above address.

ATLANTA HERITAGE ROW

Between Peachtree Street and Central Avenue at Alabama Street
Atlanta, Georgia 30303 • 523-2311

On the Upper Alabama Street level of Underground Atlanta lies Atlanta Heritage Row, a small but unique museum showcasing important events and people in Atlanta's history. Dr. Martin Luther King, Jr., Hartsfield Airport and the Civil War are all recognized in interactive exhibit halls where displays have been designed so that visitors do not merely walk passively by exhibits, but instead, find themselves right in the middle of a display, able to touch, hear or experience the presentation! We recommend a trip to this Museum for your older children.

• Special events are occasionally sponsored by the Museum such as Sunday Craft Samplers which feature demonstrations of traditional crafts.

Hours: Open Tuesdays-Saturdays from 10:00am-6:00pm; Sundays from 1:00am-6:00pm. Closed Mondays.

Admission: Cost is $3.00 for adults; $2.50 for seniors; $2.00 for students and children age 4-12 years; children under 4 are FREE.

Directions: Atlanta Heritage Row is located in Underground Atlanta at the Upper Level between Peachtree Street and Central Avenue at Alabama Street. It is two blocks west of the Georgia State Capitol Building. Exit at the MARTA Five Points Station.

ATLANTA HISTORY CENTER

Museum of Atlanta History
McElreath Hall • Tullie Smith House
Swan House • Gardens • Swan Coach House Restaurant
3101 Andrews Drive, N.W.
Atlanta, Georgia 30305 • 261-1837

The Atlanta Historical Society's Buckhead complex which presently includes McElreath Hall, Tullie Smith House, Swan House, the extensive gardens and the Swan Coach House Restaurant is getting ready for a new addition, the Museum of Atlanta History. And, in keeping with its growth, the complex has been renamed the **Atlanta History Center.** One admission ticket includes all exhibits, museums, house tours and gardens.

MUSEUM OF ATLANTA HISTORY. Scheduled to open in 1993, the newest addition to the Atlanta History Center will be a modern 83,000 square foot museum honoring Atlanta's heritage. The centerpiece of the Museum will be a permanent multi-media exhibit depicting the story of Atlanta. Also to be housed in the Museum are some 6,000 items from the Beverly M. DuBose, Jr. Civil War Collection, considered one of the finest in the country, containing items from both sides of the war; the Dickey Collection of 800 Civil War armaments; 32,000 decorative arts items, including the Shutze Collection of furniture, silver, ceramics and paintings presently housed in the Swan House; more than 2,500 costumes and accessories dating from the antebellum period to the present; and, 100 quilts and 500 textile items, including an extensive collection of lace and shawls from the 1860s. The new facility will also include two classrooms, an orientation theater and discovery rooms for hands on activities. More information about the Museum and its exhibits should be available as it nears completion.

MCELREATH HALL. McElreath Hall houses two permanent exhibits:

"Atlanta and the War 1861-1865," illustrating the events that led to Sherman's attack on Atlanta; and, "Atlanta Resurgens," the story of Atlanta and Atlantans presented through newspapers and other publications, photographs, artifacts and relics, art from all media, videotapes, antiques and educational programs. The third exhibit hall displays changing exhibits which have included presentations on *Gone With the Wind*, Georgia furniture, costumes, architecture, landscaping and gardening tradition, and Atlanta women. McElreath Hall also contains a library and archives of local and state history, which includes one of the city's largest photograph collections; the Cherokee Garden Library, which is a gardening and horticultural research collection of current and rare material; and, an auditorium and meeting rooms where lectures and special events are held year-round. These exhibits are quite appropriate for older children.

THE TULLIE SMITH FARM. The Tullie Smith Farm is an 1840s pioneer house typical of a pre-Civil War working-farm. Its outbuildings include a kitchen, a barn, wellhouse, storage house, smokehouse, corn crib, log cabin and blacksmith shop. Tours are given on the half-hour and sometimes include demonstrations of folk skills, such as basketry, open-hearth cooking, whittling and smithing. The small cabin and out-buildings provide the setting for the annual fall Folklife Festival, the spring Storytelling Festival, and Sheep to Shawl Day, the best times by far for you to bring your younger children to see this attraction. (See our chapter on "Festivals and Special Events" for more information.)

THE SWAN HOUSE. The Swan House is a Palladian-style mansion built in 1928 by an Atlanta family whose fortunes were made in railroads, cotton, banking and real estate. Tours of this oppulent home are given on the half-hour and include a look at the Philip Trammell Shutze decorative arts collection. (We're talking fragile pieces, so we suggest you don't bring younger children here!) Behind the Swan House is a Victorian playhouse filled with toys authentic to the era which may be of interest to your child.

GARDENS. There are over 32 acres of beautifully landscaped gardens and woodlands, including The Mary Howard Gilbert Quarry Garden, Frank A. Smith Rhododendron Garden, Swan and Tullie Smith gardens and the one-half mile "Swan Woods Trail" which is labeled for a self-guided study. The grounds and trails are pretty and educational, and are recommended for children, especially if they need a nice break after touring the rest of the Center.

SWAN COACH HOUSE RESTAURANT. The Restaurant is located in the former garage and servant's quarters for the Swan House. Lunch is served Mondays through Saturdays from 11:30am-2:30pm. A gift shop and art gallery open Mondays-Saturdays from 10:00am-4:00pm are also housed here.

- There are occasional one-day classes and workshops offered at the Center. Additionally, the Center hosts festivals and special events such as "An Old Fashioned Christmas," and "the Civil War Revisted: Atlanta Encampment," a living history extravaganza.

- There is a small gift shop presently housed in McElreath Hall with traditional crafts, educational toys, books, jewelry, Civil War items and *Gone With the Wind* memorabilia.

- Handicapped access to certain attractions is available, but call ahead for parking directions.

- Restrooms and water fountains are available.

Hours: Open Mondays through Saturdays from 9:00am-5:30pm and on Sundays from 12:00noon-5:30pm. Closed on Thanksgiving, Christmas Eve, Christmas Day and New Year's Day.

Admission: Cost is $6.00 for adults; $4.50 for students and seniors; $3.00 for children over 6-17; and, children under 6 are FREE. The Center is free on Thursdays after 1:00pm. Group rates are available. Yearly Family Membership is $50.00 and includes free admission.

Directions: Take the West Paces Ferry exit on I-75 to Northside Drive and go east on West Paces Ferry Road toward Buckhead for about 2.5 miles. Turn right on Andrews Drive (not West Andrews). The Atlanta History Center is the first driveway on the left.

ATLANTA HISTORY CENTER–DOWNTOWN

Information Center
140 Peachtree Street
Atlanta, Georgia 30303 • 238-0655

If you wish to explore Atlanta's history on any level, the Atlanta History Center's downtown Information Center is a logical and helpful place to begin. The friendly staff can tell you the how, what, when and where for exploring Atlanta's history with your family. The Center presents numerous videos on Atlanta's history, including a great 18-minute overview, free of charge. Numerous brochures are available which provide up-to-date and enticing details on special walking tours (guided and unguided) and major historical attractions found in Atlanta. You may also browse through their research library and view a small area of changing exhibits highlighting architecture, folk art, politics and other topics about Atlanta.

- Occasionally, the Center presents free lectures and special events, some of which might be of interest to older children, such as programs featuring cartoonists, storytellers and craftspeople.

- The Center's gift shop is small but unusual, stocked with books, toys, crafts and other memorabilia.

- Handicapped access is available to the first floor only.

Hours: Open Mondays through Saturdays from 10:00am-6:00pm. Call about holiday closing dates.

Admission: FREE.

Directions: The Atlanta History Center is located downtown in the restored 1911 Hillyer Building. It is across the street from the MARTA Peachtree Center Station (take the Ellis Street exit from the station) and is convenient to the High Museum at Georgia-Pacific Center and the Atlanta-Fulton County Public Library.

ATLANTA MUSEUM

1537 Peachtree Street, N.E. • Atlanta, Georgia 30308 • 872-8233

Housed in the historical Rufus M. Rose House (the family residence of the founders of Four Roses Liquor) and listed on the National Register of Historic Homes, this curiosity of a museum (or historical flea market?) is a hodge-podge of over 2,500 items packed into eight small rooms on the upper level. Among its more notable possessions are an original model of Eli Whitney's cotton gin, furniture, books and photographs from Margaret Mitchell's house, a cache of Confederate weapons, Indian artifacts, a Japanese "Zero" airplane, Hitler's cigar box and other Nazi memorabilia, a stone from King Tut's tomb, Emperor Haile Selassie's throne and Queen Victoria's shawl. Just a sample...there's much more!

We recommend that you think twice about taking small children to visit the Museum. (What would you do with their curious hands and wriggly bodies?). If you bring older children here, be prepared to answer a lot of questions; the collection is neither organized nor well-labeled.

•   Handicapped access and restroom facilities are not available.

•   The Museum is across the street from Crawford Long Hospital's Medical Museum.

Hours: Open Mondays through Fridays from 10:00am-5:00pm. On weekends it is open for groups of 20 or more, but by appointment only. We suggest you call ahead to make sure the Museum is open.

Admission: Admission is $3.00 for adults and $2.00 for children.

Directions: The Museum is about two blocks south of North Avenue on Peachtree Street across from Crawford Long Hospital.

BIG SHANTY MUSEUM

2829 Cherokee Street • Kennesaw, Georgia 30144 • 427-2117

Big Shanty Museum is a must for Civil War history buffs and children of all ages, but especially for children who are already train fanatics.

Big Shanty, the original name of the city of Kennesaw, was the start of the "Great Locomotive Chase" which took place during the Civil War. (Yes, Disney made a movie about it!) You can touch history here, only 100 yards from the spot where the locomotive "The General" was stolen by Northern troops on April 12, 1862, during the famous Andrews Railroad Raid debacle. The Northerners' plans were foiled when pursuers boarded the locomotive "Texas" (now enshrined at the Cyclorama), caught up with the raiders and recaptured The General for the Confederacy. The General continued to operate for the South throughout the War.

The Museum, a converted cotton gin, houses The General's restored engine and tender. And is it ever an impressive sight! After you have had a chance to walk around the General, proceed upstairs to watch a narrated slide presentation about the Raid. It will be easier for you to understand the importance of the Museum and get answers to the many questions you will be asked by your children, once you view the program. Afterwards, when you go back downstairs and look at The General again, you will see the train in a slightly different light. Next look at the far wall for several historical photographs of The General as it looked way back then. Look at the Civil War relics in the room that help make the past more concrete and understandable to children as well as adults. There are quilts, clothing worn by ordinary people and soldiers, examples of food eaten by soldiers, stone bullets, a fife, bugle, both Confederate and State of Georgia money, news articles, personal notes and a miniature replica of Kennesaw and The General as they were over a century ago.

- On your way out, walk through the gift shop, but be forewarned–the toy engines, trains and other small items are very appealing to small hands.

- First visit Kennesaw Mountain Battlefield Park for a picnic and hike. Or, walk around historic Kennesaw and go over to the Mauldin Doll Museum or the Doll Gallery. (Read more about these attractions later in this chapter.) Our family accomplished the picnic, a 2-mile hike at Kennesaw Mountain, a visit to Big Shanty and the Doll Museum, and made it back to Atlanta in just under 5 hours.

- Or visit during the Kennesaw Big Shanty Festival in April!

- Parking is free across the street by the old depot.

- For more information about "The Great Locomotive Chase" and to see the restored "Texas," we suggest you visit The Atlanta Cyclorama.

- Handicapped access is available for the downstairs portion of the Museum.

- Restrooms and water fountains are available.

Hours: Open Mondays through Saturdays from 9:30am-5:30pm for most of the year. Open Sundays, and

December, January and February from 12:00noon-5:30pm. Closed on Easter, Thanksgiving, Christmas and New Year's Day.

Admission: Cost is $2.50 for adults; $1.00 for children age 7-15 years; and children under 7 are FREE. Maximum cost per family is $10.00.

Directions: Go North on I-75 to Exit #117 (Chastain Road), and make a left on Cherokee Street. Follow the signs to Big Shanty (about 2 miles). The Museum is about 25 miles north of Atlanta.

CALLANWOLDE FINE ARTS CENTER

980 Briarcliff Road • Atlanta, Georgia 30306 • 872-5338

Callanwolde is a Tudor-styled mansion built in 1920 as the home of Charles Howard Candler, eldest son of Coca-Cola founder, Asa G. Candler. The huge mansion, which is now listed on the National Register of Historic Places, is surrounded by 12 acres of lawns, formal gardens and a small conservatory. But, most importantly, Callanwolde is DeKalb County's most unique art center.

Callanwolde presents a year-round program of concerts, performances, lectures, recitals, poetry readings, and children productions by guest artists and Callanwolde's affiliate groups–the Poetry Committee, The Young Singers of Callanwolde, the Southern Order of Storytellers, the Apprentice Dance Company and the Community Concert Band. The mansion is a marvelous location for musical performances since the sound system, which features a magnificent 3,752 pipe Aeolian organ, the largest of its kind in playable condition, was especially designed for and built into the mansion and extends to every major room in the house.

Also, housed on the second floor of the historic mansion is The Callanwolde Gallery presenting exhibits by local artists year-round, and the Art Shop, a small gift store filled with collectibles created by artists and craftspeople.

We strongly suggest that you and your children visit Callanwolde only in conjunction with a festival, performance or class. The grounds, conservancy and gardens, although quite pretty, are also formal and not the best place for a picnic or day's outing with high-spirited children.

•   Callanwolde has a large selection of classes and workshops for preschoolers through adults including offerings in dance, drama, painting, photography, pottery, writing and textiles. The Summer Arts Camp, "Kaleidoscope," for preschoolers and older children includes visual arts, puppetry, writing, movement and dramatics.

•   Callanwolde presents the annual Olde Christmas Storytelling Festival in January, and Christmas at Callanwolde every December. See our chapter on "Festivals and Special Events" for more information about these events.

•   Callanwolde is available for private parties and events. Call 872-5338 for information.

•   Handicapped access is available, but call ahead for special directions.

•   Restrooms and water fountains are available.

Hours: Callanwolde and the Art Gallery are open Mondays through Saturdays from 10:00am-3:00pm; the Art Shop is open Tuesdays through Saturdays from 10:00am-3:00pm; and, the Conservatory is open Mondays through Fridays from 10:00am-2:00pm. Closed on all legal holidays.

Admission: Admission to the grounds and Art Gallery is
FREE. A special tour of the mansion is available
by appointment for groups of 15 or more at a cost
of $1.50 for adults and 50¢ for children.

Directions: Callanwolde is located in the Druid Hills/Emory
section of Atlanta on Briarcliff Road in between
Ponce de Leon Avenue and North Decatur Road.
Take I-85 to the North Druid Hills Road exit and
head east. Turn right on Briarcliff Road and head
south. Callanwolde will be on the right side of the
road, in between North Decatur Road and Ponce
de Leon Avenue.

CARTER PRESIDENTIAL CENTER
MUSEUM OF THE JIMMY CARTER LIBRARY

One Copenhill Avenue • Atlanta, Georgia 30307 • 331-3942

Housed in the Carter Presidential Center complex, the Museum of the
Jimmy Carter Library memorializes the life, career and Presidency of
Jimmy Carter. It also offers a glimpse of the office of the American
Presidency and addresses modern day issues such as war and peace,
hunger and poverty, human rights, the environment and the economy.

The permanent exhibits in the Museum are quite interesting and highly
recommended for older children. We were also pleasantly surprised to
discover how much fun our preschoolers had here; there was much to see
and do, and enough hands-on activities to keep everyone happy. Exhibits
included a replica of the Oval Office as it appeared during Jimmy Carter's
term, an interactive video display allowing us an oportunity to participate
in one of Jimmy Carter's famous "town-meetings," a special video presentation of children's thoughts on the Presidency called "If I Were President," a glimpse into the voluminous stacks in the Jimmy Carter Library,

personal aspects of the Presidency such as a collection of elegant gifts from foreign leaders, and an exhibit recognizing Rosalind Carter's important role as "Partner of the President." The Museum also has changing exhibits which explore various historical aspects of the Presidency and eras in America's history.

After visiting the Museum, our family had a grown-up lunch at the Center's restaurant, followed by a stroll through the lovely landscaped Japanese gardens which look out over downtown Atlanta.

- Members of the public are not allowed access to the Library or the remainder of the Carter Presidential Center unless they have a legitimate research purpose.

- Handicapped access is available.

- Restrooms and water fountains are available.

Hours: The Museum is open Mondays through Saturdays from 9:00am-4:45pm, and on Sundays from 12noon-4:45pm. Tours are available by special appointment. The Museum is closed on Thanksgiving, Christmas and New Year's Day. Restaurant hours are Mondays through Saturdays from 11:00am-4:00pm, and Sundays from 12:00noon-4:30pm.

Admission: Cost is $2.50 for adults; $1.50 for seniors; and, children under 16 are FREE.

Directions: *Going South*: Take I-75/85 South to Exit #100 (North Avenue) and turn left. Continue to North Highland Avenue and turn right. Continue one block to Cleburn Avenue and turn right into the Carter Center parking lot. *Going North*: Take I-75/85 North to Exit #96A (Boulevard/Glen Iris) and turn left at dead end. Turn right at Highland Avenue and continue 1/2 miles to Cleburne Avenue and turn left into the Carter Center parking lot. Parking is FREE.

CENTER FOR PUPPETRY ARTS

1404 Spring Street • Atlanta, Georgia 30309
Ticket Office: 873-3391• 24-Hour Hotline: 874-0398

The Center for Puppetry Arts is the most comprehensive puppetry center in the entire nation, attracting masters of puppetry from all over the world! The puppeteers are serious professional students of world puppetry and its history. Their extensive knowledge of various culture's puppets, traditions and stories is demonstrated in productions of classic tales that have always appealed to American children, such as Pinocchio, Rumpelstiltskin, Tom Thumb and The Velveteen Rabbit. The productions are always unique, interesting, and fun, fun, fun! Rod puppets, full body puppets, hand puppets or marionettes might be used by black clothed puppeteers on stage in a theatre where every seat is a good seat. After each production, which lasts about an hour, the puppeteers remove their head coverings and explain to the audience just how they held and manipulated the puppets. They then act out a couple of minutes of the performance in this manner, so children can get a "behind the scenes" glimpse of the voice, rhythm and fundamentals of puppet movement.

Before or after the performance, you should visit the Center's Puppet Museum which features one of the largest exhibits of puppets in North America. There is a fascinating permanent collection of over 150 hand, string, rod and shadow puppets, including tiny pre-Columbian clay puppets, ritualistic African figures, puppets from Asia, the Soviet Union, South America, North America and Europe, and even Muppets by the late Jim Henson. One room in the Museum is reserved for special exhibits which might include a memorial exhibit dedicated to a great puppeteer, or an in-depth study and celebration of a contemporary puppetry artist. In the hands-on gallery, children may operate rod, hand, string and shadow puppets on various stages.

- "Create a Puppet Workshop" and other innovative classes are offered year-round for children age 4 and up. Workshops are held on weekdays and Saturdays and last a little over an hour. Participants have an opportunity to create a unique puppet and learn how to bring it to life. "Puppet Camp" and "Create a Big Production Camp" are offered during the summer months. Call for information, costs and reservations.

- The Family Series consists of three puppet shows offered during the regular season. The Summer Festival consists of six different shows. See our chapter on "Performing Arts for Children" for more information about these series.

- You can have a puppet-making Birthday Party in the Center's Birthday Party Room for children age 4-12 years. Combine the party with a puppet show which will be sure to delight everyone. Call for details.

- The annual "Travel Fund Benefit," in the spring features games, face painting, puppet shows, puppet making and refreshments.

- There is a small, but interesting gift shop.

- Handicapped access is available.

- There are restroom facilities and water fountains.

Hours: *The Museum* is open on Mondays through Saturdays from 9:00am-4:00pm and evenings on performance nights. *Ticket Office* hours are Mondays through Fridays from 9:00am-5:00pm, and Saturdays from 9:00am-4:00pm. *Free guided tours* of the Museum are offered Mondays through Saturdays at 11:45am and 1:45pm. Closed on major holidays and Sundays.

Admission: Center Museum cost is $2.00 per person. Shows are $4.25 per person which also includes a visit to the Museum. Reservations are required. The

31

Family Series of three shows costs $7.65 for
members, and $8.50 for non-members. A Summer
Festival pass for six shows cost $17.00 per person.
There are several levels of annual membership,
the minimum contribution being $25.00. Benefits
include a 10% discount on tickets, classes, workshops and gift shop purchases as well as preferen-
tial seating for Family Series performances.

Directions: The Center is located in midtown Atlanta. *Going
South:* Take I-85/75 South to Exit #29. Take a right
on Spring Street and the Center will be a block and
a half on the right. *Going North:* Take I-85/75 North
to the 10th Street exit and turn right. Go to West
Peachtree and turn left. At 18th Street turn left and
the Center will be a block and a half on the left.
Parking is FREE behind the Center.

CHATTAHOOCHEE RIVER NATIONAL RECREATION AREA

Park Headquarters & Information • 1978 Island Ford Parkway
Dunwoody, Georgia 30350 • 394-7912 or 394-8335 or 952-4419

The Chattahoochee River is a national treasure and luckily for us, it is
right in our backyard. The Chattahoochee National Recreation Area is a
series of beautiful park lands along a 48-mile stretch of the River. Even
if you have already been to certain portions of the Park, we strongly urge
you to visit Park headquarters and pick up a fistful of their informative
brochures to find out more about the Recreation Area.

Scenic Trails: Some brochures describe the flora and fauna that inhabit
the area, while others contain individual maps that detail scenic trails
along the River and information on trail difficulty, parking, picnicking,
telephones, restrooms, launch areas, handicapped access and horseback

riding. We can attest that the trails are well marked and for the most part, appropriate for families with young children, babies in backpacks and dogs on leashes. There are also open meadows for playing, picnic tables, grills and trash containers. All the ingredients you need for many wonderful and varied Sunday afternoons along the River!

- **Sope Creek/Historic Mill Trail** located off Johnson Ferry and Paper Mill Roads is about a 4-mile easy hike beside the creek, around the pond and through the woods. View ruins of the Marietta Paper Mill built in 1854 which manufactured newsprint, stationery and wrapping paper (something kids can relate to) and the ruins of a flour mill that operated until 1902. There is a small parking lot at the start of the trail.

- **Vickery Creek Trail** system includes an easy hike from Allenbrook (site of the Roswell Historical Society, 227 S. Atlanta Street) to the creek via the Ivy Woolen Mill ruins.

- **Island Ford Trail** begins at Park Headquarters and is an easy walk down to the Chattahoochee River. The walk alongside the river is ideal for small kids and dogs on leashes with optional forks in the path for a more moderate hike. The trails are well marked with signs indicating trail configurations and degrees of difficulty.

Fishing: Other brochures provide information about fishing on the Chattahoochee, a designated trout stream. You should be aware that a valid Georgia fishing license with a trout stamp is required for those 16 years of age and older. Also, live bait, such as minnows, may not be used. For more information about fishing, see our chapter on "Sports and Recreation," or call Park Information at 394-8335.

Canoeing and Rafting: Brochures are also available about boating, rafting, canoeing and kayaking on the River, including advice on river and land safety. Children of all ages may boat with families on the River, but a U.S. Coast Guard approved life preserver is required for each person aboard any watercraft, including inner tubes! If you need to rent a raft or other watercraft, see our our chapter on "Sports and Recreation" for more information. If you would like information on River conditions at Buford

Dam call 945-1466, and at Morgan Falls Dam, call 329-1455.

Special Programs: The Park offers free ranger guided winter walks, which we recommend for families with older children as these leisurely walks last anywhere from 2-3 hours. You can discover the many scenic trails along the Chattahoochee and learn about Indians, early settlers, plantlife and wildlife. In addition to winter walks, there are nature and cultural programs held throughout the year at all branch units of the Park.

CHATTAHOOCHEE NATURE CENTER

9135 Willeo Road • Roswell, Georgia 30075 • 992-2055

Located on the River, the Chattahoochee Nature Center is an excellent community nature preserve and a wonderful attraction for children of all ages. Walking from your car to the Nature Center building, you will first notice the native garden clearly marked with plant identification labels.

Once inside the building, you can view changing exhibits of live animals (sometimes snakes, opposums or turtles) and visit the Nature Store which stocks an extensive collection of nature books, bird feeders, bird seed, rocks, T-shirts and many other items, including small bags of duck and fish food. Be sure to pick up the Center's brochures named *Walk the Woodlands* and *Wander our Wetlands* for informative descriptions of what you will observe and hear on your nature walks.

Then go outside the back door to the duck pond where you can feed the ducks, fish and turtles inhabiting the especially serene and scenic pond near the River; and, visit the bald eagles, a small mammal habitat and a hawk and owl aviary. Marked trails through the surrounding woodlands and a boardwalk through the marshes across the road are quite manageable for preschoolers.

- "Sunday Specials" is an educational program offered every Sunday at 2:00pm for ages K-adult. After-school and weekend classes are scheduled at least two times a week. "Summer Nature Camp" for children age 6-10 years offers sessions covering different topics about nature.

- There are guided evening canoe rides during the summer down the Chattahoochee River, weekend guided walks, and moonlight prowls around the forest available for families.

- No picnicking is permitted on the grounds of the Center, but Chattahoochee River Park, which has picnic facilities and a playground is only 1/2 mile away (Azalea Drive.

- There are bins in the parking lot area for recycling newspapers, glass (sorted by color) and aluminum cans.

- Handicapped access is available.

- There are restrooms and water fountains.

Hours: Open daily from 9:00am-5:00pm. Closed on legal holidays.

Admission: Cost is $2.00 for adults and $1.00 for children non-members. Members are free. Yearly Family

Membership is $35.00 and includes free admission, discounts on classes and purchases in the nature shop, a free subscription to the monthly newsletter, "The Kingfisher," and access to special member events.

Directions: The Park is located outside I-285 in Roswell. Go north on Georgia 400 and get off at the Northridge Exit. Go west to Roswell Road. Turn right on Roswell Road and turn left on Azalea Drive (just after crossing over the Chattahoochee River). Take Azalea Drive to Willeo Road passing by Chattahoochee River Park. Take a left on Willeo Road and travel 1/4 mile to the Nature Center which will be on your right.

HISTORICAL CLAYTON COUNTY DRIVING TOUR

Clayton County Chamber of Commerce
P.O. Box 774 • Jonesboro, Georgia 30237 • 478-6549
24 hr. Info Line: 409-6806

Clayton County is rich with antebellum plantation homes and historic mansions, cemeteries, churches and courthouses. The Chamber of Commerce has compiled a brochure called *Clayton County, Georgia–The Land of GONE WITH THE WIND–Special Interest Driving Tour* which lists about twenty of the county's historic sites and attractions. Also listed in the brochure are two excellent stops for children: the Atlanta State Farmer's Market, discussed in our section on Farmer's Markets; and, the Reynolds Nature Preserve, a woodland and wildlife refuge, more fully described in our section called "Ecology, Nature, Science, History and Politics."

Most notable among the historical plantations on the tour are Ashley Oaks Mansion, Stately Oaks Mansion and Crawford-Talmadge Plantation, all of which are available for private tours and social functions, although reservations must be made well in advance. (Tours of Crawford-Talmadge Plantation require a group of 30 people or more). Stately Oaks is the headquarters for Historical Jonesboro and the site of Clayton County's annual Fall Festival, "Georgia Folklore by Moonlight" storytelling sessions, as well as other special events throughout the year. Call the Clayton County Chamber of Commerce for more information about all of the plantation tours.

This do-it-yourself tour of a portion of Georgia's Historic Heartland should be both interesting and educational for older children, and if done in moderation (with a stop at the Reynolds Nature Preserve and/or the Farmer's Market), may be even enjoyable for younger children.

CNN STUDIO TOUR

Omni Center • 100 Techwood Avenue, S.W.
Atlanta, Georgia 30303 • 827-2400

Take your older children on a tour of the international headquarters of CNN and Headline News, the two 24-hour all news networks, for a behind the scenes glimpse of T.V. news-in-the-making.

The excitement begins when you enter the CNN tour waiting area. The room is covered with bright photographs of the CNN newscasters that you may soon be seeing. Overhead, television monitors air the current programs being broadcast on the four television channels owned by Turner Broadcasting System (TBS).

As your tour begins, you leave the waiting area and travel up the world's largest free-span escalator (8-stories!) from which you have a spectacular view of the CNN Center atrium. At the top of the escalator your tour guide will give a brief introduction, after which you have an opportunity to wander around a very polished photography exhibit highlighting TBS's holdings and accomplishments. Then the tour of the studios begins....

Your tour guide will lead you around the offices of CNN until you reach the large glass windows overlooking the news floor. You get an excellent behind-the-scenes look at the entire process of producing the news program, seeing state-of-the-art technology and learning how it is used in all aspects of news production. You will watch writers, editors and producers working to produce the news broadcast, and through a clever use of mirrors, you will actually be able to see the news anchors reporting the news live. We watched as "hot" information came into the newsroom by wire from one of the station's correspondents in Eastern Europe, then traveled through the hands of writers, editors and the graphics department, and then, a few minutes later, we heard it being reported live by the news anchors!

After leaving the CNN newsroom, you proceed to the glass windows looking out over Headline News, a smaller scaled-down version of the CNN Studio. Again, we were able to view the live broadcast and learn more about how Headline News operates. We were impressed, and felt we now had an insider's view on how a television news program ends up in our living room.

- Arrive at least one-half hour early to buy your tickets because they are sold on a first come, first serve basis. Allow even more time if there are a lot of conventions in town. After you purchase your tickets, wander around the CNN Center Mall where you can look through glass windows to see and hear two different radio station's live broadcasts. Shop at the Turner Store which is stocked with T-shirts, gift items, memorabilia and mementos from the classic films owned by TBS. Store hours are Mondays through Fridays from 9:30am-6:00pm, and Saturdays and Sundays from 10:00am-5:00pm. Call 827-2100 for more information.

- This is not a tour for preschoolers. There are too many stairs and the information imparted by the tour guide will be well over their heads.

- You can combine this tour with a visit to the Federal Reserve Monetary Museum which is just two blocks away.

- Tours are available for handicapped persons, but must be scheduled ahead of time.

- There are restroom facilities and eateries in the building.

Hours: Open Mondays through Fridays from 10:00am-5:00pm, and Saturdays and Sundays from 10:00am-4:00pm. Tours are on the hour and last approximately 45 minutes. Groups of 10 or more require reservations.

Admission: The cost is $5.00 for adults; $2.50 for seniors, students and children over 5 years of age; children under 5 are FREE. Group rates are available.

Directions: The CNN Center is located in the heart of Downtown Atlanta and houses the Omni Hotel and Omni Sports Arena. The less expensive parking lots are located west of the Omni on Marietta Street.

CYCLORAMA

800 Cherokee Avenue, S.E.
Atlanta, Georgia 30315 • 624-1071 or 658-7625

Next to Zoo Atlanta lies The Atlanta Cyclorama, which brings to life the hot summer day when Confederate troops led by General John B. Hood made a desperate attempt to save Atlanta from Major General William T. Sherman's Union forces. This is an attraction like no other in Atlanta.

When you enter the Museum you are greeted by the famous steam locomotive "Texas" which chased and caught "The General" south of Chattanooga in the "Great Locomotive Chase." You can wander around the downstairs portion of the museum and look at an assortment of Civil War artifacts while you wait for the production to start. The presentation begins with an impressively produced 12-minute movie narrated by James Earl Jones which chronicles the campaigns leading to the famous July 22, 1864 Battle of Atlanta.

Next, you enter the Cyclorama itself, where a revolving seating platform slowly turns you around the massive Civil War panoramic painting (It's 42 feet high and 358 feet around-about the size of a football field!) and the 30-foot wide three-dimensional diorama below it. Simultaneously, a multi-media production complete with lights, sound effects and narration highlights the stories memorialized in the amazing painting. During a second revolution around the painting, a guide talks about the history of the painting itself and provides some amusing trivia, such as how Clark Gable's face came to appear in the diorama.

For more in depth exhibits about The Battle of Atlanta, be sure to see the upstairs portion of the museum. Here photographs of the original and reconstructed parts of the painting are displayed side by side, as well as numerous Civil War artifacts, photographs, and exhibits honoring all soldiers of the War.

A visit to the Cyclorama is a must for older children. Although the sign on the Museum door indicates that the attraction is not suitable for children under 3 years of age, we took a 2-year-old who made it through the thirty-minute production with flying colors (albeit, with some squirming and whispers).

- There is an excellent Civil War history bookstore in the Museum.

- You might want to make a day of it by visiting Cyclorama, having a picnic in Grant Park and then going on safari to Zoo Atlanta.

- For more information about "The Great Locomotive Chase" and to see "The General," we suggest you visit Big Shanty Museum in Kennesaw.

- Handicapped access is available.

- There are restrooms and water fountains.

Hours: Open daily from 9:30am-4:30pm, September through May; and to 5:30pm, May through September. Tours are given every half hour. Closed on New Year's Day, Martin Luther King, Jr. Day, Thanksgiving Day and Christmas Day.

Admission: Admission is $3.50 for adults; $3.00 for seniors; $2.00 for children ages 6-12, and FREE for children under 6. Group rates are slightly lower.

Directions: Take I-20 to the Boulevard exit (one exit east of I-85/75). Follow signs to Grant Park, Zoo Atlanta and the Cyclorama.

HISTORICAL DEKALB COUNTY

DeKalb Historical Society Museum
DeKalb Historic Complex • DeKalb Historical Tours
DeKalb Historical Society • Old Courthouse on the Square
Decatur, Georgia 30030 • 373-1088 or 373-3076

THE DEKALB HISTORICAL SOCIETY MUSEUM. The DeKalb Historical Society Museum is now housed on the first floor of the Old Courthouse on Decatur Square, and with the promise of new funds, will soon be renovated, expanding in size and increasing its exhibits.

The Museum presently features two permanent exhibits. "DeKalb: The First Hundred Years" contains artifacts, photographs, maps and memorabilia dating from turn-of-the-century Atlanta up through World War I. "Johnny Reb and Billy Yank: The Life of the Common Soldier" honors the

41

common soldier of the Civil War, displaying his uniforms, guns and weapons. The Historical Society is hoping to put together another exhibit featuring the history of DeKalb's granite industry. Also housed in the Old Courthouse are a Library and Archives which will be quadrupled in size with the coming expansion. Stop by with your older children to see this small Museum when you are in the Decatur area. Or, make a day of it and visit the Museum in conjunction with one of the historical tours highlighted below.

- Handicapped access is presently not available, but will be included in the upcoming rennovations.

- Restrooms and water fountains are available.

Hours: Open Mondays through Fridays from 9:00am-4:00pm. Closed on all legal holidays.

Admission: FREE. Donations are appreciated. A Family Membership in the DeKalb Historical Society costs $25.00.

Directions: The Old Courthouse is located on the Square in Downtown Decatur at the intersection of Clairmont Road and E. Ponce de Leon Avenue, next to the Decatur MARTA Station.

DEKALB HISTORIC COMPLEX. A little further west from the Old Courthouse on West Trinity Place, lies the Historic Complex of the DeKalb Historical Society, a collection of early DeKalb historical dwellings that have, for the most part, been restored by the Society. The center of the complex is the **Benjamin Swanton** house, home of an early entrepenuer who came South during gold-rush days. This furnished antebellum house is believed to be Decatur's oldest townhouse. Also at the complex are two log cabins–the **Biffle Cabin**, a restored log cabin built by a Revolutionary War veteran, which now serves as a kitchen for the Swanton House, and the **Thomas-Barber Cabin**, a rustic log cabin built by early pioneers. The latest edition to the complex is the **Mary Gay House**, the antebellum home of Mary Gay, whose *Life in Dixie During the*

War tells the dramatic story of Decatur's Civil War days.

- During the summer months, the Historical Society presents Wednesday morning storyhours and pioneer activity programs for children age 5 and older which include demonstrations of pioneer activities, such as open-hearth cooking and woodworking. See our chapter on "Festivals and Special Events" for more information about this storyhour.

Hours: Open on weekdays by appointment only. Call the DeKalb Historical Society well in advance to schedule your tour.

Admission: The cost is $2.00 per person. Yearly Family Membership in the DeKalb Historical Society costs $25.00 and entitles you to free admission at the Complex.

Directions: The Complex is located on W. Trinity Place about four blocks west of the Old Courthouse Square and one block west of the Decatur Police Station.

DEKALB HISTORICAL TOURS. Two different tour brochures are available for those who enjoy being tourists in our own city and are eager to explore the historical sites of DeKalb County and Downtown Decatur. Call the DeKalb Convention and Visitor's Bureau (378-2525) or the DeKalb County Historical Society (373-1088) for the brochure *Driving Tours of DeKalb County* which presents four different tours of the historic homes, cemeteries, roads, churches, log cabins, museums and art centers found in DeKalb County. And, for those who have energetic children who are up for two hours of walking, the DeKalb Historical Society's brochure *Historic Downtown Decatur, A Walking Tour* outlines a self-guided walking tour around Downtown Decatur, which begins at the Old Courthouse Square and leads you past more than twenty historic landmarks.

EMORY UNIVERSITY MUSEUM OF ART AND ARCHAEOLOGY

Michael C. Carlos Hall
(On the Quadrangle of the Emory Campus)
Atlanta, Georgia 30322 • 727-4282

Emory University's ancient art and archaeology museum is housed in a beautifully renovated marble building which is listed on the National Register of Historic Places. The interior of the building is contemporary, blending beautifully with the art and archaeological treasures found within.   An impressive expansion is in the works which will triple the Museum's existing space, and will include a cafe and lots of instructional space.

Presently, the Museum's permanent exhibits on the first floor focus on artifacts, sculpture, pottery, coins and everyday objects from the ancient cultures of the Near East and Mediterranean.   Highlights of the exhibits are the mummies and treasures in the Museum's Egyptian collection. Make sure you see the vibrant painting of The Goddess of the West. This "new" addition to the Museum was actually resting in obscurity at Emory for over 70 years. It was accidentally found in the Museum's storage room on the bottom of a fragile wooden coffin that was being moved to make room for a new exhibit. In addition to the permanent collection, special exhibits on loan from other institutions change regularly and are displayed on the second floor of the Museum.

You might be surprised to discover that children, even preschoolers, find this Museum enjoyable. Its spaciousness allows children to move freely and the exhibits, with some explanations from parents, are appropriate for children. A word of caution: Count on your energetic children running off a bit of energy on the magnificent staircases, but watch toddlers closely because the marble stairs are a real challenge.

•   Children of all ages can join the Museum's Children's Culture

44

Club, which not only puts children on the Museum's mailing list of special activities, but entitles them to invitations to the Halloween Party "where mummies come alive," membership in the Birthday Club, and invitations to special showings of all new Museum exhibits.

- The Museum offers a Family-Preschool Workshop where parents learn how to teach their preschool children about viewing the treasures of the Museum. The Museum offers storytelling and a wide selection of workshops and programs for children in archaeology and the visual and performing arts in conjunction with special exhibits. During the summer months, the Museum offers a 2-day workshop called "Dig It," where children age 5-18 years explore archaeology techniques and older children actually get to work at a local excavation site.

- The Museum's annual B.C. Fest held in the spring is a must for children of all ages. See our chapter on "Festivals and Special Events" for more information.

- Parking on weekdays is difficult. Emory University has a short age of parking space, so you may have to plan on a long walk to the Museum.

- There is a very small gift shop.

- Elevators and handicapped access are available for those who need assistance. Call ahead for directions on their locations.

- There are restrooms and a water fountain.

Hours: Open Tuesdays through Saturdays from 10:00am-4:30pm. Open on Sundays from 12:00noon-5:00pm. Closed on major holidays.

Admission: Admission is FREE although a donation of $2.00 is appreciated. Group tours are available for $10.00 with advance reservations. Call 727-4282. The cost to join the Children's Culture Club is $10.00 for members and $35.00 for non-members. Yearly Family Membership is $50.00. Call 727-0516 for more information.

Directions: The Museum is located in the heart of the Emory campus on the Quadrangle. Take I-85 to Clairmont Road and head south. Turn right on North Decatur Road and continue to Emory Village. Turn right on Oxford Road which leads into the campus. Circle to the right on Mixell Drive and bear left on Kilgo Circle. The Museum is clearly marked on the right.

FEDERAL RESERVE MONETARY MUSEUM

Federal Reserve Bank Building
104 Marietta Street, N.W. • Atlanta, Georgia 30303 • 521-8747

If you know a child who needs a lesson on the value of money, then the Federal Reserve Monetary Museum is certainly the place to visit! And, even if lessons aren't needed, this Museum will give your family an opportunity to see $100,000.00 bills, solid gold bars and many other rare and unusual currencies.

The Museum is located in the imposing Sixth District Federal Reserve Bank Building on Marietta Street. Your family will sign in with the armed guard at the front desk and get directions to the Museum. You will also be warned that the glass exhibit cases in the Museum are hooked up to a sensitive alarm system so that even a mere touch will set off the alarm. (Obviously, this is not the place to bring small children!)

The Museum is housed in a small room that looks like a board room in one of the downtown banks. The exhibits showcase the history of currency through the ages, and include a 27-pound genuine gold bar, trading beads, arrowheads, $100,000.00 bills, gemstones, salt and many other interesting and often beautiful examples of early exchange units. There is also a bowl filled with small packets of shredded dollar bills that you may take home with you. The excellent exhibits in this Museum will certainly convince your family that money is serious stuff!

• Brochures are available in the lobby of the building which may be of interest to older children and adults, including information about the Federal Reserve System, how to identify counterfeit money, and regional economic updates.

• Combine a visit to the Museum with a tour of the CNN Studio which is two blocks west on Marietta Street. Or, stop by the Atlanta Journal and Constitution which is one block east, for a quick look at their lobby exhibit. (See our section called "Ecology, Science, Nature, History and Politics" for more information about the exhibit.)

• Handicapped access is available, but it is complicated and needs to be arranged in advance by phoning 521-8747 and asking to speak with the person in charge of tours.

Hours: Open Mondays through Fridays from 9:00am-4:00pm. Closed on Federal holidays.

Admission: FREE.

Directions: The Museum is located in the heart of Downtown Atlanta two blocks east of the CNN Center. Inexpensive parking is located west of CNN Center on Marietta Street.

FERNBANK SCIENCE CENTER

DeKalb County School System • 156 Heaton Park Drive, N.E.
Atlanta, Georgia 30307 • 378-4311

FERNBANK EXHIBITION HALL. Fernbank Science Center's Exhibition Hall displays various exhibits on the natural environment and animal habitats of the Southeast from prehistoric times to the present. Highlights of the permanent exhibits include a reproduction of plants and animals of the Okefenokee Swamp, dinosaurs, meterological exhibits, dioramas of insects, interactive computer display terminals, an authentic Apollo spacecraft, and a Cave Art exhibit with dioramas with hands-on activities. Special exhibits change regularly. Most of the exhibits in the Hall are appropriate for preschoolers, others are more interesting to older kids.

• Special science and nature enrichment programs, workshops, lectures, film series and open-houses for children and families are offered throughout the year, as well as an exciting roster of summer programs and courses in astronomy, birding, science, gardening, forestry and meteorology which should not be missed. Most of the programs are FREE.

• A good time to visit is during the fall Science Book Fair.

• There is a small gift shop stocked with T-shirts, dinosaurs, posters, books and other small items relating to science and nature. The shop does not have regular hours.

• Handicapped access is available.

• There are restrooms and water fountains.

Hours: Open on Mondays from 8:30am-5:00pm; Tuesdays through Fridays from 8:30am-10:00pm; Saturdays from 10:00am-5:00pm; and Sundays from 1:00pm-5:00pm. Fernbank has extended holiday closings, so call ahead before visiting.

Admission: FREE. Sign up to be on the mailing list of events. Membership is Free.

Directions: Fernbank is located south of Emory University in Decatur off Ponce de Leon Avenue. *Going east* on Ponce de Leon turn left on Artwood Road (a few miles past Briarcliff Road) and follow the signs to Heaton Road. Then turn right into the parking area. *Going west* on Ponce de Leon turn right on Artwood Road (about 1 mile past Clairmont Road) and follow the signs to Heaton Road. Turn right into the parking area. Parking is free.

LIBRARY AND LABORATORIES. Housed within the Science Center is one of the leading science reference libraries in the Southeast open to the public. There is also a Media Distribution Center with slide sets, instructional media kits and traveling exhibits for use by schools, libraries and other non-profit organizations; a Meterological Laboratory; an Electron Microscopy Laboratory; and, a Human Development Classroom, all of which periodically conduct open-houses for individuals and families.

Hours: The Library is open to the public Mondays and Fridays from 9:00am-5:00pm, Tuesdays, Wednesdays and Thursdays from 8:00am-9:00pm, and Saturdays from 10:00am -5:00pm.

Admission: FREE.

Directions: See above.

FERNBANK FOREST. Outside the Science Center, lies Fernbank Forest which consists of two miles of paved trails, ponds, look-out points and instructional shelters amid a 65-acre forest. The trails are perfect for younger children who, by following a simple map, can wander through at their own pace and enjoy the area's original, undisturbed vegetation. Of special interest is the "Easy Effort Trail" for those with physical impairments. Tape narrations and Braille recorders are available for the visually impaired.

- The paved trails make it easy to take babies and toddlers along in strollers.

- No running, jogging, picnicking or recreational activities are allowed in the forest. No pets are allowed. Children under 12 must be accompanied by an adult.

Hours: The Forest is open to the general public on Sundays through Fridays from 2:00pm-5:00pm and Saturdays from 10:00am-5:00pm. The Forest is open to school groups by special appointment daily from 8:30am-5:00pm. Fernbank has extended holiday closings, so please call ahead before visiting.

Admission: FREE.

Directions: See above.

THE PLANETARIUM. Fernbank's Planetarium is the largest in the Southeast, boasting a 70-foot diameter projection dome, a Zeiss Mark V projector and seating for 500! Celestial theater-in-the-round shows are presented year-round for children ages 5 and up, and there are special children's productions year-round. Children under 12 must be accompanied by an adult.

Hours: Showtimes vary and Fernbank has extended holiday closings, so please call ahead before visiting.

Admission: The cost is $2.00 for adults; $1.00 for students; Senior citizens are free. Summer children shows are 50¢/person.

Directions: See above.

THE OBSERVATORY. Fernbank's Observatory houses the largest telescope in the world dedicated primarily to public education. The 36-inch reflecting telescope is open to the public to view celestial objects, and older children will thrill at an opportunity to use such a powerful telescope.

Hours: Open Thursday and Friday on clear evenings only, from darkness-10:30pm. On cloudy evenings, the Observatory is open by appointment only. Fernbank has extended holiday closings, so please call ahead before visiting.

Admission: FREE.

Directions: See above.

FERNBANK GREENHOUSE. The Fernbank Greenhouses have moved from Clifton Road and are now located off Briarcliff Road inside the DeKalb Addiction Center. The Greenhouses are small but filled with many varieties of labeled plants, cacti, small trees and herbs. At the end of the visit, children are invited to pot a small plant to take home, complete with instructions about its care. A short but sweet visit!

Hours: Open on Sundays only from 1:00pm-5:00pm. Closed on all holidays.

Admission: FREE.

Directions: The Greenhouses are located inside the DeKalb Addiction Center at 1260 Briarcliff Road (in between Ponce de Leon Avenue and North Decatur Road). Take I-85 to the North Druid Hills Road exit and head east. Turn right on Briarcliff Road and the DeKalb Addiction Center will be on your right just past North Decatur Road.

FOX THEATRE DISTRICT TOUR

660 Peachtree Street • Atlanta, Georgia 30365
522-4345 • Ticket Information: 881-2000

During your guided tour of the Fox Theatre conducted by the Atlanta Preservation Center, you will hear all about how this absolutely unique 1920s Moorish/Egyptian/Art Deco fanatasy of a movie palace was "saved" by the efforts of Atlantans, and how it came to be designated as a National Landmark. The tour is excellent for older school-age children who will enjoy seeing the stars on the ceiling, hearing about the amazing organ and thrill at the opportunity to go backstage.

- The 1-1/2 hour tour also includes a trip to the Ponce de Leon Apartments, the Carlton Bachelor Apartments and the restoration-in-progress of the Georgia Terrace Hotel. You may choose to opt out of this portion of the tour.

- Musical productions, ballets and movies are shown at the Fox Theatre throughout the year which will delight children of all ages. Keep your eyes open for these performances, as this is an excellent way for children who are too young for a formal tour to be able to see and enjoy this imaginative building.

Hours: Tours are available year-round and begin at the Kiosk in the Fox Theatre Arcade. During the months of *February through November*, tours are held on Mondays and Thursdays at 10:00am; and, on Saturdays at 10:00am and 11:30am. During the months of *December and January*, tours are held on Mondays and Thursdays at 10:00am. No reservations are necessary. Groups tours are by appointment only.

Admission: Each regularly scheduled tour is $4.00 for adults, $2.00 for senior citizens and children and $2.50 for groups of 20 or more attending a regularly scheduled tour. Special group tours cost $5.00 for each adult with a $50.00 minimum.

Directions: The Fox Theatre is accessible by the North Avenue MARTA Station, #N-3. It is located at the intersection of Peachtree Street and North Avenue.

THE GEORGIA GOVERNOR'S MANSION

391 West Paces Ferry Road, N.E.
Atlanta, Georgia 30305 • 261-1776

A few mornings each week, the public rooms of Georgia's executive residence are open to the public. Volunteer guides stand at roped entrances to each of the formal rooms on the first floor level (You are not allowed to actually enter the rooms.) and explain the historical significance of the nineteenth century furniture, art, carpets, crystal, silver and other elegant period furnishings found in each of the rooms. The tour is short, pleasant and appropriate for older school-aged children.

• Many school groups visit the Mansion during the holiday season to see the Christmas decorations, so be prepared for crowds during this time.

• The annual celebration of the lighting of the State Christmas Tree is held in December; it is the best time to visit with younger children. See our chapter on "Festivals and Special Events" for more information about this event.

• Handicapped access is available.

Hours: Tours are given on Tuesdays, Wednesdays and Thursdays between the hours of 10:00am and 11:30am. Closed on all legal holidays.

Admission: FREE.

Directions: Take the West Paces Ferry exit from I-75 and go east on West Paces Ferry Road toward Buckhead for about 2 miles. The Georgia Governor's Mansion will be on your left. The guard at the gate will direct you to the parking area.

GEORGIA STATE CAPITOL BUILDING
GEORGIA STATE MUSEUM OF SCIENCE AND INDUSTRY

Capitol Square, N.W. • Atlanta, Georgia 30334 • 656-2844

THE GEORGIA STATE CAPITOL BUILDING. The first thing everyone notices about Atlanta's skyline when driving up Interstate I-85/75 is the brilliant dome of our State's Capitol Building, the largest gold dome in the United States. The gold leaf covering the dome was mined near Dahlonega, the site of America's first gold rush, and brought to Atlanta by wagon train in 1958, and later in 1978 when the dome was reguilded.

As you approach the Capitol, your children might get anxious to go inside, but see if you can take a few minutes to tour the Capitol grounds. There are many impressive statues, a replica of the Liberty Bell, a monument to the Spanish War Veterans and a sculpture on the northeast side symbolizing Black Georgian's struggle for political power.

Upon entering the building through the main entrance, you will pass right by the Governor's office (This is really where he works!) and into the beautiful marble interior of this massive building. The 237-foot high central rotunda is filled with marble busts and portraits of past governors and other famous Georgians. The north and south wings of the building are hung with the flags of the fifty states as well as all of the different flags that have flown over the State of Georiga. Also, in the north wing is a portrait of Dr. Martin Luther King, Jr., civil rights leader and Nobel Peace Prize recipient.

The many legislative chambers are located on the third and fourth floors of the Capitol and the entrance to the galleries of the Senate and House are on the fourth floor. If your children are old enough, and the legislature is in session (January through March), be sure to go in for a few minutes. Prepare your children in advance not to expect to understand very much as it is really difficult to figure out what is going on on the floors of the legislative bodies.

GEORGIA STATE MUSEUM OF SCIENCE AND INDUSTRY. The Museum of Science and Industry is located primarily along the halls and corridors of the fourth floor of the Capitol, and consists of extensive exhibits and dioramas about the State's wildlife, including deer, fowl, native fish, birds and a large whale. Also showcased are hundreds of rocks and minerals from every county in Georgia, including an exhibit of rocks which glow under fluorescent lights. A Native American heritage exhibit includes Indian artifacts and dioramas depicting four cultural periods dating back over 2,500 years. On the first floor of the Capitol, children can view tattered and torn flags of Georgia regiments from various wars and four cases of model airplanes depicting the history of aviation.

- Do not miss Indian Heritage Week each November.

- Tours for the hearing and sight impaired are available. Contact the Capitol Guide Service at 656-2844. Handicapped access is available.

- Restrooms and water fountains are available.

Hours: Open Mondays through Fridays from 8:00am-
5:30pm. Tours are conducted at 10:00am, 11:00am,
1:00pm and 2:00pm. Group tours are available by
appointment.

Admission: FREE.

Directions: The State Capitol is located in Downtown Atlanta
across the street from Underground Atlanta, the
New Georgia Railroad and The World of
Coca-Cola.

HISTORICAL GWINNETT

GWINNETT COUNTY MUSEUM, 455 Perry Street, Lawrenceville,
Georgia 30245 (822-517). The one-room Gwinnett County Museum
(formerly the Lawrenceville Female Seminary) is packed with early
educational material, furniture, books, clothing, dolls, antique school
desks, historical documents, veteran's memorabilia and other similar
items collected from all over Gwinnett County. If Gwinnett County
historian Marvin Nash is available during your visit, he will be more than
glad to supplement the exhibits with stories and information that will help
bring to life the history and heritage of the County. The Museum is
somewhat unusual and probably best enjoyed by your older children.
Stop by during your historic tour of Gwinnett County.

*   There is no handicapped access. The Museum is on the second
    floor of the historical building.

*   Restrooms are available.

Hours: Open Mondays through Fridays from 10:00am-
3:00pm. Group tours need to schedule an appointment.

Admission: FREE.

Directions: Take I-85 North to GA 316 to the Lawrenceville
exit. Turn right off the exit and head to the Square.
At the Old Courthouse turn right on Perry Street
which leads to the Museum.

PLANTATION HOUSES OF GWINNETT COUNTY, P.O. Box 261,
Lawrenceville, Georgia 30246 (822-5174). For a do-it-yourself driving
tour of historical antebellum plantation homes in Gwinnett County, write
to the Gwinnett Historical Society for a copy of their brochure *Plantation
Houses of Gwinnett County–Self-Guided Driving Tour.* The brochure is full
of information about the history of Gwinnett County (e.g. Did you know
that Gwinnett County is named after Button Gwinnett, one of Georgia's
three signers of the Declaration of Independence, even though he never
actually set foot inside the county?) and provides directions and information about seventeen historical homes and plantations in Gwinnett
County.

Most of the homes on the tour are privately owned and not open to the
public, so please respect the privacy of the property owners and stay in
your vehicle. The following homes are available for tours by appointment
only: the Wynne-Russell House (1826), now owned by the Lilburn Women's
Club (call 921-2210); the Bowman-Pirkle House (1818) operated by
Gwinnett Parks and Recreation (call 945-3543); and The Elisha Winn
House (1812), which was the County's first courthouse (call 822-5174).
Or visit the Elisha Winn House the first weekend of October during the
traditional Elisha Winn Fair. See our chapter on "Festivals and Special
Events" for more information about this fair.

This do-it-yourself tour lets you proceed at your own pace and gives you
an opportunity to take an historical drive into the past.

VINES BOTANICAL GARDENS, 3500 Oak Grove Road, Loganville,
Georgia 30249 (822-8840). The 90-acre park recently donated to Gwinnett
County Parks and Recreation by Myrna and Charles "Boe" Adams
features over 25-acres of developed gardens, a 3-acre lake which is home
to a family of swans, an 18,000 square-foot elegant manor home (presently
not open to the public), fountains, statues galore, and flowers, flowers,

and more flowers. A visit to this lovely, serene attraction is a must for any family visiting the Gwinnett County area.

- Most paths at the Gardens are easily accessible to strollers (excluding those paths arounds the home).

- The grounds may be rented for weddings and other special events.

- There is a small picnic area, a water fountain and soft drink vending machine at the main entrance, but no food or drink are allowed beyond the picnic area. Presently there are only portable "restroom" facilities.

Hours: Open on Tuesdays-Saturdays from 10:00am-5:00pm; Sundays from 1:00pm-5:00pm. Open additional hours during peak blooming seasons. Call 466-7532.

Admission: Cost is $2.00 for adults; $1.00 for children 5-12 years; Children under 5 are FREE.

Directions: I-85 North to Highway 316, exit at Route 120 and turn right. Continue until you reach GA 20 and turn right. Contine on GA 20 about and make a right on to Oak Grove Road. The Gardens are about one mile on the left.

THE HERNDON HOME

587 University Place, N.W. • (Near Clark Atlanta University)
Atlanta, Georgia 30314 • 581-9813

Alonzo Franklin Herndon was Atlanta's wealthiest Black person and one of America's foremost businessmen and philanthropists. A former slave from Social Circle, Georgia, Alonzo Herndon came to Atlanta in the late 1800s, and in 1905 founded Atlanta Life Insurance Company. After his death in 1927, his son, Norris Bumstead Herndon, carried on the family's tradition of business prominence leading Atlanta Life to prosperity and making it the largest black-owned insurance company in the United States. The Herndon family's tradition of community service and philanthropy to Black schools, churches and social agencies is now continued by The Herndon Foundation which owns and operates Atlanta Life and The Herndon Home.

The Herndon Home is a Beaux Arts Classical mansion designed by Alonzo Herndon and his first wife Adrienne McNeil, a drama teacher at Atlanta University. The mansion was built by skilled Black craftsmen, and throughout the years has stood as a symbol of Black achievement. Norris Herndon's collection of antique furniture, Roman and Venetian glass, silver, Oriental rugs and other decorative artwork completed the impressive home. A tour of the mansion begins with a short videotape about the Herndon family, followed by a comprehensive tour of the home.

Although we feel that a trip to the mansion by older children is a must, we recommend that you not take preschoolers. The mansion is full of valuables, the videotape and tour would be hard for a young child to follow, and your attention (and the rest of the tour group's) would probably be directed to amusing your child throughout the visit rather than to the enjoyment of the home.

- The annual Christmas Open-House and Kwanzaa Celebrations in December are good times to visit the house.

- Handicapped access is available only for the first floor of the home.

- Restrooms and water fountains are available.

Hours: Open Tuesdays through Saturdays from 10:00am-4:00pm. Closed on all legal holidays. Reservations are required for groups.

59

Admission: FREE.

Directions: Take I-85/75 to the Martin Luther King Drive, Jr. exit and travel west until you reach Vine Street. Turn right at Vine Street, and right again at University Place. The Home is located near Clark Atlanta University.

HIGH MUSEUM OF ART

Robert Woodruff Arts Center
1280 Peachtree Street, N.E., Atlanta, Georgia 30309 • 892-3600

The High Museum of Art is a modern, light-filled architectural master-piece, which houses Atlanta's permanent art treasures and special exhibits from the Museum's collection and other institutions. The Museum offers children an opportunity to discover art in a spacious and attractive facility.

SPECTACLES, on the lower level of the Museum, is the current permanent exhibit for children. The exhibit introduces children to the creative process involved in making and looking at art and allows them to explore line, motion, light, space, illusion, point of view, color and material. They are invited to participate in "hands-on" activities which allow them an opportunity to touch, draw and create on their own. Some of the fun exhibits are a shadow room where children's body positions are frozen on a wall for a brief period of time, a wall with stick-on shapes for constructing three-dimensional art, and light boxes where primary-colored shapes can be manipulated to create different colors. A trip to the High Museum of Art and SPECTACLES is recommended for children of all ages.

•   The High Museum conducts "Art Explorers," a weekend work shop which combines gallery visits with discussions and hands-on experimentation in drawing and painting, printmaking, mobile construction, sculpture, textiles and mixed media. Also offered are workshops tied into special exhibits and/or seasonal holidays. "Parent/Preschool" workshops allow parents and children an opportunity to work together with paint, clay and collage. The summer camp program, "Art Quest," focuses on a variety of art media including sculpture, printmaking, textiles, drawing and painting.

• Storytelling hours, puppet shows, children's films and family festivals are scheduled year-round, including the Children's Festival held annually in the spring, and a Christmas Holiday Family Festival. Look in our chapter on "Festivals and Special Events" for more details.

• There is an excellent Museum book and gift shop stocked with unusual books, toys and art project kits for children.

• Handicapped access is available.

• Restrooms and water fountains are available.

Hours: *Museum*: Open Tuesdays-Saturdays from 10:00am-5:00pm, and Sundays from 12:00noon-5:00pm. On Fridays the Museum is open to 9:00pm. Closed on Mondays. Closed on all legal holidays.

SPECTACLES: Open TuesdaysFridays from 2:00pm-4:30pm, Saturdays from 10:00am-4:30pm, and Sundays from 12:00noon-4:30pm. Closed on Mondays. Closed on all legal holidays.

Admission: Except during special exhibits when admission costs may be increased, the cost is $4.00 for adults; $2.00 for students and seniors; $1.00 for children age 6-17 years; children under 6 are FREE. The Museum is free on Thursdays from 1:00pm-5:00pm. Yearly Family Memberships are available at a cost of $50.00 and include free admission, discounts on classes, workshops and summer programs, discounts in the gift shop and many other privileges.

Directions: The High Museum of Art is located on Peachtree Street between 12th and 13th Streets, and next to the Woodruff Arts Center. Parking is available behind the building for a small fee. The MARTA Arts Center Station is behind the building.

HIGH MUSEUM AT GEORGIA–PACIFIC CENTER

133 Peachtree Street, N.W. • Atlanta, Georgia 30303 • 577-6940

This small, attractive "extension" to the High Museum of Art is located in the heart of downtown Atlanta inside the Georgia-Pacific Center. The Museum is compact and can easily be traversed by the youngest of preschoolers. Rotating exhibits have, for the most part, been appropriate for children. For example, "Moving: The Folk Art of Mattie O'Kelley" received a lot of good reviews by our children because they loved the familiar details and bright colors of the paintings. Also, at the same time, the exhibit "Cool Abstractions: American Art Since the Sixties," including Andy Warhol's "Marilyn," received a lukewarm review from our small critics. Keep an eye on the Saturday *Weekend* section of the *Atlanta Journal and Constitution* for information on current exhibits, or call the Museum to get more details if you need help in deciding whether an exhibit is appropriate for your child.

•   Some special exhibits have workshops or classes associated with them, most of which are free. For example, a 1991 exhibit, "Traditional Crafts of Saudi Arabia," was accompanied by storytelling sessions and a program on belly dancing.

- Guided tours are available for students on Tuesdays through Thursdays from 10:00am-11:30am in the months of October through May. Teachers for grades K-2 may schedule "Learning to Look" tours that use gallery games and activities to learn about the artist's vocabulary of line, shape, color and texture. Tours for grades 3-12 consist of a guided tour of the special exhibits, an introduction to Atlanta's urban architecture and an exploration of "Dawn's Forest," a sculpture by noted American artist Louise Nevelson.

- There is handicapped access.

- Restrooms and water fountains are available.

- The Museum is across the street from the Atlanta-Fulton County Public Library and the Information Center of the Atlanta History Center.

Hours: Open Mondays through Fridays from 11:00am-5:00pm. Closed on legal holidays.

Admission: FREE.

Directions: *Going South* on I-75/85, get off at the Butler Street exit and turn right on Houston Street. *Going North* on I-75/85, get off at the Edgewood/Houston Street exit and turn left on Houston Street. Pay parking is available at nearby lots. The Museum is near the MARTA Peachtree Center Station. (Use the Ellis Street exit from the station.)

KENNESAW MOUNTAIN NATIONAL BATTLEFIELD PARK

Old Highway 41 and Stilesboro Road
P.O. Box 1167 • Marietta, Georgia 30061 • 427-4686

Kennesaw Mountain National Battlefield Park is an enjoyable place to go for a family picnic, to hike and to learn more about the Civil War. To start off your visit, first go by the Visitor's Center and pick up some brochures about the Park. You can also view a slide presentation which provides introductory information about the 1864 Campaign and the Battle of Kennesaw and explains that the Park was established to commemorate this major Civil War battle.

The Park has two different picnic areas complete with tables, trash cans and barbeque facilities. The area near the Visitor's Center has a small creek running by which provides another fun place for children to explore.

There are also several marked trails that begin at the Visitor's Center. Round-trip distances are 2-miles, 5-miles, 10-miles and 16-miles. We took the 2-mile hike to the top of Kennesaw Mountain and it was a nice, wide trail of moderate steepness. There is an overlook at the summit of the Mountain that provides a panoramic view of the Battlefield. Our children loved running back down the trail! Take note–THERE IS NO WATER, FOOD or SHELTER along the trails.

- During the summer months, living history demonstrations and programs are often presented at the Park.

- Parking is in short supply at the Visitor's Center.

- There are restrooms and water fountains at the Visitor's Center.

- Bicycles are not permitted. Dogs must be on a leash.

Hours: Open daily from 8:30am-5:00pm. Open later in the summer months.

Admission: FREE.

Directions: The Park is located 3 miles north of Marietta. Take I-75 to Exit #116 (Barrett Parkway). Turn left on Barrett Parkway which dead-ends at Cobb Parkway (US 41). Turn right on Cobb Parkway and go to the first light. Turn left at the light and continue about 2 1/2 miles until you reach the Park.

MARTIN LUTHER KING, JR. HISTORIC SITE

CENTER FOR NONVIOLENT SOCIAL CHANGE, 449 Auburn Avenue, N.E., Atlanta, Georgia 30312 (524-1956). The Center is the only official national and international monument dedicated to the life of Martin Luther King, Jr. Its goal is to preserve and advance Dr. King's mission by applying his principles of nonviolence to all areas of human activity.

A small Exhibition Hall at the Center displays photographs and memorabilia depicting Dr. King's personal and public life. For a small fee ($1.00), you can view a movie on the life and message of Dr. King. In the courtyard of the Center, in a simple reflecting pool, lies the marble crypt of Dr. King engraved with the words from his famous speech, "Free at last, free at last, thank God Almighty, I'm free at last!" His grave, the nearby eternal flame, and the Chapel of All Faiths stand as moving reminders of the life and mission of Dr. King.   A visit to this monument is important for children of all ages.

The Center sponsors numerous conferences, training programs, internships, workshops, community services and cultural events, and actively promotes nonviolent solutions to family, local governmental, national and international problems. It also houses a Library and Archives containing the world's largest collection of primary source material on the Civil Rights Movement and Martin Luther King, Jr.

• The Center sponsors King Week in January, a Nonviolent Film Festival, original theater productions, and KingFest, a summer-long series of musical and cultural performances. See our chapter on "Festivals and Special Events" for more information.

• There is a snack area in the Center and gift shop with books, posters, postcards and other items.

• Handicapped access is available.

• There are restrooms and water fountains.

Hours: Open daily from 9:00am-6:00pm with later closing hours during summer months and the peak tourist season.

Admission: FREE.

Directions: Located 1/2 mile east of Peachtree Street on Auburn Avenue Parking is available behind the Community Center.

EBENEZER BAPTIST CHURCH, 407 Auburn Avenue, N.E., Atlanta, Georgia 30312 (688-7263). Just a block down from the Center for Nonviolent Social Change lies the church where Dr. King, his father and his grandfather preached. Walk in and see the historical sanctuary. You are also welcome to attend Sunday services at 7:45am and 10:45am, although this may not be the best activity for preschoolers and children who are not accustomed to religious services.

• Tours are offered Mondays-Fridays from 10:00am-4:00pm..

• Handicapped access to certain areas of the Church is available but call ahead for directions. There are restrooms and water fountains.

Hours: The Church is open to the public on Mondays through Fridays from 9:30am-12:00noon and from 1:30pm-4:30pm. Call for Saturday hours.

Admission: FREE. Donations are always welcome.

Directions: The Church is a block west of the Center for Nonviolent Social Change.

MARTIN LUTHER KING, JR. BIRTHPLACE, 501 Auburn Avenue, N.E., Atlanta, Georgia 30312 (331-3919). About one block east of the Center for Nonviolent Social Change lies the simple Victorian birth home of Martin Luther King, Jr. The 1895 home has recently been restored, and tours are scheduled every fifteen minutes. Walk down the street and see this historic home, even if just from the outside.

• Handicapped access is not available. There are no restrooms or water fountains.

Hours: Open daily from 10:00am-4:30pm from June to Labor Day, and from 10:00am-3:30pm from Labor Day to May.

Admission: FREE.

Directions: The home is about one block east of the Center for Nonviolent Social Change. There is an American flag out front.

HISTORICAL MARIETTA

Marietta Welcome Center
Marietta National Cemetery
No 4. Depot Street • Marietta, Georgia 30060 • 429-1115

MARIETTA WELCOME CENTER AND HISTORICAL TOURS.
The Marietta Welcome Center occupies part of the original Marietta Railroad depot and offers historic films, slide presentations, walking tours, historic exhibits and information about the community and county.

When visiting the Center, be sure to pick up the brochure called *Historic Marietta Walking/Driving Tour* which outlines both a walking and a driving tour of historic Marietta. Featured are a sampling of historic parks, churches, homes, businesses, hotels and cemeteries in downtown Marietta. The brochure provides a brief historic narrative about each of the fifty stops on the tour and a general synopsis of the history of Marietta. You can rent a portable cassette player and tour guide tape at the Welcome Center for $4.00 to supplement the brochure. Almost all of the homes and businesses on the tour are privately owned and not open to the public, although some can be seen during the Christmas holiday tour of homes.

•	Drive the new "Cannonball Trail," a 17-mile, two hour tour of Civil War sites.

•	Plans are presently underway to create a museum at the historical **Root House**, one of the stops on the tour.

•	Handicapped access is available. There are restrooms and water fountains.

Hours:	The Welcome Center is open Mondays through Fridays from 9:00am-5:00pm, Saturdays from

10:00am-3:00pm, and Sundays from 1:00pm-4:00pm. Closed on all legal holidays.

Admission: FREE.

Directions: Take I-75 North to Exit #113 (N. Marietta Parkway). Turn left on to North Marietta Parkway and go 2.3 miles to Mill Street. Turn left of Mill Street and the Depot will be immediately on your right.

MARIETTA NATIONAL CEMETERY. One of the stops on the tour is Marietta National Cemetery. Henry Cole, a Marietta citizen who remained loyal to the Union throughout the Civil War, originally offered land for a cemetery to be used as a burial ground for both Union and Confederate soldiers. He hoped that by honoring those who had fallen together, the living might learn to live together in peace. Unfortunately, this peace offering was rejected by both the North and the South, so Henry Cole donated the land to be used as a national cemetery (and a Confederate Cemetery was later built nearby). Approximately 10,000 Union soldiers (almost 3,000 of which are unknown) from 23 states are buried in the 24-acre Marietta National Cemetery along with veterans of the Cherokee Indian War of 1836, Revolutionary War, Spanish American War, and five subsequent wars—over 17,000 gravesites in all! The Veterans Administration maintains the Cemetery and has an excellent collection of historical literature at the Cemetery office.

Hours: The Cemetery is open daily 24-hours a day. The Office is open on weekdays from 8:00am-5:00pm. Call 428-5631 for more information.

Admission: FREE.

Directions: Located at the corner of Washington Avenue and Roswell Street in downtown Marietta.

MAULDIN DOLL MUSEUM

2238 Whitfield Place
Kennesaw, Georgia 30144 • 426-8818 or 428-4931

Mrs. Mauldin began collecting Cupie dolls over fifteen years ago, and it didn't take long for her to discover the joy of collecting. (Not to mention the monetary value!) She and her husband soon became avid collectors and now the Museum is home to over four thousand dolls! The walls of their six-room house are lined from floor to ceiling with all sorts of dolls. If your children are doll enthusiasts then a visit to this Museum will surely astound and delight them.

• The Museum is only a couple of blocks from Big Shanty, so you can plan on visiting both in the same day.

• Handicapped access is available, but restrooms are not accessible to wheelchairs. There are water fountains.

• When in Kennesaw, you can also visit **The Doll Gallery** which is located at the KOA Campground behind the Crown Gas Station on U.S. 41. Mrs. Bygall is the proud owner of this 6-room house which is the home to thousands of dolls. She has carefully arranged her dolls in Mother Goose settings and is very happy to discuss the history of the dolls with you. Please call for an appointment. (Home: 422-8584 or Office: 427-2406)

Hours: Open Tuesdays through Saturdays from 10:00am-4:00pm. Phone ahead in the winter to make sure it is open.

Admission: Cost is $3.00 for adults and $2.00 for children.

Directions: Take I-75 North to Exit #118 and turn left on

Cherokee Street. Go over the railroad tracks and take an immediate right on Main Street. Turn right on Whitfield Place.

MEDICAL MUSEUM–CRAWFORD LONG HOSPITAL

550 Peachtree Street, N.E. • Atlanta, Georgia 30365 • 686-4411

The lobby of Crawford Long Hospital of Emory University houses a very small museum of medical memorabilia and hospital artifacts. The hospital is named after Crawford Williamson Long, the first doctor in the United States to use anesthesia (ether) in surgery. The Museum's collection has furniture from Dr. Long's office and some of his original papers. Also displayed are early medical and surgical equipment, Confederate memorabilia and an exposé leading us to believe that George Washington's death may have been caused by medical malpractice! A small, interesting exhibit — for older children, only. Take a quick peak if you happen to be in the neighborhood.

•   The Atlanta Museum is across the street from the hospital.

•   Handicapped access is available. Restrooms and water fountains are available in the hospital.

Hours: The Museum is only open on Mondays, Tuesdays and Wednesdays from 10:00am-2:00pm.

Admission: FREE.

Directions: Crawford Long Hospital is about 2 blocks south of North Avenue and Peachtree Street in midtown Atlanta, across from the Atlanta Museum.

THE NEW GEORGIA RAILROAD

The Georgia Building Authority • 1 Martin Luther King, Jr. Drive
Atlanta, Georgia 30334 • 656-0769 or 656-0768

All aboard! Take your children for a wonderful ride on the New Georgia Railroad. You may ride the 18-mile Atlanta loop which lasts about an hour and a half, or take the 16-mile excursion to Stone Mountain Village and Park, stay and play awhile and return to Atlanta.

We took our families on the Atlanta loop and did we ever have fun! The ride was very comfortable as the train is climate controlled, has soft seats and spacious legroom. On the journey we heard all about the sites we were passing and about the history of the steam engines which were pulling our train. We took a lot of picnic food (but there is a snack bar on the train for those of you who come empty-handed), and our children ate their way around Atlanta.

During the ride, passengers are entertained by a singing banjo player who invites kids and adults alike to join in. Near the end of the trip, all children get free balloon animals of their choice.

- Free parking is available at 90 Central Avenue, near the entrance to Underground Atlanta.

- The railroad depot has railroad items for sale, such as engineer hats.

- Restrooms and water fountains are available at the depot and on the train. The train has a snack bar which sells hot and cold snacks and beverages.

- There are occasional spring excursions to Macon, Savannah and

Brunswick, and a special caroling train execursion in December. Call for more details.

• Adults can enjoy the luxurious dinner train to Stone Mountain which runs on weekend evenings. Call for more details.

• Private parties for up to 900 people can be arranged!

Hours: The Atlanta Loop usually runs three Saturdays a month, the Stone Mountain excursion one Saturday a month. Call for the current schedule. The Atlanta Loop trains depart at 12:00noon and 2:00pm. The Stone Mountain Run departs at 10:00am and 2:00pm. Reservations are not required, although they are recommended. You must arrive at least 10 minutes before departure time.

Admission: The Atlanta Loop costs $10.00 for adults, $5.00 for children, and children under 2 are FREE if they do not occupy a seat. The cost of the Stone Mountain Run is $12.50 for adults, $5.00 for children, and children under 2 are FREE if they do not occupy a seat. Group rates are available.

Directions: The New Georgia Railroad is located next door to Underground Atlanta and The World of Coca-Cola and across the street from the Georgia State Capitol Building. The MARTA Five Points Station is two blocks away.

OAKLAND CEMETERY

248 Oakland Avenue, S.E. • Atlanta, Georgia 30312 • 688-2107

Established in 1850, historic Oakland Cemetery was the only municipal burying ground in Atlanta, so nearly everyone, rich or poor, was buried here until 1884. Now listed in the National Register of Historic Places, the 88-acre Victorian cemetery is filled with a large collection of Gothic and Classic Revival mausolea, ornate statutory and the graves and monuments of many famous Atlantans, including: golfer Bobby Jones; Atlanta's first mayor Moses Formwalt; author Margaret Mitchell; and, Morris Brown College founder Bishop Wesley Gaines.

A visit to Historic Oakland Cemetery is not for everyone, and is certainly not for every child. Full of important historical information, the cemetery is an open-air museum and presents an opportunity for your children to learn about the history of Atlanta. Yet any child's trip to a cemetery is sure to raise questions about death and mortality, so be sure you are ready to discuss the questions and concerns that your children have.

- The annual Sunday in the Park usually takes place in October and includes picnic lunch, storytelling, carriage rides, a Victorian boutique, bands and other history-oriented events.

- A note about security: Although there is a security guard present, it is recommended that you take the Atlanta Preservation Center's tour (522-4345) or schedule your visit at active hours.

Hours: Open from dawn to dusk, daily. The Cemetery Office is open Mondays through Saturdays from 9:00am-5:00pm, but it is closed for lunch. Group tours for 10 people or more are available by appointment.

Admission: FREE. A Walking Tour Brochure is available at the Cemetery Office for $1.25.

Directions: Take I-85/75 to the Martin Luther King, Jr. Drive exit and go east on the Drive until it dead ends at the Cemetery.

HISTORICAL ROSWELL

BULLOCH HALL, 180 Bulloch Avenue, Roswell, Georgia 30075 (992-1731). The Hall is the antebellum home of Mittie Bulloch, President Theodore Roosevelt's mother and Eleanor Roosevelt's grandmother. This historic home which was built in 1840, is now listed in the National Register of Historic Places.

During your walk around the home, you will see period and museum rooms, gallery space, a reference library and antebellum gardens. Permanent exhibits include photos and documents from the James Stephens Bulloch and Theodore Roosevelt families, a collection of artifacts left in Roswell by the federal troops encamped in the area during July 1864, and a Roswell Textile Mills exhibition.

An excellent tour for children is available for school groups which includes a guided tour of Bulloch Hall; demonstrations of folk skills, such as open-hearth cooking, candle-dipping, soap-making, basketry and quilting; a hands-on experience with a Heritage Trunk (filled with articles used in everyday life during the 1800s); and a slide presentation about life in historical Roswell. The cost per child is approximately $1.50.

•   Bulloch Hall also serves as a cultural center in Roswell. Special events are scheduled year-round, including lectures, readings, fine arts and crafts shows, storytelling, musical concerts, historical exhibitions, literary perspectives, theater performances, special festivals and lliving-history demonstrations. See our chapters "Festivals and Special Events" and "Performances for Children" for more information about those events which are appropriate for children.

- Workshops and classes are offered for children year-round in folk crafts and history. "Camp Bulloch" is a one-of-a-kind summer camp offering children an opportunity to experience first hand the way of life and recreation of children of the 1800s. Camp activities include arts and crafts, stories, songs and games, Indian lore, hikes and architectural explorations.

- Handicapped access is available.

- There are restrooms and water fountains.

Hours: Tours are scheduled Tuesdays through Fridays from 11:00am-2:00pm with special appointments available for larger groups.

Admission: Cost is $3.00 for adults; $2.00 for senior citizens; $1.00 for children age 6-16 years. Children under 6 are FREE. Yearly Family Memberships cost $25.00 and entitle you to free admission, special invitations to events, newsletters and discounts on classes.

Directions: Take I-285 to the Roswell Road exit. Head north on Roswell Road and across the Chattahoochee River until you reach the Town Square in Roswell. Turn left at GA 120, then right on Mimosa, and then left on Bulloch Avenue. There are signs directing you to Bulloch Hall.

ROSWELL HISTORICAL SOCIETY TOUR, Roswell Historical Society, Inc., 227 S. Atlanta Street, Roswell, Georgia 30075 (992-1665). Roswell is a beautiful city and a walk around the historic downtown area can be quite pleasant, even for younger children. Your walking tour should begin at Allenbrook, headquarters of the Roswell Historical Society. View a slide show of the history of Roswell and its homes, and pick up a copy of the brochure entitled *Historic Roswell* (or write ahead to the Roswell

Historical Society) for a do-it-yourself walking tour of the city. The tour takes you past historic homes, squares, churches, businesses, cemeteries and of course, the cotton and woolen mills of the Roswell Manufacturing Company.

One of your stops along the way will be Bulloch Hall which is open to the public. The rest of the homes are private, some of them still occupied by descendants of Roswell's founding families, and are only open at certain times and by appointment.

- Allenbrook is the site of many special events during the year including the Fall Arts and Crafts Festival and Christmas open-houses. See our chapter on "Festivals and Special Events" for more information on these and more festivals in Roswell.

- Stop by **Roswell Mill Square**, 85 Mill Street at Roswell Square (552-8716). Currently housing a large multi-artist **Arts Pavilion** with a cooperative gallery and working studios, the Mill expects to open many shops in the already constructed buildings. Children may view art demonstrations in up to ten active studios. Closed Mondays and Tuesdays.

- Park your car at Founder's Cemetery (where Roswell King and Teddy Roosevelt's grandfather Bulloch are buried), which is about 25-feet beyond the trail entrance to **Vickery Creek Park–Roswell Mill Ruins Trail,** and begin a very interesting walk on a wide, well-designed trail of steps and flat creek walks. Along the way are interpretive markers explaining the unique history of the cotton mill and the ruins that you can literally touch. All along the walk you hear the suspenseful roar of the waterfall that powered the Mill, and at the base of the trail you are rewarded for your patience by being able to walk right up to the top of the falls. The water is polluted as the signs warn, so do not come prepared for a dip in the creek.

Hours: Allenbrook is open Mondays through Fridays from 10:00am-4:00pm. The Society conducts free guided tours on Wednesday mornings from April through October.

Admission: FREE.

Directions: Take I-285 to the Roswell Road exit. Head north on Roswell Road and across the Chattahoochee River. Allenbrook will be on the right about 1/10th of a mile after the River.

ROSWELLL FIRE MUSEUM, 1002 Alpharetta Street, Roswell, Georgia 30075 (641-3730). This fun antique museum houses early firefighting equipment, including a fire rattle (used to wake up the residents during a fire), a leather fire helmet, old tools, fire wagons once pulled by horses, a uniform and more. Children are welcome to ring a 19th century fire bell and sit in a 1940s red pumper truck! Take your camera. School and other groups are welcome by the very friendly firefighters. FREE

SCITREK

The Science and Technology Museum of Atlanta
395 Piedmont Avenue • Plaza Level
Atlanta, Georgia 30308 • 522-5500

SciTrek, Atlanta's hands-on museum, is recognized as one of the country's top ten physical science museums.   Children are invited to explore, create and problem-solve in this exciting laboratory of physical sciences, technology and mechanics. The main portion of the Museum is divided into three different areas: Mechanics and Simple Machines, Light and Perception, and Electricity and Magnetism.   Each section provides visitors with an opportunity to learn and experiment with state-of-the-art exhibits. There is also a special exhibit area where visiting shows are housed. Throughout the day, the Museum offers free "Mr. Wizard" like demonstrations of principles of physics and chemistry. This section of the Museum is guaranteed to capture the rapt attention of anyone over the age of five.

The spectacular Kidspace is a separate area for children under the age of seven, where scientific principles and experiments are learned through play. Among the many work stations are a construction site with bricks, electricity and plumbing material, a television weather desk with video camera, computer terminals with educational programming, a puppet show area also with video cameras, face-painting, a puzzle area and more. By far the most popular area is the water play section, complete with water hoses, dam construction, bubble-making and a selection of water toys that will insure that your children will not leave the area dry!

- There are workshops, family programs and walking tours centered around the physical sciences and architecture which are offered in conjunction with special exhibits at the Museum, including "Science Around the Clock," an overnight program for families and groups. SciTrek sometimes hosts a Science Fair in conjunction with World of Wonderment offering a forum for science displays submitted by children from Atlanta and Fulton County Schools, and a Toy Fair featuring educational toys from about 50 different toy manufacturers.

- A Summer Day Camp Program may be offered during the months of July and August which has themes related to the physical sciences, architecture, creative thinking, inventing or exploration. Additionally, a Summer Film Festival may also be offered which features full-length feature films, animated shorts and science fiction for the whole family.

- SciTrek is available for birthday parties.

- The Museum gift shop is excellent, filled with unusual puzzles, books, toys, kites and more, but the merchandise is not cheap. (Museum members do get a discount).

- There is a small food concession area with tables and chairs.

- Handicapped access is available.

- There are restrooms and water fountains.

Hours: Open Tuesdays-Saturdays from 10:00am-5:00pm, and Sundays from 12noon5:00pm. Monday mornings are available for school groups. Closed on Easter, Thanksgiving, Christmas and New Year's holidays.

Admission: Admission is $6.00 for adults; $4.00 for children ages 3-17 years; children under 3 are FREE. Special rates are available during specified hours of the day. Discounts for groups of 12 or more, with reservations. Yearly Family Memberships cost $45.00 and entitle you to free admission.

Directions: SciTrek is in the Atlanta Civic Center on Piedmont Road. *Going South* on I-85/75 get off at the Courtland Street exit. Turn left on Harris Street; then turn left onto Piedmont Road. At the first light, turn right onto Ralph McGill Boulevard. At the first light turn into the parking lot. *Going North* on I-85/75 get off at Pine Street (Exit #98) and at the second light turn right onto Courtland Road. Go to the second light and turn left onto Ralph McGill. Turn left into the parking lot. Parking fees are $3.00 for cars and $9.00-$12.00 for buses and recreational vehicles.

SIX FLAGS OVER GEORGIA

7561 Six Flags Road, S.W. (at I-20 West)
Mableton, Georgia 30059 • 948-9290

Six Flags is a 331-acre amusement park that has over 100 rides, attractions and shows. The Park is named for the six flags that have flown over

Georgia. (Quick! What are they? Spain, France, England, Georgia, the Confederacy and the United States.) It is clean, well-managed and full of cheerful young attendants.

For young children, there is a mini-zoo, train ride, Yosemite Sam's Playfort, featuring rope climbs, slides and ball baths, Looney Tune Land and Bugs Bunny Land, both of which have lots of great rides and play areas.

For older and braver children, there are, of course, the amazing roller coasters: The Great American Scream Machine, Z-Force and the newest thriller, The Georgia Cyclone, a replica of the legendary Coney Island Cyclone. You can also enjoy Ragin' Rivers, a raft ride down four slides, the "The Great Gasp," a parachute that drops 210 feet in a matter of seconds, Splashwater Falls, the Looping Starship and the many other exciting and fun rides at the Park.

And, don't forget the shows, musical concerts, magic, fireworks and the daily stunts of the U.S. High Diving Team which entertain children of all ages.

•   Discount tickets can be found all over Atlanta. Look for them at Krogers, in newspapers and at other metro-Atlanta locations.

•   General Admission covers the cost of all rides and performances except for a few special evening concerts which may have a surcharge.

•   The Park reopens for "Fright Nights" during certain weekends in October so that Atlantans can celebrate the Halloween holiday. Rides are sometimes operating. During the months of November and December, the Park opens in the evenings for "Holiday in the Park," with special performances, sledding and ice skating. The rides are generally not operating.

Hours: The Park is open at 10:00am daily from Memorial Day to late August. Closing hours vary but are usually around 10:00pm. From about mid-March

to Memorial Day, and late August through
October, the Park is open on most weekends.
Call for the current schedule.

Admission: A one-day pass to the Park costs $20.95 for adults;
$14.95 for children age 3-9 years; FREE for kids 2
years and under; $10.48 for seniors over the age of
55 years. The best buy is a 2 consecutive day ticket
which cost $24.95. A season's pass cost $54.95 a
person or $150.00 for a family of four.   Parking is
$4.00. Call for other prices.

Directions: Six Flags is located 12 miles west of downtown
Atlanta directly off of I-20. You can see the Park
from the expressway and there are signs to direct you.

SOUTHEASTERN RAILWAY MUSEUM

3966 Buford Highway • Duluth, Georgia 30316 • 476-2013

If your children like trains, you simply must explore this one-of-a-kind
outdoor museum for retired railroad cars. Some of the cars at this 12-acre
trainyard have been restored by the Atlanta Chapter of the National
Railroad Historical Society and are in top condition, while others are in
various stages of decay. All are interesting. Kids can climb on some of the
cars including a working, shiny black steam engine, freight cars, a
Pullman dining car and a few good-old red cabooses. (Haven't you always
wanted to go inside a real caboose?) Watch your children carefully while
they explore, since a few of the cars are not safe to climb on due to their
severe state of disrepair. Be sure to peak into the busy "Corner Shop" to
view engine and rail cars being restored. Some of the restored locomo-
tives are now part of the New Georgia Railroad.

On the third Saturday of each month (May-October), children can take an irresistable 10-minute ride on miniature trains, lovingly and painstakingly built by the North Georgia Live Steamers. Riders sit in gondolas built to scale which are pulled by powerful steam engines along 5,000 feet of railroad track with a little tunnel and bridge. Call ahead to make sure that the trains are operating on the day you plan to visit.

On certain Saturdays, you can also get on board a restored train and take a Southern Steam Excursion pulled by "Old 97" or a diesel locomotive. Ride in a caboose around the grounds, or take a longer excursion to Toccoa and Chattanooga. Call the Museum for the weekend steam-up schedule.

- The Museum volunteers urge everyone to use safety precautions. Avoid walking on the rails and keep a safe distance from moving equipment.

- The Museum's library, housed in a U.S. Post Office railroad car, is a repository of over 7,000 items of railroad memorabilia. Among the more interesting documents for children are a train register with the real Casey Jone's signature, old signal lanterns, rail spikes and telegraph equipment.

- Dogs are welcome on a leash.

- There are a few picnic tables.

- There are snacks, beverages and souvenirs for sale in the Central of Georgia Baggage Car No. 405.

- The terrain is gravel, so this is not a good place for strollers and wheelchairs.

- There are many interesting free brochures about the history of the Southern Railway System and on safety. There are also activity sheets just for kids.

Hours: Open on Saturday from 9:00am-5:00pm, except

on days set aside for the longer Southern Steam
Excursions and holidays. Call ahead to make
sure it's open.

Admission: The Museum is FREE, but donations are welcome.
Short Southern Steam Excursions are $2.00 for
adults and $1.00 for children. Longer excursions to
Toccoa and Chattanooga average $60.00. Call 416-6292
for more information.

Directions: Take I-85 north to the Pleasant Hill Road exit. Turn
left and go to Buford Highway. Take a left on
Buford Highway and continue for about 1/4 mile.
The Museum will be on the left, immediately after
a railraod spur.

STONE MOUNTAIN PARK

P.O. Box 778 • Stone Mountain, Georgia 30086
498-5600 or 498-5690

Stone Mountain Park's 3,200-acres are filled with activities for the whole family. The focal point is, of course, Stone Mountain, the world's largest exposed granite outcropping, the north side of which proudly displays Confederate Memorial Carving, a monument honoring Confederate President Jefferson Davis and Generals Robert E. Lee and "Stonewall" Jackson.

Families of all ages hike to the summit of the Mountain year-round for a breathtaking, panoramic view of Atlanta and its surroundings. (Our 3-year-old makes it all the way, no problem.) During every summer evening, families picnic and enjoy the one-of-a-kind, hour-long laser show on the Carving, complete with popular music, dancing laser beams and fireworks.

ATTRACTIONS. The larger of the Park's attractions include the Antebellum Plantation, a re-creation of a typical Southern plantation of the 1800s; the Antique Auto and Music Museum, a collection of vintage cars and musical instruments, including an authentic Tucker automobile; the Skylift, whose Swiss cable cars lift you to the top of Stone Mountain to see, among other things, the Theater in the Sky Movie House; the Scenic Railroad Ride around the base of the mountain; the Paddlewheel Riverboat on Stone Mountain Lake; The Grist Mill; and our family's favorite, the Wildlife Trails and Trader's Camp Petting Farm, which has over 20-acres of natural woodland filled with cougar, elk, bison and other animals that were once indigenous to Georgia. Plans for the future include rennovating the TRR Cobb House as a center of Civil War history memorabilia.

RECREATIONAL ACTIVITIES. The Ice Chalet Complex has full skating facilities and instruction. Boating, fishing, tennis, golf, hiking, camping, bicycle rentals, batting cages and minature golf are also available. The Waterworks Beach Complex includes two white-sand beaches, a tube water slide, a playground, game room, bathhouse and snack bar. And wait, there's more ... Stone Mountain Park has the city's largest and best play structure for children: a wonderful maze of slides, tunnels and climbing challenges. Adjacent to the structure is a toddler's play structure and lots of picnic tables, outhouses and a drinking fountain. A perfect place for a birthday party!

- There are restaurants, snack bars and picnic areas galore.

- Special events year-round bring families to the Park, including the Old South Celebration, Springfest, Fantastic Fourth and the famous Yellow Daisy Festival. See our chapter on "Festivals and Special Events" for a complete description of the Park's annual events.

- Stone Mountain offers an excellent Summer Day Camp Program where children can enjoy all of the attractions in the Park as well as activities in arts and crafts, nature lore, tennis, fishing, hiking, sports and swimming.

- For information on fishing, boating and the sports facilities at the Park, see our chapter on "Sports and Recreation."

Hours: The Park is open daily year-round from 6:00am-12:00midnight. Attractions and recreational facilities have varied hours, but most attractions open at 10:00am and close early evening hours during the summer, and late afternoon during the rest of the year. Call the Park for more detailed information. The Laser Show starts at 9:30pm every evening from early May through Labor Day and on special fall weekends.

Admission: There is a vehicle parking fee of $5.00 per family car or $20.00 for an annual permit. Special rates are available for buses. Admission to most of the attractions cost extra as do the recreational facilities.   Call the Park for more detailed information.

Directions: Take I-285 to U.S. 78 (The Stone Mountain Freeway) going east. The Park Exit is clearly marked.
When you enter the Park you will be given a map
and information brochure.

SWEET AUBURN DISTRICT

**AFRICAN AMERICAN PANORAMIC EXPERIENCE (THE APEX
MUSEUM),** Collections of Life & Heritage, Inc., John Wesley Dobbs
Building, 135 Auburn Avenue, N.E., Atlanta, Georgia 30303 (521-APEX).
The APEX is a permanent collection of exhibits that depicts the cultural
heritage of African-Americans and recognizes their contributions and
achievements in helping to build America. Displays include a re-creation
of the Yates & Milton Drug Store; the Paul Jones Collection of African Art,
representing aspects of African culture through media such as masks
and sculpture; a state-of-the-art trolley with a video production called
"Sweet Auburn, Street of Pride;" and special exhibits chronicling black
achievements in history and science. (Find out where the question "Is it
the real McCoy?" came from!)   The Museum also has exhibits which
honor Atlanta's black community.

A visit to the APEX is recommended for all school-age children. The
Museum is small, but full of interesting things to do and see.

*   Tours are available for groups at a reduced rate and by
reservation. We strongly recommend the tour; the guides
are excellent.

*   Handicapped access is available.

*   There are restrooms and water fountains.

Hours: Open Tuesdays through Saturdays from 10:00am-5:00pm; on Wednesdays from 10:00am-6:00pm.

Admission: Cost is $2.00 for adults, $1.00 for senior citizens and students, and children under 5 are FREE. Yearly Family Memberships are available for $50.00 and entitle you to free admission and the newsletter.

Directions: The APEX is located on Auburn Avenue about 3 blocks east of Peachtree Street in downtown Atlanta.

ATLANTA LIFE INSURANCE COMPANY, Herdon Plaza, 100 Auburn Avenue, Atlanta, Georgia 30303 (659-2100). Atlanta Life Insurance Company, the largest black-owned insurance company in the United States, was founded in 1905 by Alonzo Herndon. The atrium of the modern high-rise houses a permanent exhibit on the Herndon family and the history of Atlanta Life Insurance as well as a magnificent corporate collection of African-American art which is featured during an annual art exhibit. A quick stop into the building is worth your while before or after a trip to the APEX.

• Handicapped access and restrooms are available.

Hours: Open to the public on weekdays during regular business hours.

Admission: FREE.

Directions: The Atlanta Life Insurance building is directly across the street from the APEX Museum.

SOUTHERN CHRISTIAN LEADERSHIP CONFERENCE HEADQUARTERS, 334 Auburn Avenue, Atlanta, Georgia 30312 (522-1420). The SCLC was founded by Dr. Martin Luther King, Jr. over thirty years ago, and the organization, now headed by Reverend Joseph Lowrey, still plays an important role in the Civil Rights Movement. Stop by and take a quick tour of the headquarters and office in which Dr. King and his

Hours: Open Mondays through Fridays from 9:00am-
4:30pm.   Call ahead for an appointment if you
would like a guided tour.

Admission: FREE.

Directions: The SCLC is a few blocks east of the Atlanta Life
Insurance Company on Auburn Avenue.

THE TELEPHONE MUSEUM

Southern Bell Center, Plaza Level
675 W. Peachtree Street, N.E. • Atlanta, Georgia 30375 • 529-7334

The Telephone Museum is a rare find and highly recommended for people of all ages. This small Museum traces the history of the telephone from its earliest inception to the creation of telestar and fiber-optic technology. Your self-guided tour begins with an exhibit about Alexander Graham Bell and the significant events leading up to his invention of the telephone.   (What were the first, now famous, words spoken over a telephone?) Next, children will marvel at the collection of telephone sets dating from the beginning of World War II and an old-fashioned switch-board which some of us have only seen on television shows! (If you happen to look overhead, don't be surprised by the life-size figure of a lineman, hard at work on the top of a telephone pole!)

There is a mini-theatre with a 15-minute movie about the history of the telephone. (You can keep your younger children occupied by having them keep track of how many times they see the "jumping monk" in the presentation!) Exiting the theatre and continuing around the Museum hall, you will enter the modern age of fiber optics and digital technology. The fun hands-on displays helped all of us understand the complexities of communication a little better.

- You can park behind the Museum and go to lunch at the Varsity one block west of the Southern Building for a very unusual experience in fast-food eating. Or, you may eat at one of the several eateries on the Lower Level of the Southern Bell Center.

- Amnesty International's Human Rights Gallery is one block north of the Museum.

- Handicapped access is available, but please call ahead for directions. Restrooms and water fountains are available in the Southern Bell Center.

Hours: Open Mondays through Fridays from 11:00am-1:00pm. Closed on all legal holidays.

Admission: FREE.

Directions: The Southern Bell Center is located on West Peachtree Street at the intersection of North Avenue and behind the Fox Theatre.

UNDERGROUND ATLANTA

Between Peachtree Street and Central Avenue at Alabama Street
Atlanta, Georgia 30303 • 523-2311

The former business center of historical Atlanta is again alive with activity. Retail stores, restaurants, night clubs, street vendors and street performers populate the below-the-street levels. Above-the-ground, fountains, pedestrian promenades, Heritage Row, park benches and a soaring 10-story light tower complete this miniature city. The new Underground has become a major retail and entertainment center in Atlanta with a historical twist.

Underground offers something for everybody–beautiful retail stores for the spenders in the family, and clowns, mimes, street performers and balloons for those younger family members who expect more out of life than just shopping.

- On the Upper Alabama Street level of Underground Atlanta visit Atlanta Heritage Row, a small but unique museum.

- There is a large selection of excellent restaurants as well as a huge food court specializing in international fast food. Restaurant and club hours vary.

- A good time to visit Underground is during one of its many year-round special events. Quite a few are geared to families and children. See our chapter on "Festivals and Special Events" for more information.

- Handicapped access is available, but call ahead for directions. There are restrooms and water fountains.

Hours: Open Mondays through Saturdays from 10:00am-9:30pm, and on Sundays from 12:00noon-6:00pm. Closed on Christmas Day.

Admission: None.

Directions: Underground is located between Peachtree Street and Central Avenue at Alabama Street, next to The New Georgia Railroad and World of Coca-Cola . It is two blocks west of the Georgia State Capitol Building. Exit at the MARTA Five Points Station.

WHITE WATER PARK

250 North Cobb Parkway • Marietta, Georgia 30062 • 424-9283

White Water is the largest and most visited water park in the Southeast. Yes, it is crowded. You can expect long waits for some attractions, but they are well worth it! There are over 35 acres of water adventures, including White Water Rapids, The Atlantic Ocean (a water pool), and for the daring, the Gulf Coast Screamer, Bermuda Triangle, Bahama Bob-Slide and Black River Falls. For young children, there is Little Squirts Island with more than 25 activities, including water and tube slides and water guns. For those who want to cool off in the summer heat, this attraction can't be beat!

• The Park is adjacent to the American Adventures amusement park complex that offers rides, miniature golf, play areas and a penny arcade.

• "Dive-in" movies are featured on Wednesdays and Fridays in July.

• Only appropriate swim attire is allowed. There are locker and shower facilities.

• There are five restaurants/snack bars and gift shops. Picnicking is permitted in the parking lot area, but there are no picnic tables.

• Food, alcoholic beverages and glass containers may not be brought into the Park.

Hours: Open weekends in May, and then daily from Memorial Day through Labor Day. The Park opens at 10:00am and closes around 9:00pm with occasional late night openings.

Admission: Daily admission for adults–$14.99 plus tax, children under 48"–$9.99 plus tax, children under 4 years and seniors are FREE. Daily combo ticket with American Adventures for adults–$16.99 plus tax, and for children $11.99 plus tax. Season pass for family of 2–$79.99 plus tax, for a family of 3–$99.99 plus tax, and each additional member is $29.99 plus tax.

Directions: Take I-75 North to Exit #113, and follow signs to North Cobb Parkway and the Park. It is about 8 miles north of downtown Atlanta.

THE WORLD OF COCA-COLA PAVILION

(Next to Underground Atlanta) • 55 Martin Luther King, Jr. Drive
Atlanta, Georgia 30303 • 676-5151

Coca-Cola has erected a stunning 45,000 square-foot pavilion that offers a fascinating multi-media tour of the century-plus history of the world's favorite soft drink. Merchandise, memorabilia, interactive displays, radio and television commercials and state-of-the-art technical displays glorify Coca-Cola's influence in over 160 countries.

To enter the Pavilion you walk under an 11-ton red and white neon sign which Coca-Cola believes will become one of Atlanta's most famous landmarks. Your tour is self-guided, though there are cheerful hosts and hostesses who speak a variety of languages to answer your questions. Your one to two hour tour will take you past rare and invaluable artifacts from the archives of the company such as the original prototype for the first Coca-Cola bottle, trays, magazine ads, photographs and Dr.

Pemberton's original book describing the Coca-Cola formula–a formula that is still top secret!

The Pavilion also has a modernistic soda fountain that shoots a 20-foot stream of soft drink into your cup, unlimited samples of soft drinks from around the world, an 18-foot high Coke bottle, a simulated bottling demonstration (which one of our preschoolers thought was real) and a store honoring the Coca-Cola trademark, stocking the world's largest selection of Coca-Cola brand merchandise. You may shop at the Trade Mart for free if you choose not to take the tour.

No matter how you feel about the taste of Coke versus its rivals, or whether or not you want your children drinking soft drinks, Coke is certainly part of our pop culture; and, this attraction celebrates that in a tasteful, fun presentation.

- There is a passenger drop-off in front of the Pavilion and nearby parking decks.

- Handicapped access is available. Certain video presentations are close-captioned for the hearing impaired.

- Restrooms, water fountains, and lots of soft drinks are available.

Hours: Open Mondays through Saturdays from 10:00am-9:30pm and Sundays from 12:00noon-6:00pm. Closed Easter, Thanksgiving Day, Christmas Eve, Christmas Day and New Year's Day. Tours start at 30-minute intervals and tickets are sold for specific entrance times. Reservations can be made Mondays-Fridays from 9:00am-5:00pm by telephone by charging your credit card. There is a $2.00 additional fee per transaction.

Admission: The cost is $2.50 for adults, $2.00 for seniors, and $1.50 for children age 6-12 years and children under 6 are FREE. Admission includes complimentary soft drinks. Discounts are available for groups of 25 or more.

Directions: The Pavilion is located next to Underground
Atlanta and the New Georgia Railroad and near
the Georgia State Capitol Building. It is two
blocks from the MARTA Five Points Station.

THE WREN'S NEST

1050 Ralph David Abernathy Boulevard, S.W.
Atlanta, Georgia 30310 • 753-7735 or 753-7736

The Wren's Nest is a living tribute to Joel Chandler Harris (1848-1908),
author of the Uncle Remus tales (Br'er Rabbit and Br'er Fox). Most
importantly, it is Atlanta's main stage for the art of storytelling.

This National Historic Landmark houses the original Harris family memorabilia, books, photographs and furnishings. During your guided tour of
the Nest, you will see a slide presentation about Mr. Harris and learn how
his writing was heavily influenced by listening to his friend, Uncle Bob
Capers, a black slave who told him irresistable folktales and animal
stories. Later another slave, George Terrell, enchanted the young Joel
with more African folklore. Harris' stories, which are written in the
authentic middle Georgia dialect, tried to recapture these tales which had
been changed and refined through the many tellings. For a period of time
in the 1960s, his writings were deemed racist, but are now appreciated as
a valuable contribution to African-American history and culture.

The art of storytelling that so deeply moved Mr. Harris is perpetuated at
the Wren's Nest to the delight of children and adults alike. Members of
the Southern Order of Storytellers perform every Saturday at 2:00pm and
involve the audience in each presentation. During our visit, children were
invited on stage to play the part of various characters (prompted and
coached by the storyteller). All of the children had a marvelous time!

•   The annual Wren's Nest Fest is held in May and includes storytelling, theatrical performances, puppet shows and a parade. $2.50 includes admission to all performances and events.

- The Christmas Festival and Open House at the Wren's Nest takes place on the Sunday in December closest to Joel Chandler Harris' birthday. You can see the Nest decorated in Victorian Christmas finery, hear storytelling, school choral groups and enjoy refreshments.

- Located in the West End, Atlanta's oldest neighborhood, the Wren's Nest is featured on an Atlanta Preservation Center Walking Tour (522-4345).

- There are picnic grounds, a gift shop, restrooms, water fountains but no handicapped access.

Hours: Open Tuesdays through Saturdays from 10:00am-4:00pm, Sundays from 1:00pm-4:00pm, with the last tour conducted at 4:00pm. Closed on major holidays and Mondays.

Admission: Cost is $3.00 for adults, $2.00 for seniors and teens, $1.00 for children from age 4-12 years, and children under 4 are FREE. Group rates are available.

Directions: From I-85/75, take I-20 West to the Ashby Street exit. Turn left on Ashby Street, then a right on Gordon Street. There are signs to assist you in locating the Wren's Nest.

YELLOW RIVER GAME RANCH

4525 Highway 78 • Lilburn, Georgia 30247 • 972-6643

Along the banks of the Yellow River, sprawled over 24 wooded acres, are families of trusting deer waiting to be carressed and fed crackers from your children's hands. There are also a lot of chubby rabbits who live in Bunny Burrows, waiting to be petted and given some fresh carrots and lettuce.

Wildlife trails lead you past all sorts of animal exhibits, including buffaloes, bears, mountain lions, birds-of-prey, foxes, owls, skunks,pheasants, porcupines, ground-hogs and bobcats, to name a few. The large farm area houses cows, ponies, goats, sheep, donkeys, chickens, pigs, ducks and geese, all of whom make a lot of noise and show how pleased they are to see you and more food!

The trails are natural, the animals abundant, and the woods rustic. It is not hard to figure out why Yellow River Game Ranch is a favorite for children of all ages.

- We recommend that you bring your own snacks for the animals. Carrots, greens and crackers are favorites.

- There is a souvenir shop (try to get through it without stopping), a concession stand, a small playground, picnic areas, restroom facilities and old-fashioned mechanical horse-and-wagon rides.

- During certain months, Yellow River Game Ranch offers hayrides and a special log cabin for birthday parties.

- The paths are rustic, making handicapped and stroller access a bit difficult.

Hours: Open daily from 9:30am-6:00pm, and from Labor Day to Memorial Day from 9:30am-Dusk.

Admission: Cost is $3.50 for adults, $2.50 for children age 3-11 years, children under 3 are FREE. Discount rates apply for groups of 15 or more children.

Directions: Take I-285 to US 78 and go east toward Stone Mountain. Stay on US 78 past the Stone Mountain Park exit for 4 traffic lights. The Farm will be on your left.

ZOO ATLANTA

800 Cherokee Avenue, S.E. • Atlanta, Georgia 30315 • 624-5678

You never know which animal will be the "star" of your next visit to Zoo Atlanta. The Zoo is undergoing a multi-million dollar redevelopment program and every visit brings more new animals and exhibits, in all natural environment habitats. Everything is being done right here, and the Zoo is a real delight to visit.

The newest exhibits open at Zoo Atlanta are The Ford African Rain Forest featuring Willie B. and the Yerkes gorilla families housed in a re-creation of a West African tropical rain forest; Masai Mara, a re-creation of the savannahs of Kenya and Tanzania starring giraffes, ostriches, gazelles, lions, zebras, impalas, East African birds and black rhinos; the Orangutans of Ketambe, an Indonesian rain-forest habitat filled with families of high-climbing orangutans; the Elephant Show, with Starlett, Victoria and Zambezi showing-off their special tricks; the Wildlife Show, featuring endangered species, birds of prey and other small animals; the Children's Railroad Train circling the Children's Zoo area; Flamingo Plaza, where you can be sure to see baby Pink Chilean flamingos; and, the Sumatran

Tiger exhibit, displaying two rare cats. The newest exhibit at the Zoo is the Small African Primate Center. And don't forget the Reptile House, one of the largest reptile collection in the United States!

Exhibits for the future include The Arctic Coast and Sea Lion Cove which will feature polar bears, sea lions and birds; the Okefenokee Swamp/ Georgia Coast displaying wolves, bears, alligators, otters and eagles; International Farms, which will be a petting farm of domestic animals from around the world; and, South American Tropics, a jungle addition to the Reptile House showcasing anteaters, tamarins, sloths and other animals from the Amazon. Thank you Friends of Zoo Atlanta for a job well done. Year-after-year, this attraction has been voted #1 in our household.

- Times for the Elephant Show, Wildlife Show and feeding of the sea lions and gorillas vary. Call ahead as you don't want to miss these events.

- Zoo Atlanta sponsors all sorts of special events throughout the year for children. See our chapter on "Festivals and Special Events" for information about the annual events. Also, be sure to keep your eyes open for many other special days offered each year.

- The Zoo has a large selection of educational programs, classes, workshops and summer camp programs for children. "Night Crawlers," a great overnight program includes behind-the-scenes tours, wildlife films, a night hike and fun and games. "Summer Safari Day Camp" also includes behind-the-scene visits as well as hands-on wild encounters with small animals, art and other activities.

- "Project Discovery," for groups only, consists of a visit to the Zoo and introduces children to the zoo world using live animals, artifacts and suplemental materials. Other programs for schools include several unusual "Wildlife Shows" and the "Zoomobile" which will visit preschools as well as schools for older children.

- Concession stands and snack bars are plentiful as are restroom facilities and water fountains.

- Handicapped access is available.

- Strollers are available for rental at a cost of $2.00/day with a refundable $3.00 deposit.

- The Zoo has an attractive gift shop filled with T-shirts, stuffed animals, small animal items and beautiful jewelry, pottery and woodcarvings from Africa.

Hours: Open weekdays from 10:00am-5:00pm and on weekends from 10:00-6:00pm during daylight savings time. Closed on New Year's Day, Martin Luther King, Jr. Day, Thanksgiving Day and Christmas Day.

Admission: The cost is is $6.75 for adults, $4.00 for children age 3-11 years, and children 2 and under are FREE. Seniors pay $5.75 on weekdays. Yearly Family Memberships cost $45.00 and entitle you to free admission and many other benefits. Discount rates for groups are available. The ZooTrain ride costs $1.00 per person.

Directions: Take I-20 to the Boulevard exit (Exit #26), one exit east of I-85/75. Follow signs to Grant Park, Zoo Atlanta and The Cyclorama. Parking is free.

3. Tidbits: More Good Things To Do

T his chapter includes smaller, sometimes more unusual places to go with children than described in the previous chapter. This does not mean that outings to these locations will be any less important or enjoyable for your family. Quite the contrary. Because of the uniqueness of some of these places and ideas, you may discover some real treasures. And, best of all, most of the activities in this chapter are FREE or of nominal cost! We recommend that you look through this chapter, experiment and visit some of the unusual places that we describe.

ECOLOGY, NATURE, SCIENCE, HISTORY AND POLITICS

Many, many places to go with children on the topics of ecology, nature, science, history and politics are described in our chapter "Places To Go." What is different about this section is that it contains tidbits of information on places to take children that few people know about, or that sometimes slip parents' minds or that, without this information, you may not have deemed worth a visit at all. Some places and activities are for children of any age, such as Earth Day events, The Nature Company and nursery visits. Other places are for the more sophisticated or older child, such as Amnesty International and Rhodes Hall. Peruse these listings, for we are certain there are many places here your family will want to visit!

——— ECOLOGY, NATURE AND SCIENCE ———

ATLANTA CITY GREENHOUSES
1139 North Avenue (Across from Maddox Park)
Atlanta, Georgia 30318 • 658-7919

Atlanta's new greenhouse facility grows plants for the City's parks. *Hours:* 7:00am-3:30pm on weekdays for small groups; larger groups by appointment only. These directions may be helpful: Take Northside Drive to Bankhead. Past Ashbury Street go under the trestle. Take a left under the trestle and the loop goes around the park. Take the road down to the right. You might want to call before you go–rumor has it, they may be closing soon. FREE.

BRADLEY OBSERVATORY AND PLANETARIUM
Agnes Scott College
East Hancock Street and South Candler Street
Decatur, Georgia 30030 • 371-6294

Bradley Observatory is open to the public on the first Friday of every month during the academic year at 8:00pm. There is a brief lecture and a planetarium show, after which anyone may gaze through the telescopes. The program is geared for children 8 years and older and adults. Be sure to call ahead as the schedule is subject to change. FREE.

BUFORD TROUT HATCHERY
Trout Place Road • Buford, Georgia 30518
404/889-1150

This well-stocked fish hatchery is open for families to visit, and between the hours of 8:30am and 4:30pm someone will be there to answer your questions. Buford has a brood stock but also receives 3-inch fingerlings from federal hatcheries to raise to adults. The fish are released into the Chattahoochee when they are about 10-inches long. Approximately 190,000 trout are released each season. The hatchery is located on Highway 20 between Cumming and Buford. Coming from Buford, cross over the river, go about 1.3 miles to Pruitt Road and take a right, then take the next turn onto Trout Place Road. FREE.

BUSH MOUNTAIN OUTDOOR ACTIVITY CENTER
1442 Richland Road, S.W.
Atlanta, Georgia 30310 • 752-5385

Only 3 miles from downtown Atlanta, the Outdoor Activity Center is aptly named "Atlanta's Forest in the City," as it offers 3 miles of hiking trails running through a 26-acre Piedmont forest. The Center offers guided Nature walks, a discovery learning room, a traveling nature show, workshops, adventure teaching gardens, puppet shows, scout programs, Christmas in the Woods, Arbor Day educational programs, birthday parties, birdseed sales, a nature shop, a picnic and playground area, a treehouse classroom and, its newest addition, Naturescapes, an outdoor environmental learn-and-play sculpture designed to teach children about different habitats in the forest community. Groundbreaking has begun for a new nature center scheduled to open in early 1992. *Hours*: Mondays-Fridays from 9:00am-4:00pm or by appointment. The park is FREE, but there are small fees for the tours, traveling nature shows and discovery craft projects.

COMPUTER SCIENCE AND ACADEMIC ACHIEVEMENT

Some of the Atlanta colleges and universities offer programs for children in computer sciences and advanced academic skills. *DeKalb College Continuing Education*, 3251 Panthersville Road, Decatur, Georgia 30034 (244-5050). DeKalb College offers summer classes introducing children to computer sciences. *Emory University Tennis and Computer Sports Camp*, Woodruff Physical Education Center, Emory University, Atlanta, Georgia 30322 (972-8241 or 727-6545). Emory's summer program offers children age 8-17 years an opportunity to learn and improve their computer and tennis skills. Session instruction is designed for a child's individual needs, and courses include Introduction to the Computer, Caring for the Computer, Computer Programming and Enhancement of Verbal Skills and Math Skills Utilizing Simulation Games. *Georgia Institute of Technology*, Academic Affairs, 225 North Avenue, Atlanta, Georgia 30332 (894-8994). Georgia State offers "Summerscape," an excellent summer science and computer enrichment program for rising 7th and 8th graders. *Georgia State University Saturday School for Scholars and Leaders*, Department of Early Childhood Education, 917 Urban Life Center, University Plaza, Atlanta, Georgia 30303 (651-2840 or 651-2581). Saturday School for Scholars and Leaders is an extensive program of extracurricular topics for gifted children offered year-round. On five consecutive Saturdays, "gifted" children (having an IQ of 120 or above or results in school indicating a 90th percentile or higher ranking on a standardized achievement test) attending kindergarten through 12th grade are eligible to attend. Courses encompass a wide range of subjects - computer, sciences, math, architecture, physiology, humanities, creative writing, journalism, art, music, dramatics, movement, ballet and foreign languages. There is also a preschool program. ***Kennesaw College**, Division of Continuing Education, Professional Development and Extension, P.O. Box 444, Marietta, Georgia (4236765). Year-round, Kennesaw College offers workshops promoting study skills and classes in computer proficiency. During the summer, the College offers a dazzling array of summer camp programs in computers, rockets, chisanbop, music, foreign languages and cultures, calligraphy, business, visual arts, nature, sports, science, mythical monsters and superheroes.

EARTH DAY

Earth Day has become a very important time of year in Atlanta as well as elsewhere in the country. Participating in Earth Day events, whether attending festivals or planting a seed in your yard, is a yearly lesson for children in the possiblities of people working together to better the human condition. It is an opportunity to discuss ecological issues of pollution (air, water, sound, visual), to discuss conservation and recycling, to get involved in politics by writing to government representatives and companies, to study about endangered species, hazardous products and toxic wastes, pesticides, alternative forms of energy, the destruction of rain forests, and acid rain. The subjects and educational discussions and projects your family can get involved in are endless. Earth Day events are advertised well in advance. Look in the *Atlanta Journal and Constitution*, especially the *Weekend* section, and *Youth View* and *Creative Loafing*. Newsletters from your library and places of interest, such as the Atlanta Botanical Garden, Chattahoochee Nature Center, Fernbank Science Center, SciTrek, Zoo Atlanta and participating book stores, will all detail their special events.

GEORGIA DEPARTMENT OF NATURAL RESOURCES
205 Butler Street, S.E. • Suite 1352
Atlanta, Georgia 30334 • 656-3530

The Georgia Department of Natural Resources sponsors numerous special events, workshops and programs at all of the Georgia State Parks and Historic Sites. Programs include hiking and backpacking activities, nongame and wildlife classes, music and dance, folk skills and living history demonstrations, fishing, wildflower programs, canoe excursions, Native American activities and holiday programs. Send away for the Department's brochure entitled *GEORGIA STATE PARKS AND HIS-TORIC SITES - SPECIAL EVENTS* which provides a comprehensive list of the year's scheduled activities.

HARD LABOR CREEK OBSERVATORY
Hard Labor Creek Park
Rutledge, Georgia • 404/557-2863

Georgia State University opened this observatory in Hard Labor Creek Park which is about an hour west of Atlanta (off I-20 near Madison). The observatory is open to the public during evenings about once a month. Please call the Observatory to find out the date of the next open house.

MONASTERY OF THE HOLY SPIRIT
Highway 212
Conyers, Georgia 30207 • 483-8705

If serenity is what you seek, take your family on a sojourn to this monastery set in beautiful natural surroundings. You may visit unannounced or you may call ahead to arrange a group tour which includes a slide presentation and time at the bookstore and gift shop. A special treat is the bread that is baked on the premises every Thursday and sold at the gift shop all week long until sold out. The monks suggest you bring a sack lunch (minus the bread, of course) and spend an afternoon visiting the monastery and picnicking by the lake.

THE NATURE COMPANY
Lenox Square Mall Shopping Center
3393 Peachtree Road
Atlanta, Georgia 30326 • 231-9252

Part of a nation-wide chain, this store has many items of interest to children as well as adults. Children are fascinated by the stunning museum-like displays and science toys (some of which may be touched) all over the store. For example, in the back of the store are drawers full of rock and mineral specimens for sale. A sign encourages you to open the drawers and look. Other items include magnifying glasses, puzzles, posters, jewelry and bug collecting kits, and the children's science book section is tremendous. The Nature Company is a fun and interesting place to go, especially on a rainy day when you need a special indoor activity. Also, keep this store in mind when you need to buy a child a special birthday gift. The store offers year-round workshops for children and a special Summer Nature Series for preschoolers. *Hours*: 10:00am-9:30pm, Monday-Saturday; 12:30pm-5:30pm, Sunday.

NURSERIES

Even without spending a cent, nurseries can be visited and enjoyed for their displays of outdoor seasonal plants and interesting houseplant varieties. Visit at least once each season (not just springtime!) to get a sense of what grows in this part of the world, with our kind of climate. For less than one dollar per child, seeds may be purchased to plant indoors or out for an individual science lesson. Toddlers can plant a seed in a glass between a wet paper towel and the inside of the glass and watch the roots and stem grow. Older children can choose a particular plant they like best and go to the library to learn more about it. Develop a project by keeping a journal, identifying parts of the plant, or describing the many uses of the plant. Planning a serious flower or vegetable garden, or growing specialty plants such as Bonsai, takes many visits to nurseries and libraries to do a good job. Just go for a spontaneous visit when your family needs something to do together. There is something for everyone at a nursery.

PANOLA MOUNTAIN STATE PARK
2600 Highway 155, S.W.
Stockbridge, Georgia 30281 • 389-7801

Located 18 miles southeast of Atlanta off of I-20, this 100-acre granite monadnock is a beautiful conservation park sheltering rare plants and animals. It has a picnic area and nature center with interpretive exhibits that young children enjoy. There are six miles of hiking trails, but bicycling is not permitted. Saturdays and Sundays throughout the summer, there are films, a slide show, and/or storytelling related to nature. Special early bird and moonlight walks are scheduled year-round as are nature programs, workshops and demonstrations on such diverse topics as wildflowers, birds of prey, bats and mushrooms. The hikes are FREE, as are most of the other programs. The Park occasionally runs a summer "Environmental Discovery Program" for children. *Park Hours*: 7:00am to dark. *Interpretive Center Hours*: 10:00am-6:00pm, Monday-Friday; 10:00pm-4:00pm, Saturday, and 1:00pm-5:00pm, Sunday. Closed Mondays except for major holidays. FREE.

RECYCLING

Surely there is no longer anyone left who needs to be convinced that recycling is a good thing, even a necessary thing. Everyone knows recycling conserves natural resources, landfill space and energy, generates revenues, and enhances the quality of the environment. But it can be a bit of a bother to do. Fortunately, County governments are increasing their curbside recycling, local schools have paper drives, many popular locales (such as Your DeKalb Farmer's Market) have bins, and companies such as Mindis Recycling have recycling centers around town. Also visit Mindis Mart (973-2312) in Marietta, which pays for recycled items. Drive up and helpers will remove your recyclables. Walk in the unique store which offers games, posters, stationery, garden supplies, T-shirts and other items with a recycling theme. Children really enjoy participating in recycling. My son loves taking his red wagon to the neighbors to collect their newspapers. Every little bit helps and we feel better when we do it. Above all, we are teaching our children to care, and to care is to take an active role. The Sierra Club Atlanta Group has a comprehensive publication, *Recycling Directory for the Extended Atlanta Metropolitan*

Area, that lists recyling places by area, notes what kinds of materials they accept and when. The book is available at most area book stores and costs $2.00.

W.H. REYNOLDS MEMORIAL NATURE PRESERVE
5665 Reynolds Road
Morrow, Georgia 30260 • 961-9257

This 120-acre preserve is a fine place to go for a short hike in the forest among ponds and streams. Four miles of trails begin and end at the Visitor's Center, ensuring that no one can get lost! The Center also houses an interpretive nature exhibit and is the site of many interesting nature classes for children and families throughout the year. There are two large picnicking areas, and it is run by the Clayton County Department of Parks and Recreation. _Preserve Hours_: 8:30am to dark. _Visitor's Center Hours:_ 8:30am-5:30pm, Monday-Friday; 11:00am-3:00pm, Saturday; 1:00pm-5:00pm, Sunday. Admission is FREE.

SOUTHFACE ENERGY INSTITUTE
158 Moreland Avenue, N.E.
Atlanta, Georgia 30307
Mailing address:
P.O. Box 5506, Atlanta, Georgia 30307 • 525-7657

This institute is a non-profit public interest group that has promoted renewable energy resources through education and research of alternative technologies for over a decade. Your family can take a very interesting self-guided tour through their Southface Alternative Energy Center and see such innovations as toilets that dramatically reduce water usage, special insulated window coverings ("window quilt"), ellipsoidal reflector lamps and occupancy sensors that automatically turn on or off a light when someone enters or leaves a room. There is always someone available to answer your questions, plus a sizeable library for public use. There are numerous free energy publications of interest to adults and to upper elementary kids who might be doing a special project in this field. _Hours_: 9:30am-5:30pm, Monday-Friday. FREE.

SPACE CAMPS

Challengers Club Space Camp, Dr. Ronald E. McNair Foundation, P.O. Box 54392, Atlanta, Georgia 30308 (872-2333). Children age 10-14 years can sign on as one of the space camp crew for Challengers Club Space Camp which is a five day summer program offering children hands-on exposure to space and science education. The program may include a field trip to the U.S. Space Center in Hunstville, aerospace experiments at Six Flags Amusement Park, space demonstrations at SciTrek, meetings with NASA scientists, rocket building workshops or an overview of careers in space. ***U.S. Space Camp**, P.O. Box 1680, Huntsville, Alabama 35807 (205/837-3400) (For Reservations: 1/800/63SPACE). Although not local, we could not resist including this listing! Year-round, children from all over the world can attend a one-week program at U.S. Space Camp to learn how they can become involved in science and space technology. Hands-on experiences in rocket propulsion, spacesuits, simulated space walks, astronaut training activities and Space Shuttle mission simulations are all a part of the program. In Alabama, camp is offered for children in grades 4-6; in Florida, camp is offered for children in grades 4-7. Older children in grades 7-12 can attend U.S. Space Academy and the Aviation Challenge which offer more advanced programs. There is also an Adult Space Academy and a special Teacher Program. Special parent/child sessions are now available on certain holiday weekends for children age 6-12 years. Call for details and costs.

SWEETWATER CREEK STATE CONSERVATION PARK
Lithia Springs, Georgia • 944-1700
Mailing address:
P.O. Box 816, Lithia Springs, Georgia 30057

Located in Douglas County about 25 minutes from Atlanta, Sweetwater Creek is a beautiful, lush forest with lakes, streams and a reservoir. You can spend the better part of a day hiking on five miles of trails, picnicking in one of many picnic shelters, boating, fishing, or playing in one of the playgrounds. Not only is this vast area conserved for its natural resources, but it is also a site of historical significance: there are ruins of the New Manchester Manufacturing Company, a textile factory burned by Sherman's troops during the Civil War. Programs on nature, history and boating safety as well as other special events are offered throughout the year, as well as a Summer Jr. Ranger camp and an annual New Manchester Days Celebration in July. Most activities are FREE, but boat rentals are available for a fee. *Hours*: 7:00am-10:00pm daily. Park admission is FREE.

CATOR WOOLFORD MEMORIAL GARDEN
1815 South Ponce de Leon
Atlanta, Georgia 30307 • 377-3836

Located on the grounds of **REACH, INC.** (formerly the Cerebral Palsy Center), this beautiful garden is open to the public until dark each day. Through a cooperative effort between REACH, Inc. and Fernbank Science Center, high school students enrolled in a vocational horticulture program (Occupational Education Center-Central campus) take meticulous care of the garden, the stream, and the paths and plant all of the flowering bulbs and plants. If your family would like to take a quiet stroll through a beautiful garden, try this one. FREE.

━━━━━ HISTORY and POLITICS ━━━━━

In addition to the larger institutions we discussed elsewhere in this book related to history and politics that appeal to a mass audience, there are more esoteric places you might be interested in.

AMNESTY INTERNATIONAL /
HUMAN RIGHTS GALLERY OF ATLANTA
740 W. Peachtree Street, N.W.
Atlanta, Georgia 30308 • 876-5661

Amnesty International's gallery addresses the issue of human rights on an international level. Past exhibits focused on the failed revolution at Tiananmen Square and the dilemma of refugees world-wide. Call to find out what the current exhibit is. *Hours*: 9:00am-4:00pm, Monday-Friday. FREE.

ATLANTA JOURNAL AND CONSTITUTION
72 Marietta Street
Atlanta, Georgia 30303 • 526-5286

The lobby of the Atlanta Journal and Constitution has a small showcase of historic newspaper front pages; a special display featuring Ralph McGill, Margaret Mitchell and other individuals who have worked on the newspaper; and a large linotype machine. The exhibits are small and a bit out-dated, but a quick stop by the newspaper lobby if you are already in the neighborhood would be worth your while. (The newspaper is next door to the Federal Reserve Bank's Monetary Museum and down the street from the CNN Center). *Hours*: 8:00am-5:00pm, Monday-Friday. FREE.

ATLANTA PRESERVATION CENTER TOURS
84 Peachtree Street, N.W.
The Flatiron Building, Suite 401
Atlanta, Georgia 30303 • 522-4345

The Atlanta Preservation Center is a non-profit association dedicated to promoting historic preservation in Atlanta through advocacy and education. Members provide assistance to people interested in preserving historical buildings and neighborhoods. The Center has a newsletter, a speaker's bureau and conducts walking tours of Atlanta as a means of increasing public awareness of and appreciation for the City's architectural heritage. Most of the tours offered by the Center are probably too long and detailed for young children to enjoy; however, the year-round guided tour of the Fox Theatre, an exotic Moorish and Egyptian revival movie palace, would be enjoyed by older children. For information on and a description of the Fox Theatre tour, see **FOX THEATRE** in our chapter called "Places To Go." Other tours offered by the Preservation Center are the Historic Downtown Tour, Inman Park Tour, Oakland Cemetery Tour, Underground and Capitol Area Tour, and West End and Wren's Nest Tour. These tours are only offered during the months of April through November. The cost of the tours is $4.00 for adults and $2.00 for children. The Center offers a unique "Heritage Education" program for elementary school children. Call the Center for current information on this program and other new ones being developed.

COBB COUNTY YOUTH MUSEUM
649 Cheatham Hill Drive, S.W.
Marietta, Georgia 30064 • 427-2563

The Cobb County Youth Museum is unlike traditional museums where children can only walk by exhibits. Here, children actually get to participate in the Museum's exhibits by dressing in costume, using period props, and interacting with the Museum's staff in skits, puppet shows, parades and narrations centering on the exhibit's theme. For example, a recent program was called "Quest," which used skits, costumes, narration and a puppet show to highlight the accomplishments of Clara Barton and Jacques Costeau. Children had an opportunity to learn all about government in this unusual setting. The Museum is primarily for groups of school children from the second grade and up, but it is open to the public on a limited basis. _Hours_: Tours are open to the public on Mondays through Fridays at 9:30am and 11:00am, mid-June through mid-July and on the first Sundays of October, Novemb er, March, April, May and June. Phone for exact dates and times. School tours are offered Mondays through Fridays from 8:30am-2:00pm during the school year. Teachers must schedule a visit in advance. A fee is charged for school groups. Admission is FREE to the general public. (The Museum is located in the Cheatham Hill section of Kennesaw Mountain National Battlefield Park.)

FORT PEACHTREE
2630 Ridgewood Road, N.W.
Chattahoochee Water Treatment Plant Facility
Atlanta, Georgia 30318 • 355-8229

Fort Peachtree, located to the rear of the property of the Chattahoochee Water Treatment Plant, is a replica of the original fort built by the British on the shores of the Chattahoochee River as the first non-Indian establishment in Georgia. The original "Fort Peach Tree" served as a stronghold against the Creek Indians, and was also a strategically located trading post and ferry landing on the river. All that remains now is this replica of the original fort. (There are no exhibits, artifacts or documents other than two signs explaining the historical significance of the site). Down the road from the Fort is a pretty picnic area near the shores of the Chattahoochee. Although it would be difficult to expect a child to be able to imagine the original Fort Peachtree or the historical significance of the site, it is an unusual site for a picnic or fishing expedition. (There are no restroom facilities. Finding the Fort is quite difficult, so be sure to call ahead for directions.) *Hours*: 8:00am-4:00pm, Monday- Friday. FREE.

GEORGIA DEPARTMENT OF ARCHIVES AND HISTORY
330 Capitol Avenue, S.E.
Atlanta, Georgia 30334 • 656-2350

This striking building, a 17-story, windowless "ice cube" of marble, houses official records, state documents, census data, photographs, prints and maps dating from 1733. There is not much here for the casual sightseer, but some of the displays on the main floor might be of interest to older children such as the maps on permanent display and occasional special exhibits on geneology. Tours by appointment. *Hours*: 8:00am-4:30pm, Monday-Friday; 9:30am-3:00pm, Saturday. FREE.

HAPEVILLE DEPOT MUSEUM
620 S. Central Avenue
Hapeville, Georgia 30354 • 669-2175

Housed in Hapeville's rennovated train depot (originally built in 1890), the Hapeville Depot Museum is small and jam-packed with memorabilia from the 1900's. Exhibits highlight the role of airplanes, cars and trains in Hapeville's history. (Hartsfield Airport is nearby, the Ford Assembly Plant in Hapeville opened in 1947, and the Museum is in the old train depot.) A whole room of the Museum is devoted to a Model Railroad. Installed by the Hapeville Central Model Railroad Club, it has about 400 feet of track with tiny trains running through a village and mountains. *Hours*: 11:00am-3:00pm, Tuesday-Friday; 1:00pm-4:00pm, Sunday. FREE.

RHODES HALL
Georgia Trust for Historic Preservation
1516 Peachtree Street, N.W.
Atlanta, Georgia 30309 • 881-9980

Rhodes Hall is a Victorian structure, built in the Romanesque Revival style. Constructed in 1903 as a home for the Rhodes family, the design was inspired by Rhineland castles. It is currently owned by the State of Georgia and is the headquarters for the Georgia Trust for Historic Preservation. In the spring of 1990, restoration began with the installation of the original carved mahogany staircase and stained glass windows. Nine Tiffany glass panels depict the "Rise and Fall of the Confederacy." _Hours:_ 11:00am-4:00pm, Monday-Friday. _Cost:_ $2.00/adult; 50¢ per child.

THE SANDY SPRINGS HISTORIC SITE
6075 Sandy Springs Circle
Sandy Springs, Georgia 30328 • 851-9111

A visit to the Sandy Springs Historic Site includes a very informative guided tour of the Williams-Payne House (Learn where the expression "Sleep tight" came from!), a restored 19th-century Sandy Springs farmhouse, furnished in period antiques, and an opportunity to view an authentic local 1860's fully restored milk house, a 19th-century "privy," and the natural springs for which Sandy Springs is named. The Historic Site is also the location for the annual fall Sandy Springs Festival featuring folk craft demonstrations, music, vintage car shows and other living history activities. _Hours:_ 10:00am-4:00pm, Mondays-Fridays. _Cost:_ $2.00/ adult; $1.00 children 12-18 years, students and senior citizens. Children under 12 are FREE.

ZACHOR HOLOCAUST CENTER
Jewish Community Center-Lower Level
1745 Peachtree Street, N.E.
Atlanta, Georgia 30309 • 873-1661

The Center houses a permanent exhibit of Holocaust history, photography and survivor's memorabilia. _Hours:_ There are regularly scheduled hours, including on Sundays, but because the Museum is staffed by volunteers, coverage is not always certain. We suggest you phone ahead to make an appointment. FREE.

```
┌─────────────────────────────────────────┐
│            FARMERS MARKETS                │
│                  &                        │
│            PICK  YOUR OWN                  │
└─────────────────────────────────────────┘
```

FARMERS MARKETS

Food shopping is a weekly chore that cannot be avoided. We can try to add a little spice to the routines by frequenting the different grocery stores in our neighborhood, but even so, children (and parents, too), still get bored. Luckily, Atlanta offers a variety of alternatives to ordinary super-market shopping that children and families will find fun, and in certain instances, educational.

THE ATLANTA STATE FARMERS MARKET
16 Forest Parkway
Forest Park, Georgia 30050 • 366-6910

The Atlanta State Farmers Market is located about 15 minutes south of downtown Atlanta in Forest Park (off I-75). It is the second largest wholesale market for fruits and vegetables in the United States. The huge complex is filled with farmer's produce, plants, shrubbery and local specialties such as honey, relishes, pickled vegetables and peanuts. During the summer and fall, the complex is filled with eye-catching displays of seasonal produce. During the winter months, the market sells Christmas trees and other holiday greenery. The market also houses an egg processing plant, a hamper house stocked with crates and baskets, and a cannery. *Hours:* The complex is open 24-hours a day, every day of the week, but the majority of the farmers' booths are set up and open for business from 8:00am-5:00pm. On site is a Davis Brother's Cafeteria which serves up southern style meals using produce purchased from the market. Stop by for a country style breakfast or a meal of fresh vegetables, fruits, meats and southern desserts–a fitting end to your shopping. The cafeteria is open daily from 6:00am-8:30pm. Call 366-7414 for more information.

SWEET AUBURN CURB MARKET/
THE ATLANTA MUNICIPAL MARKET
209 Edgewood Avenue
Atlanta, Georgia 30303 • 659-1665

The newly rennovated Atlanta Municipal Market is located near the Martin Luther King, Jr. Historical District and Grady Hospital. This old-fashioned market operates in the same manner as when it first opened in 1923, and it is filled with vendors selling massive quanitites of meat, fresh fruit and vegetables, as well as a selection of cheese and grocery items. For your first visit, we recommend that you not expect to do much food shopping - this market's rustic style may not appeal to everyone. Just plan on looking around at the displays and getting used to the unique atmosphere. Even if you decide not to buy any food at the market, we guarantee you that your children will nevertheless long remember the visit. *Hours*: 8:00am-5:45pm, Monday-Thursday; 8:00am-6:45pm, Friday and Saturday.

YOUR DEKALB FARMERS MARKET
3000 E. Ponce de Leon Avenue
Decatur, Georgia • 377-6400

Your DeKalb Farmers Market is a small city unto itself filled with fresh meats, fish, produce, cheeses, flowers, spices, dairy products, baked goods, deli items, coffees, and if that weren't enough, ethnic foods, nuts, dried fruit, wine, beer and gourmet groceries. Each department is filled with eye-opening selections of unusual and varied products–all reasonably priced. Free samples of seasonal fruit, baked goods, sparkling juices and chunks of cheese are available for sampling, but if you still feel hungry, you can visit the snack area which features fresh baked goods, samosas and piping hot coffee. No matter how sophisticated your tastes, you can be sure that you will find something in the market that you have never eaten before—Be brave — experiment and eat well! Bring sweaters for the children–the market is chilly! *Hours*: 10:00am-9:00pm, Monday-Friday; and 9:00am-9:00pm Saturday and Sunday.

HARRY'S FARMERS MARKET
1180 Upper Hembree Road
Roswell, Georgia 30076 • 664-6300

Now that Harry's Farmers Market is open, the northern suburbs have a fantastic farmers market of their own. Similar to Your DeKalb Farmers Market, Harry's stocks a large selection of farm fresh produce, meats, fish, cheese, flowers, spices, dairy products, coffees, dried fruits and nuts, all reasonably priced. Unlike the DeKalb market, it does not have as large a selection of ethnic and gourmet foods. But nowhere in Atlanta will you find a better bakery–the selection and variety of the market's baked goods will titillate your palate. The delicatessen in the market is well worth the trip to Roswellespecially for you Northerners who are wondering where you can find a great selection of Kosher deli meat, pickles, Passover foods and other delicacy items! Less crowded and more spacious, Harry's offers an equal alternative to Your DeKalb Farmers Market. To make your summer shopping with your out-of-school kids more fun, Harry's celebrates its July birthday with two weeks of free daily activities for children. Enjoy jugglers, face painting, pie-eating contests, magicians, a stilt walker, and much more! *Hours*: 9:00am-8:00pm, Monday-Thursday; 9:00am-9:00pm, Friday; 9:00am-8:00pm, Saturday; 10:00am-7:00pm, Sunday.

NORTH FULTON COOPERATIVE MARKETS
730-7000

Purchase fresh produce at tailgate markets operated through the North Fulton Cooperative Extension Service on Tuesdays, Thursdays and Saturdays from 7:00am-12noon during the summer months. Locations are the Roswell Mall parking lot, Mount Vernon Presbyterian Church in Sandy Springs, and Wills Park Recreation Center in Alpharetta.

Look out for: Two new large farmers markets are scheduled to open in Gwinnett County in 1992 - **Fresh Market Festival** at I-85 and Steve Reynolds Boulevard and **Harry's Farmers Market** at Satellite Boulevard in Duluth.

GEORGIA CERTIFIED FARM MARKETS
Georgia Farm Bureau Federation, Commodity Department
P.O. Box 7068
Macon, Georgia 31298 • 912/474-8411

For those who may want to take a ride in the country, venturing out beyond the metro Atlanta area, you can write to the Georgia Farm Bureau Federation, at the address above, for a copy of their brochure called *GEORGIA CERTIFIED FARM MARKETS*. The brochure lists over 40 retail farm markets in Georgia certified by the Bureau, and for each farm provides directions, telephone numbers, months of operation and, most importantly, a description of the seasonal produce available at the farm. The descriptions are mouth-watering–peaches, plums, berries, apples, watermelons, butter beans, collards, Vidalia onions, pecans, honey, relish, peanuts, jams, jellies, pumpkins, syrup, corn, gourds, fried pies, firewood, cured hams and bacons, muscadine grapes, ciders, dairy products, sausages, Christmas trees, candies, hanging baskets, country crafts, quilts, soaps–take your pick!

———— PICK YOUR OWN FOOD ————

Wouldn't it be wonderful if we all had the time and space to have our own gardens in the backyard filled with our favorite seasonal produce? And while we're dreaming, let's throw in a few fruit trees, berry patches and an herb garden. Our children could run outside and in a few minutes be back with everything we'd need for the evening dinner. Well, we may not be able to fulfill our fantasies, but we are lucky to have farmers who allow us, for a few hours (and a few bucks), to pretend their farms are our own and welcome us to pick vegetables, fruit and berries.

Equally as much fun as the gathering of food is deciding as a family what foods to cook and letting the children participate in the preparation. Not only will children of all ages develop a deeper understanding and appreciation of farming and where food really comes from, but the lesson of *The Little Red Hen* will be most clearly understood!

•   The brochure published by the Georgia Farm Bureau Federation called *GEORGIA CERTIFIED FARM MARKETS* (described above) also lists farms that are "PYO"–Pick Your Own.

LAKE LAURA GARDENS, Burnt Hickory Road, Marietta, Georgia (427-1774). Lake Laura Gardens is a small garden that is perfect for preschoolers and younger children, complete with dog, cats and hammock. Families may wander about and pick seasonal vegetables, flowers, fruits, herbs and berries. And, for the patient child, there is also a small trout pond stocked with large fish. Call for hours and directions.

FARMERS AND CONSUMERS MARKET BULLETIN. The *Farmers and Consumers Market Bulletin* is a weekly publication of the Georgia Department of Agriculture. Certain of its summer and fall issues list the names, addresses, telephone numbers and information about farms that allow you to "Pick Your Own" produce. The main branch of your library system should have a copy of the Bulletin or you can call the Department of Agriculture (656-3722) which will be glad to send you a FREE copy. Below is a summary of the farms often listed in the May, July, and August issues of the Bulletin which are within an hour and a half drive from the metro-Atlanta area.

REMEMBER - Always call ahead to find out:

- **What crop is in season**
- **The availability of the produce**
- **Picking times**
- **If you will need to provide your own containers**
- **Cost**
- **Detailed directions**
- **Bathroom facilities**

BARTOW COUNTY

C.E. Morrison, Kingston, Georgia (404/336-5708). Corn, peas, beans, okra and tomatoes are available for picking.

Glen Cove Nursery, 1/4 north of Etowah Indian Mounds, Cartersville, Georgia (404/386-0207 or 404/386-3656). This farm is a great one to visit in conjunction with a trip to the Etowah Indian Mounds and Museum. The farm's specialty is raspberries and blackberries.

CHEROKEE COUNTY

Aaron & Pat McLain, 18040 Union Hill Road, Alpharetta (475-6836). Blueberries are available for picking in the months of July and August. Open 8:00am-Dark on Tuesday, Thursday, Saturday and Sunday. Bring your own containers.

Berry Patch Farms, 786 Arnold Mill Road, Woodstock (926-0561). The owners of this Certified Farm say they do not use any chemical spray on their berry plants so you may eat as you go without concern. They are really very nice to children and encourage them to both pick and eat. Besides seasonal berries, they also have apples, pumpkins and Christmas trees. Picnicking is available nearby. Open 8:00am-Dark, Tuesday-Sunday. Containers provided.

Cagle's Milk House, Rt. 12, Box 362, Stringer Road, Canton (404/345-5591). Dairy products are produced and processed here. Open Monday-Friday, 9:00am-5:30pm; Saturdays, 10:00am-2:00pm year-round.

Dan Merrefield, Route 13, Canton (404/479-9608). This farm grows white half-runner beans and tomatoes.

CLARKE

Fleming's Farm, Frank Fleming, U.S. 78 East at Clarke/Ogelthorpe County line (404/353-3011). Corn, butterbeans, butterpeas, field peas, melons, squash and bell peppers are available for picking. Open 8:00am-6:00pm. Call ahead.

COBB

Salacoa Valley Farm, 3050 Ellis Road, Kennesaw (422-9318). This farm specializes in blackberries.

COWETA

Don L. Stambaugh, 2 miles from Peachtree City (404/251-7161). The farm has blueberries, blackberries, tomatoes, cucumbers and squash.

FAYETTE

Adams Farms, 1486 Hwy. 54W, Fayetteville (404/461-7814). Pick corn, tomatoes, greens, peas, beans and other vegetables in season at this Certified Farm. Tours are available.

David Richardson, 701 Goza Road, Fayetteville (404/461-7814). Thornless blackberries and purple hull peas are available for picking.

Harp's Farm Market, Jammie Harp, 1692 Hwy. 92 South, 4 miles south of Fayetteville (404/461-1821). Pick muscadine grapes, berries, pumpkins, Christmas trees, and more at this Certified Market. Take a hayride around the farm and picnic nearby. There is a roadside country store with jams, jellies, flowers and more for sale. Containers provided. Open daily.

FORSYTH

Bill Callaway, Route 1, Cumming (404/887-4443). Produce at this farm is Certified Organic. Sweet corn, beans, peas, cucumbers, squash, tomatoes, blueberries and raspberries are available. Call for an appointment a day or two ahead.

FULTON

Ralph Dangar, 710 Cox Road, Roswell (993-6621). Cabbage is available.

Whimsy Haven Farm, 552 Hwy. 279 (Old National Hwy.), Fairburn (404/461-6742). Berries, vegetables, herbs, shittake mushrooms, worms are available here. Picnic in shade. Portable toilets and Spanish speaking staff are some of the amenities at this Certified Farm.

William Brown, 1055 Jones Road, Roswell (993-6866). Seasonal blueberries may be picked here.

GWINNETT

Green Acres Farm, Bill Isaacs, 2839 Lenora Road, Snellville (979-1336 and 972-6865). Besides blackberries, boysenberries, tayberries and strawberries, this farm has barns, horses, water wells and tractors to delight young children.

Pine Ridge Berry Farm, John Craddock, 311 Scenic Highway, Lawrenceville (963-0937). Pick blackberries on Wednesday and Saturday from 7:00 am- Dark when in season.

HENRY

Bond's Peach Orchard, 1315 Fairview Road, Ellenwood (404/474-4160). Pick peaches by appointment July and August.

Gordon's Berry Patch, Gordon Olmstead, 490 Dorsey Road, Exit #70 off I-75, Hampton (404/946-3525). Blueberries and blackberries are available during summer months. Open 8:00am-8:00pm on weekdays but please call ahead before coming.

Gardner Farms, P.O. Box 177, Locust Grove (404/957-4912/2113). Peaches, blueberries, blackberries and local produce are available for picking daily from 7:00am-7:00pm, May through September.

H.C. Seabolt, 2323 Legion Mill Road, Locust Grove (404/957-3196). Pick blackberries June-July. Call for an appointment.

NEWTON

Margaret Dimsdale, 4300 Salem Road, Covington (404/786-4687). Blueberries are available for picking from 8:00am-8:00pm on Monday through Saturday. Bring your own containers.

OCONEE

A.W. White, Jr., High Shaols Road, Watkinsvillle (404/769-6237). Ten kinds of plums available daily June-July.

B.A. Thomas Peach Orchard, 5850 Macon Highway, Bishop (404/769-6472). Peaches, muscadines, plums, nectarines, scuppernongs and seasonal vegetables are available at this orchard. Open 7:00am-6:00pm daily (except Friday and Saturday mornings) from mid-May through mid-September.

David H. Malcolm, 4250 Hog Mountain Road, Watkinsville (404/769-5706). Concord grapes, scuppernongs and figs are available for picking. Open daily from 8:00am-8:00pm.

Doug Felder, 1010 Pete Dickens Road, Bogart (404/725-9489). Blackberries available daily in June and July.

James Miller, 1371 Union Church Road, Watkinsville (404/769-6359). Eight to nine varieties of blueberries available June through August. Bring your own containers. Open daily.

Jodies S. Patton, Sr., 1501 McNutt Creek Road (2 miles south of Bogart) (404/725-7424). Corn (yellow sweet and white sweet), peas (silver hull, purple hull), okra, butterbeans, squash, tomatoes, butter peas, cucumbers and green beans are available for picking. Open daily from 7:00am-8:00pm. Bring your own containers.

SPAULDING

Buck Creek Farm, Milt and Pauline Jellum, 175 Chappell Mill Road, Orchard Hil (404/228-2682). Blueberries, blackberries and raspberries are available for picking, and fresh tomatoes may be purchased on Tuesday, Thursday and Saturday from 8:00am-8:00pm.

Futral Farms Peach Orchard, 5061 Jackson Road, Griffin (404/228-1811). Pick your own peaches daily from 8:00am-7:30pm in June through mid-August. Ice water and portable toilets are available.

Bill Ison, Highway 16, 10 miles west of Griffin, 6 miles east of Senoia (404/599-6970). Blueberries and blackberries are available June through August. Containers are furnished. Open 7:00am-7:00pm on Monday through Friday; 9:00am-4:00pm on Saturday, September-November. Call for an appointment on Sunday.

WALTON

Gerald Shelnutt, Jersey Road, Loganville (404/466-8917). Lima beans, green beans, squash, okra, purple hull peas and corn are available during the summer months. Call for picking times and availability.

Hard Labor Creek Blueberry Farm, Bill and Carolyn Kitchen, Knox Chapel Road, Social Circle (near Hard Labor Creek State Park) (404/464-2412). Blueberries are available during summer months on Monday, Wednesday and Saturday from 8:30am-Dark.

Nepenthe Farms, Cynthia Perkins, 4 miles south of Monroe on Liberty Hill Church Road (404/267-7951). Blueberries are available during summer months daily. They provide containers. Call for picking times and availability.

—————————— **CHRISTMAS TREES** ——————————

Cut your Own Trees at the Following Tree Farms:
Bethany Tree Farms, 606 Old Jackson Road McDonough (404/957-5608); **Berry Patch Farms**, 786 Arnold Mill Road, Woodstock (926-0561); **Berries Christmas Tree Farm**, 90 Mount Tabor Road, Covington (404/786-1880); **Buchanan's**, Grantville (583-2398); **Farmer Red's**, 2296 Jacsonville Road, Lithonia (482-6049); **Harp's Farm Market**, 1692 Highway 92 South, Fayetteville (404/461-1821); **King's**, Wilhelmina Drive, Cobb County (948-3051); **Santa's**, Saw Mill - Smithtown Road, Gwinnett County (945-1027); and, **Worthington Tree Farm**, 145 Twin Oaks Drive, Hampton (404/478-4355).

STORYTELLING, LIBRARIES AND BOOKSTORES

STORYTELLING

Storytelling is an art form that is almost extinct in our era of television and videos. We may diligently read stories to our children, but the art of storytelling is something quite different. Fortunately this marvelous means of communication that combines story, drama, personal presence and sometimes audience participation, can be enjoyed by children and parents alike in Atlanta.

A group of professionals–the **Southern Order of Storytellers (SOS)**-performs regularly throughout Atlanta at **Bookstores**, such as Borders Book Shop, the Oxford Bookstores and the Children's Book & Gift Market. The SOS also presents the **Olde Christmas Storytelling Festival** every January at Callanwolde Fine Arts Center, the **Atlanta Storytelling Festival** every spring at the Atlanta History Center and performs weekly at **The Wren's Nest**. (See our chapter "Places To Go" for more information about this attraction.) Some members of the SOS perform at **Art Centers** and are also available to perform at birthday parties, in classrooms and other group situations. The Wren's Nest has a list of professional storytellers and their phone numbers and will be glad to provide you with the information. Call 753-7735.

A few of Atlanta's professional storytellers, necessarily being multi-talented, are teachers of creative dramatics. The **Alliance Theatre** School offers a Storyteller's class in the summer for children age 8-16 years. Call 898-1131 for information. Professional and amateur storytellers perform regularly at public library storytimes. These programs are FREE and open to the public. Call or drop by your local library for storytime schedules.

Hear a story told by a member of the Southern Order of Storytellers on **Tele-Tale**, a 24-hour telephone story telling service offered by the DeKalb County Library System. A different story is featured every day. Call 270-8238.

Listed below are more locations to alert you to the fact that storytelling happens all over Atlanta all year long!

Bulloch Hall (992-1731)
Chattahoochee Nature Center (922-2055)
DeKalb Historical Society's Log Cabin Story Hour (373-1088)
Emory Museum of Art and Archaeology (727-7522)
High Museum of Art (892-3600)
National Black Arts Festival (biennial) (730-7315)

LIBRARIES

Groundbreaking ceremonies are being held for new libraries in the metropolitan Atlanta area every year and many older libraries have been or are currently being renovated. Newer libraries have attractive reading areas for children, such as the **Chamblee Branch of the DeKalb Public Library System** which has installed stationary, decorative carousel horses in the center of the reading area for children to sit on while pouring over their books.

Besides just offering a comfortable place for children to enjoy the pleasure of books, Atlanta-area libraries offer diverse programs and services for children ranging from sleepytime **Storytimes** in the evenings to after-school **Film** specials, craft and even skateboarding **Workshops**! There are occasional workshops for adults on enhancing parenting skills. The materials available to children go beyond the tremendous children's book and reference sections to foreign language books and periodicals, magazines, records, films, videos and cassettes. Every summer libraries have **Reading Clubs** and contests for school-age kids.

Keep an eye out for the **Auburn Avenue Branch of the Atlanta-Fulton Public Library System** scheduled to open at the end of 1992, which will be a research facility dedicated solely to African-American studies. The impressive collections for the library have been gathered from all over the nation and include private papers, rare books, an extensive photography collection and other sophisticated and rare research materials. The branch will also have a huge auditorium with a full schedule of lectures, workshops and children's films. There will be storytelling hours for elementary age children.

Mark your calendar for the **Friends of the Library Annual Book Sale** held at the main branch of the Atlanta-Fulton Pulic Library System in June.

You might also be interested to know that libraries provide services to homeless shelters, voter registration, and hospital kits ... and that in DeKalb County, in 1989, the cost through taxes to each individual to support the entire county library system was less than 3 cents per day. Go to your local library today, pick up their brochures, ask questions, and find out what's going on.

Not all branch libraries provide all the services of the county's system. Contact your main branch to locate special items such as foreign language materials or videos and the branch nearest you:

Atlanta-Fulton Public Library System Central Headquarters
1 Margaret Mitchell Square N.W.
Atlanta, Georgia 30303
730-1700

Clayton County Libraries
865 Battle Creek Road
Jonesboro, Georgia 30236
477-9740

Cobb County Public Library Headquarters
266 Roswell Street
Marietta, Georgia 30060
528-2320

DeKalb County Public System Main Library
133 E. Court Square
Decatur, Georgia 30030
370-3070

Gwinnett County Public Library System
822-4522

BOOKSTORES

There are many bookstores throughout Atlanta that have tremendous children's book sections or cater solely to children. Some have programs for children, such as storytelling hours or science and nature workshops; others have toys for sale and/or playstructures and lofts for children to enjoy while reading. We cannot list all of the fine bookstores in the

Atlanta-area; however, the following are some of the more popular choices and examples of what you might find elsewhere.

Borders Book Shop, 3655 Roswell Road, N.E. (near Piedmont Road), Tuxedo Festival Shopping Center, Atlanta, Georgia 30342 (237-0707). This serene and spacious bookstore has the ambience of a library. You really get the feeling that books are very special and important–things to be revered. I like to think that the calm I feel when walking into Borders is also felt by children. The large, well-displayed children's section is easy to negotiate with a stroller. (This cannot be said of all bookstores.) A variety of events are planned throughout the year especially for kids, such as storytelling, group songs, and nature programs. A gift-wrapping service is available, and you can subscribe to the Borders Newsletter free which will tell you, among other things, about upcoming events in the Kid's Corner. *Hours:* 9:00am-9:00pm, Monday-Saturday; 11:00am-6:00pm, Sunday.

Children's Book & Gift Market, 375 Pharr Road, N.E., Atlanta, Georgia 30305 (261-3442). This is about as comprehensive a children's bookstore as you will ever find, and the staff is as knowledgeable about children and children's books as you could ever hope for. Besides a wonderful selection of books, the owners have developed a diverse program of events throughout the year, including the award-winning "Summer of Saturdays" program that offers professional storytelling, puppet shows, magic shows, science and nature activities, musicians, multi-cultural events, creative party ideas, and much, much more. There are book signings, story hours, a book club (after 10 purchases you get a book free), as well as educational toys and games. *Hours:* 9:00am-6:30pm, Monday-Friday; 9:00am-6:00pm, Saturday.

Kiddie City, 6285 Roswell Road, Sandy Springs, Georgia 30328 (252-2904). Kiddie City continues to reign as North Atlanta's premier institution for children's products of all kinds. Whether you're in the market for unique children's wear, toys, maternity fashions, baby furnishings or gifts, this store is sure to have what you need. Their impressive book section features story books, unique non-fiction for young readers and parenting books. *Hours:* 10:00am-6:00pm, Monday-Saturday.

131

My Storyhouse. Three Locations: Merchants Festival, 1401 Johnson Ferry Road (at Highway 120), Marietta, Georgia 30062 (973-2244) 3000 Old Alabama Road, Alpharetta, Georgia 30302 (664-8694) and Galleria Mall, 1 Galleria Parkway, Atlanta, Georgia (984-8734). My Storyhouse has a large selection of books for children of all ages, the best name brands in educational toys, plus cassettes, videos, art supplies, and miscellaneous toys that are particularly good for taking on trips "to help wile away the miles." A Brio train set as well as building toys are available for children to play with while parents shop. *Hours:* 9:30am-6:00pm, Monday-Saturday.

Oxford Book Store at Peachtree Battle, 2345 Peachtree Road, N.E., Atlanta, Georgia 30324 (364-2700). This huge bookstore is literally packed with an incredible number of children's (as well as adult's) books. But don't let the cramped aisles daunt you. It really is quite fun to be in the midst of so many books, and the store has a very knowledgeable person in the children's section ready and willing to help you find what you are looking for. There is a climbing structure to provide a cozy place to read and to help keep your children occupied, but my youngsters find the books and the maze of aisles interesting enough. A free summer storytelling series by professional storytellers, book signings and other special activities are designed just for children. Visit Cup and Chaucer upstairs for a special dessert with your chidlren. *Hours:* 9:00am-12:00 Midnight, Sunday - Thursday; 9:00am-2:00am (Yes, 2:00am), Friday and Saturday. Open 365 days. On the other side of Peachtree Battle Shopping Center is **Oxford Too**, 2395 Peachtree Road, Atlanta, Georgia 30324 (262-3411), which carries publisher remainders, discounted and used books, a large children's section, and also offers a summer storytelling series and year-round special activites for children. *Hours:* 9:00am-11:00pm, Sunday-Thursday; 9:00am-12:00 Midnight, Friday and Saturday. Open 365 days. Downstairs visit **Oxford Comics, Games and More** (233-8682). *Hours:* 11:00am-9:00pm, Sunday-Wednesday; 11:00am-11:00pm, Thursday-Sunday.

Oxford Book Store at Buckhead, 360 Pharr Road, N.E., Atlanta, Georgia 30305 (262-3333). This bookstore is touted as "the largest in the southeast," and we believe it! Yet, as big and comprehensive as it is, the atmosphere is warm and friendly. The woodsy, nook-and-cranny design

132

makes you feel like you are in a medium-sized specialty store in any section. The children's section has a special play/reading cave built under a staircase. Upstairs is the pleasant Oxford Espresso Cafe with a menu that includes sandwiches, desserts and ice cream, and the Arts Connection, an intimate gallery which offers workshops for children year-round. The bookstore services and hours are the same as at Peachtree Battle.

Oxford at West Paces Ferry, 1200 West Paces Ferry Road, Atlanta, Georgia 30327 (364-2488), has a large children's book section with a climbing structure, but the bookstore is not as large and comprehensive as its sisters. _Hours:_ 9:00am-10:00pm daily.

And be sure to visit these other book and/or toy stores that have many unique and hard to find children's books, or see the _Yellow Pages_ under **Book Stores** and **Toy Stores** for telephone numbers and addresses for these and other stores in you area.

ABC Parent/Teacher Learning Center
African American Book Shop
Ansley Mall Bookstore
B. Dalton Bookseller
Bookstar
Brentanos
Chapter 11
Children's Hour Toys
Doubleday Book Shop
Early Learning Centers
Father Goose's International Toys
Final Touch Gallery and Books
First World Book Store
Hakim's Book Store (African-American children's books)
Hammett's Learning World
International Bookstore (Spanish language children's books)
J & R Educational Supplies
Lenox Toys and Hobbies
The Renaissance Book Shop
Scribner's
Shrine of the Black Madonna Bookstore and Cultural Arts Center

Southwind Book Co.
Tall Tales Bookshop
The Teacher's Place
The Toy School
The Toy Store
Waldenbooks

For fellow catalogue shoppers, **World of Reading, Ltd.** (233-4042) offers books, cassettes and language learning materials in over 6 different languages.

TOURS OF THE WORKING WORLD

Below is a list of tours available around town (and a bit beyond). Although a few of these tours do allow individual families to join up with other groups, you will still have to call ahead and make reservations. You might consider a tour for your child's next birthday party for an unusual celebration. All of the listed tours are FREE.

ATLANTA BAKING COMPANY, 165 Bailey Street, S.W., Atlanta, Georgia (653-9700). Take a guided tour through the production plant of this large bakery to observe the bread-making process. Watch the dough being mixed and readied for baking, and next see the loaves being baked, sliced and wrapped. Proceed to the shipping department where you can watch the bread being loaded onto trucks. The tours lasts about 1/2-hour. Please call ahead to schedule your tour. FREE.

ATLANTA POLICE DEPARTMENT, 165 Decatur Street, Atlanta, Georgia 30303 (658-6795). Tours for children age 8 and older include the fingerprinting, identification and communication departments of the police station and a trip to the courthouse. Tours are available Monday through Friday from 8:00am to 4:00pm for groups of no larger than 15 children. There are no tours during the summer months. Write well in advance for reservations (Community Services, 2001 MLK, Jr. Drive NW, Atlanta 30310). FREE. Call your local police department to see whether or not tours are available.

ATLANTA–FULTON COUNTY PUBLIC LIBRARY, 1 Margaret Mitchell Square, N.W., Atlanta, Georgia 30303 (730-1700). The Children's Department conducts tours of the downtown branch of the Atlanta-Fulton County Library for children in the 4th through the 7th grades. Groups must include at least 10 children. The tour consists of a floor to floor walk through the library with explanations geared to the age group along with a stop at the Margaret Mitchell exhibit. Call in advance for reservations. FREE.

CHANNEL 2–WSB TELEVISION, 1601 West Peachtree Street, N.E., Atlanta, Georgia 30309 (897-7369). Tours of the television station are offered Tuesday and Thursday at 9:30am and 10:30am for children age 8 and up. Groups can be as large as 40 children, and individual families are also welcome. Call in advance to schedule your tour. FREE.

CHANNEL 5–WAGA TELEVISION, 1551 Briarcliff Road, N.E., Atlanta, Georgia 30306 (875-5551). Tours are offered Monday, Tuesday and Wednesday at 10:00am for children in the 2nd grade and older. This is a very popular field trip for school children, so we suggest that individual families make an appointment for a tour on a school holiday. Call at least 2 weeks in advance for reservations. FREE.

CHANNEL 46–WGNX, 1810 Briarcliff Road, NE, Atlanta 30306 (325-4646). This news-oriented tour is offered to groups of children over age

8 from Sundays-Thursdays. The one-hour tours are booked months in advance so plan ahead! FREE.

CHATTAHOOCHEE WATER TREATMENT PLANT, 2532 Bolton Road, N.W., Atlanta, Georgia 30318 (355-7310). Children age 5 and older can see how water is collected and treated to make it safe to drink. Tours are given Monday through Thursday from 9:00am to 2:00pm for any size group. Call in advance for an appointment. FREE.

THE COCA-COLA BOTTLING COMPANY, 1091 Industrial Park Drive, Marietta, Georgia 30062 (424-9080). Group tours of the Coca-Cola Bottling Plant are given on Wednesday at 10:00am for groups no larger than 35 children. This popular tour is usually booked six months in advance, so plan ahead. FREE.

DELTA AIRLINES, Atlanta-Hartsfield International Airport, South Terminal Information Counter, Atlanta, Georgia 30320 (765-2554). Delta Airlines conducts tours of the technical operations area for children 12 and older on Tuesday, Wednesday and Thursday at 9:30am. The minimum group size is 10 and the maximum group size is 35 people. Groups are booked months in advance so call well ahead of time. FREE.

DUNKIN DONUTS. Locations throughout Atlanta. Your local Dunkin Donut store encourages you to bring your children to the store to watch the hand-baking of a large variety of donuts and muffins. Each store has a glass window for viewing the baking area. It's FREE to watch, but samples must be purchased!

FEDERAL BUREAU OF INVESTIGATION, 275 Peachtree Street, N.E., Atlanta, Georgia 30303 (521-3900). Group tours for children age 6 through 12 with a maximum of 20 children per group, are available on Tuesdays and Thursdays at 10:00am. The tour is tailored to the age of the children, but usually includes a talk about the history of the FBI, a visit to the gun vault and computer room, a film about drugs and sometimes a demonstration explaining fingerprinting and surveillance. Call ahead to make reservations. FREE.

FIRE STATIONS. Your local fire station will be more than glad to schedule a tour of the station. Some will even let you host your child's birthday party at the station. FREE.

GEORGIA DEPARTMENT OF TRANSPORTATION, 15 Kennedy Drive, Forest Park, Georgia 30050 (363-7510). The Georgia Department of Transportation's tours are for children 10 years of age and older. The tour provides a view of the equipment and procedures utilized to test the materials used in highway construction, and can be arranged on Monday through Friday during normal working hours. Maximum group size is 15 children. FREE.

G.M. ASSEMBLY PLANT, Doraville Assembly Plant (455-5255). Tours are offered on Tuesdays at 12noon for school groups over age 16. Maximum group size is 40. There are no age restrictions on families. Call for reservations.

GOREE'S ICE HOUSE, 5425 Buford Highway, Doraville (451-2765). This small older building houses an ice-block factory that also makes ice carvings for hotels on ocassional Saturdays. Families are welcome to come and watch ice being artistically carved. We suggest you call ahead before visiting.

KRISPY KREME DOUGHNUT COMPANY. Locations throughout Atlanta. Visit one of the Krispy Kreme locations for a FREE look through the viewing windows. But remember, samples must be purchased!

LITHIA SPRINGS WATER & BOTTLING, CO., INC., 2910 Bankhead Highway, Lithia Springs, Georgia 30318 (944-3880). Children can tour the historic company that bottles the medicinal water rich in lithium (thus, the name of Lithia Springs). This rare metal is found in only three other springs in the world. Visit the Family Doctor Museum, Medicinal Gardens and "Frog Rock." Tours are given Monday through Friday from 9:00am to 4:00pm and on Saturdays from 10:00am to 12:00noon. Families are welcome to join a group. FREE.

McDONOUGH/ATKINSON POWER PLANT, 5551 South Cobb Drive, Smyrna, Georgia 30080 (792-5368). The tour of this coal-fired plant includes a slide presentation and a chance to see the motors, pumps and generators used in producing power. Children should be at least 10 years old and groups must be no larger than 30 children. Schedule your tour well in advance. FREE.

MARIETTA DAILY JOURNAL/NEIGHBOR NEWSPAPERS, 580 Fairgrounds Street, S.E., Marietta, Georgia (428-9411). The tour begins with a brief discussion about the history of this newspaper and how news is made. Your guide then leads you past the busy newsroom, the typesetters, the composition room and then, the tour highlight, the press room in operation. At the end of the tour, each child receives a newspaper hot off the press! The tour lasts about 30-45 minutes and is appropriate for children ages 8 and older. FREE.

NEWS-SUN NEWSPAPERS, 739 DeKalb Industrial Way, Atlanta, Georgia (292-3536). Your tour begins in a conference room where newspaper staff members give a brief introductory talk on how a newspaper is produced. You are then taken into the production plant to view the cameras and the printing press. The tour takes about one hour. The maximum size for a group is 20 children and they suggest a minimum age of 8. Generally, tours are given on Thursdays and Fridays at 10:30am or 3:30pm, but this varies. Call well in in advance to arrange a tour. FREE.

UNITED STATES POST OFFICE, Federal Annex, 77 Forsyth Street, Atlanta, Georgia 30304 (765-7400). Children in the 4th grade and younger can take tours of a local branch of the U.S. Post Office where they can see postal workers, mail trucks and the inner workings of the branch. Groups of children (minimum size 10 children), 5th grade and older may tour the downtown Federal Annex Building, where the machines and the process by which mail travels through the building can be seen. The tour takes about an hour and a half and is FREE.

―――――――― **TOURS FOR OLDER CHILDREN** ――――――――

ATLANTA JOURNAL AND CONSTITUTION, 6455 Best Friend Road, N.W., Norcross, Georgia 30071 (263-3971). Tours of the Gwinnett printing plant of the Atlanta Journal and Constitution are only available for children age 13 and older.

CHATEAU ELAN, LTD. VINEYARDS, Route 1, Box 563-1, Hoschton, Georgia 30548 (404/867-8200 or 800/233-WINE). A visit to this replica of a 16th-century chateau can include a tour of the winery, lessons on wine-making, a wine history museum, nature trails, picnic areas, golf, an elegant restaurant and many special events throughout the year. Tours are offered Monday through Thursday from 10:00am-4:00pm; Friday and Saturday from 10:00am-10pm; and Sunday from 12:30pm-6:00pm. Tours are FREE. (The Winery is located about 30 miles northeast of Atlanta.)

NEELY NUCLEAR RESEARCH CENTER, 900 Atlantic Drive, N.W. (Georgia Tech Campus), Atlanta, Georgia 30332 (894-3600). Tours of the research center are usually given only for children over 16 years, although they will sometimes allow younger children to tour the facility. The tour includes the research labs and a visit to the viewing gallery to see the hot cell and reactor containment building. Tours are given Monday through Friday during normal working hours for groups no larger than 30 children. Tours must be scheduled in advance and are FREE.

TRANSPORTATION
CARS, BOATS, TRAINS AND PLANES

Children are fascinated by anything that moves. Most of the conversation in our car revolves around the different vehicles we pass along the way. Be it cars, buses, mail trucks, trains, taxis, ambulances, fire engines, police cars, backhoes, cherry pickers, boats, airplanes, jets, or helicopters, they all get noticed. Preschoolers love to imitate the noises the vehicles make; they want to know everything about the vehicle and can't wait for a chance to be behind the wheel. Older kids can't understand why we won't let them really drive as they indignantly argue, "But I can reach the pedals!" Any trip which brings your child within arm's reach of transportation is sure to be a big hit.

TRAINS AND BUSES

Why not leave the car behind the next time you go to a game at Fulton County Stadium? The **MARTA Train Station** is a few blocks away and you won't have to deal with parking. Or, take your child for a short trip on a **MARTA Bus** the next time you have to run a simple errand. If you're really at a loss for something to do, take a MARTA train ride to Hartsfield Airport or Peachtree Center or Underground Atlanta and treat your child to an ice cream cone when you get there. The fare is inexpensive, and an otherwise boring day will turn into a little adventure. Call 848-4711 for MARTA schedule information.

The **AmTrak Train Station** is the only passenger train station in Atlanta. Although small, it is the only show in town for those embarking on an old-fashioned railroad journey. If you plan ahead, you may be able to schedule a visit to the station during boarding or arrival time. The station is located at the intersection of Peachtree Road and Deering Road, near Pershing Point. Call 872-9815 for schedule information.

Also, be sure to look in our chapter "Places To Go" for information on these great places: **Big Shanty Museum, Cyclorama, New Georgia Railroad, Southeastern Railway Museum, Stone Mountain Railroad** and other metro-Atlanta attractions which feature trains.

Don't miss Fernbank Planetarium's annual Christmas show "The Christmas Express" in which a little engine named Casey saves the day for the children in a small mountain village.

For the more serious train collectors, railroad memorabilia abounds at **Gandy Dancers** on Peachtree Road in the Chamblee Antique District. (A gandy dancer was a laborer on a railroad gang.) Look for the **Model Train Show** at the Cobb Civic Center in Marietta each March featuring displays, demonstrations, dealers and advice for the novice and advanced model builders. **The Atlanta Train, Model Car, Collectible Toys and Railroadiana Show** (325-3000) held every spring features over 200 tables of trains, models and toys for trade or sale. In August attend the annual **Railroadiana Sale** (233-7991) at the Georgia International Convention and Trade Center in Atlanta where over 300 tables display model trains and collectibles for sale or trade.

──────────────── **AIRPLANES** ────────────────

Big airports or small, Atlanta has plenty of opportunities for children to get close to jets and airplanes.

Hartsfield Airport has it all MARTA trains, buses, taxis, motorized transportation carts, moving sidewalks, people movers, elevators, long escalators, baggage claim areas, security checks and of course, big jets. Try to plan ahead and take the Delta Airlines Tour of the airport. (See our section in this chapter, "Tours of the Working World"). For a change of pace, stop by the International Arrivals escalator and watch the reunions of families and friends who have not, in some cases, seen each other for years. There are a hundred stories to imagine and watching all of the hugging and kissing will bring tears to your eyes (or at least a lump to your throat). Take MARTA to the airport and give your children a full day of "moving" experiences.

For a visit to a smaller airport, try our favorite, **DeKalb–Peachtree Airport** located on Clairmont Road in Chamblee. The historical airport use to be part of Fort Gordon, established during World War I to house the Emory Division of the 82nd Regiment, later the 82nd Airborne Division. Now, it is a busy commuter airport with airplanes and small jets taking off and landing continuously. The airport has built a large observation deck overlooking the runways, and next to the deck is a large grassy area complete with picnic tables and family swings. Bring a picnic lunch and enjoy this perfect lunch spot. The airport is open to the public 24 hours a day. Call 457-7236 if you need more information. See our chapter on "Festivals and Special Events" for information about Neighbor Day held in June of each year.

And, for an extra special Sunday brunch, eat at the **57th Fighter Group Restaurant** located at 3829 Clairmont Road right at the edge of one of the runways of DeKalb-Peachtree Airport. This restaurant, although not cheap, contains lots of memorabilia and artifacts that airplane lovers and military buffs will enjoy. Inside the restaurant are headphones which allow you to listen in on the Air Control Tower at the airport. Outside is an old fighter plane, several jeeps, and a convoy truck which add authenticity to the World War II fighter theme. Call 457-7757 for more information.

Stone Mountain Britt Memorial Airport, located on Bermuda Road in Stone Mountain, is open to the public daily from 8:00am to dusk. The airport is home to the **Georgia Historical Aviation Museum,** displaying four World War II fighter planes in various states of repair, including a TBM Avenger (the same kind of plane flown by George Bush during World War II). In addition to the Museum, there is a small grassy area where children can view the activity on the runways. Call 469-7604 for more information.

Fulton County Airport–Charlie Brown Field, located off Fulton Industrial Boulevard (close to Douglas County), is open to the public daily 24 hours a day. There are a few benches and a small grassy area where children can observe the airplanes and jets. Call 699-4200 for more information.

Gwinnett County Airport, Briscoe Field, is located off of Highway 316 on Airport Road in Lawrenceville. The airport offers tours by appointment, 8:00am to 5:00pm daily. Call 995-5592 for more information.

McCollum Airport is located on McCollum Parkway, off of Highway 41 in Marietta, and is open to the public by appointment only. The tour of the airport includes a visit to the hangars and a chance to go inside a small aircraft. Call 528-1615 to schedule an appointment.

South Expressway Airport, located on Tara Boulevard in Jonesboro, has a small fenced in grassy area with a few benches for viewing the runway activity. It's open to the public from 8:00am to 8:00pm. Call 471-0534.

See our chapter on "Festivals and Special Events" for information about **Lockheed/Dobbins Air Force Base's** open-house in June. Up in Calhoun is **Mercer Air Museum** (404/629-7371) a "roadside collection of aircraft" you can see from I-75. Also be sure to check our chapter "Day Trips" for information on the **Air Acres Museum** in Cartersville.

HORSE-DRAWN CARRIAGE RIDES

Now, this is really touristy! Take a 20-minute horse and buggy tour of historical downtown from Five Points to Underground Atlanta. The cost is about $12.50 a person and rides are given from 6:00pm to midnight. Look in the _Yellow Pages_ under "Carriages-Hire" and call ahead for reservations, or just hire one on the spot.

CARS

For those of you who have automobile enthusiasts in your family, keep your calendar free for the **Atlanta International Auto Show** held at the Georgia World Congress Center in March of each year (656-7600) and the spectacular **World of Wheels,** also held at the Georgia World Congress Center in December (491-0155). These mega-shows feature domestic and foreign cars, as well as vintage classics and cars that have made it to the movies. Also, check the _Weekend_ section of the _Atlanta Journal and Constitution_ and the monthly editions of _Entertainment Atlanta_ for information about smaller automobile collector shows, motorcycle shows, and auctions that are scheduled throughout the year. Information about championship race car driving and motorcycle racing at Road Atlanta and elsewhere, can be found in our chapter "Sports and Recreation," and information about the **Antique Auto and Music Museum** at Stone Mountain Park can be found in our chapter on "Places to Go."

BOATS

Other than the **Paddlewheel River Boat Ride** at **Stone Mountain Park** and **SciTrek Museum,** there are no attractions for children in Atlanta which give children a hands-on experience with boats. However, you can rent canoes and other watercraft for fun family boating and fishing on the Chattahoochee River, Lake Allatoona and elsewhere. See our chapter on "Sports and Recreation" for more information.

There is also the annual **Atlanta Boat Show** held at the World Congress Center in March of every year (998-9800), and what a show it is! This is the largest inland Marine Show in the United States, featuring over 350 exhibitors and over 500 boats. There is also the smaller **Boat Expo** held in January of each year at the Lakewood Exhibit Center (622-4488), and the **Summer Boat Show** held at the World Congress Center in August of each year (656-7600).

... AND MORE

Don't forget the obvious, but sometimes overlooked visit to your local

Fire Station
Post Office
Police Station
Neighborhood Construction Sites

PETS AND ANIMALS

If your household already has a family pet, then you know how much pleasure an animal can bring to a child. As further proof, visit Zoo Atlanta, Yellow River Game Ranch and the Wildlife Trails at Stone Mountain Park which are filled with excited children eager to get close to the animals. The petting areas of these attractions are, by far, the favorite part of each visit. Children can touch the furry bodies and figure out ways to get wet tongues to lick their hands. Read on to find out about other places in Atlanta where children can discover other animals who also deserve enthusiastic attention.

ANIMAL SHELTERS AND HUMANE SOCIETIES

The best animal petting can be found at the animal **Shelters** and **Humane Societies** in Atlanta. Playful kittens, puppies, cats and dogs (and in some instances, rabbits, hamsters and mice) are glad to see friendly faces. They seem to know instinctively just what to do to successfully audition for a new home. Your children will have plenty of hands-on opportunities with these animals. (A word of caution—make

144

sure your children understand ahead of time whether or not you are going home with a new pet. We didn't deal with this issue very well during our first visit, and our children got very upset when they watched other families leave with pets. They could not understand why they were leaving empty handed!)

Buying a Pet. If you are in the market to buy a pet, the Animal Shelter or Humane Society is the right place to be. The animals are healthy (most come wormed, with their first shots, and with a coupon good for a discount on spaying and neutering). And, most importantly, these pets are in need of a good home.

Learning About Animals. Animal shelters and humane societies offer an excellent opportunity for your children to learn more about animals. Almost all of the metro-Atlanta area animal shelters and societies listed below offer **Guided Tours** of the facilities for elementary age children. These tours often include **Films and Discussions** relating to the care of animals. The Atlanta Humane Society has an excellent series of **Educational Touring Programs** on a variety of topics that can be presented at your child's school FREE of charge. Humane Societies also sponsor special **Animal-Adoption Events** at local shopping malls, as well as **Amateur Pet Shows** and **Fund-Raising Art Contests**.

Call the numbers below for more information about visiting hours, tours and pet adoption. Also, look in *Creative Loafing* for the names and addresses of other non-profit animal shelters.

Atlanta Humane Society
981 Howell Mill Road, N.W.
Atlanta, Georgia 30318
875-5331

Cobb County Humane Society
1060 County Farm Road, S.E.
Marietta, Georgia 30060
428-5678

DeKalb Humane Society
5287 Covington Highway
Decatur, Georgia 30035
593-1155

DeKalb Animal Control Shelter
845 Camp Road
Decatur, Georgia 30032
294-2930

Clayton County Animal
Control Shelter
7810 N. McDonough Street
Jonesboro, Georgia 30236
477-3509

Gwinnett Humane Society
Highway 316 and Hi Hope Road
Lawrenceville, Georgia 30243
662-9566

PET STORES

Metro-Atlanta has an excellent selection of **Pet Stores** which have a large variety of species on display–iguanas, snakes, tame and talking birds, spiders, hamsters, guinea pigs, mice, tropical fish and even monkeys - sort of **"Mini-Zoos"** in their own right. There are also those stores that specialize in exotic birds and tropical fish - some of their displays rivaling aquarium attractions in other cities. Look in the *Yellow Pages* for **Pet Shop** listings near your home. Some of our favorite stores are: **The Aviarium** at Market Square (fish and birds) - 634-5930; **Pickadilly Pets** (fish, birds, reptiles, small animals) at Ansley Mall–892-2473, at Buckhead Crossing–261-6902, and in College Park–768-3816; **JunglePets** (923-0752) on Lawrenceville Highway in Gwinnett County (birds, reptiles, fish and small animals)–923-0752; **Tropiquarium** on Piedmont Road in Atlanta (fish galore!)–875-6121; and, **For Birds Only** in Buckhead (fish and birds)–851-1800. Most pet store owners do not encourage you to touch the animals unless you are serious about buying a pet; but, if you are interested in some inexpensive animal-watching, then a visit to a pet store is a sure-fire way to please children.

PET SHOWS

Year-round, Atlantans are showing off their pets, whether it's at a nationally recognized **Purebreed Championship Show** sponsored by the Greater Atlanta Cat Club, the Atlanta Kennel Club, or one of the many other championship purebreed clubs; or, an amusing **Amateur Pet Show or Pet Parade** sponsored by your local Humane Society or Parks and Recreation Department. Wills Park Equestrian Center in Alpharetta also is the location for two national dog shows held in the spring and fall of each year. The championship shows are not inexpensive. They are serious competitions with little opportunity for a child to get close to or actually touch the animals. But, if your child is really interested in animals, then the shows are a fascinating way to see them. (The shows may not be a good idea for preschoolers. Mine were really not welcome at a cat show; they had too much energy for the already nervous pets.) Amateur shows, on the other hand, such as the frisbee catching dogs at the **Stone Mountain Frisbee Championships** are great events for children to watch. Check with your local Humane Societies and Parks and Recreation Departments for a schedule of upcoming events.

And, don't forget the annual **Fish Show and Auction** spc ısored by The Aquarium Society of Georgia, or the **Exotic Bird Mart** held yearly at the Farmers Market Exhibit Hall. Check *Creative Loafing* and *Entertainment Atlanta* to keep up with the many shows scheduled year-round.

ANIMAL FARMS

COBB COUNTY PETTING FARM, 1060 County Farm Drive, Marietta (499-4136). You will need an appointment to visit this farm that features sheep, goats, a pig and a pond filled with ducks that eagerly await your tidbits. Families and groups are welcome to arrange a visit on Monday through Saturdays, but call well in advance.

THE RED BARN, 800 Old Rucker Road (near Harry's Farmers Market), Alpharetta (442-1617). Feed and pet animals, collect eggs from the hens, and ride ponies at this working farm! Pre-arranged group visits only, please, as this farm is a family home. There is a per child fee for groups with the exception of the 2-hour birthday party program which has a set Fee. Hours and days are flexible.

NOAH'S ARK REHABILITATION CENTER, 1425 Locust Grove Drive, Locust Grove (957-0888). Children are encouraged to touch the 500 animals that frolic in the 10-15 acre yard at this rehabilitation center for wild and exotic creatures. If your children seem to be a bit wild, they are welcome to romp, too! Open Tuesdays-Saturdays, 12noon-5:00pm. Donations are welcome. You might consider stopping to pick seasonal berries at Gardner Farms nearby (957-2113).

SMALL ART MUSEUMS, GALLERIES AND ART CENTERS

Visiting a gallery can be a special activity, even a regular event, for a family on a rainy or cold day. Artists tell us that children exposed to art at a young age and on a regular basis, will develop a fine appreciation of art that will enrich them throughout their lives.

Atlanta has a large number of **Small Art Museums and Galleries** scattered throughout the city. The Saturday *Weekend* section of the *Atlanta Journal and Constitution* is the best source to find out what is being exhibited at the various museums and galleries in Atlanta, and to figure out if the current exhibits would be enjoyable for your child. During the **National Black Arts Festival** (held in July and August biennially) numerous galleries have special showings of outstanding art work by Black artists. The July issues of *The Atlanta Tribune* and *Creative Loafing* are good sources for locating these galleries as well as other festival events.

Below are descriptions of some small art museums and galleries that are worth noting, either because their exhibits can always be appreciated by children, or because the museum or gallery has tried in the past to offer at least one exhibit each year for children. All of the listings below are **FREE**.

There are also numerous **Community Art Centers** spread throughout the Atlanta area. In addition to offering a broad range of exciting activities for children throughout the year, many have galleries which frequently exhibit art work done by children or art work that a child would enjoy. We have included all of the Community Art Centers, even those without galleries, so you will have an idea of where to look for interesting visual **Art Classes** for your children. You will find a wide range of offerings here from fun explorations for preschoolers to classes for serious young students.

ABERNATHY ARTS AND CRAFTS CENTER
254 Johnson Ferry Road
Sandy Springs, Georgia 30328 • 303-6172

The Arts Center is a program of the Fulton County Department of Parks and Recreation offering classes in the visual arts. Its small gallery periodically exhibits the art work of its students, so children and adults attending the classes have a forum to display their creations. Afternoon and early evening youth classes in drawing and painting, portraiture, pottery and sculpture are available year-round as well as a summer program "Art in the Park" held at Chattahoochee River Park. *Gallery Hours*: 9:00am-5:00pm, Monday-Friday; 10:00am-2:00pm, Saturday.

A.R.T. STATION, INC.
5384 Manor Drive
Stone Mountain, Georgia 30086 • 469-1105

A.R.T. Station is one of the four not-for-profit art centers in DeKalb County. The renovated Center holds two art galleries, a theater, a dance studio and six classrooms. The Center presently offers a wide variety of youth classes in the visual, literary and performing arts, and a performing arts series includes family-oriented productions. The Summer Arts Camp has programs in creative dramatics, drawing, painting, multi-media and music. *Gallery Hours*: 9:00am-5:00pm, Monday-Friday, and on Saturday for special exhibitions.

THE ARTS EXCHANGE
750 Kalb Street, S.E.
Atlanta, Georgia 30312 • 624-4211 or 624-1572

The Arts Exchange is a multi-cultural, multi-disciplinary arts resource center located near Zoo Atlanta. The Center houses a Municipal Gallery with art exhibits sometimes geared to children. A wide variety of class offerings for children include creative dramatics, voice, piano, dance, visual arts (mixed media), martial arts and Tai-Chi Chuan. A special all day Summer Arts Enrichment Program runs for 6 weeks, and the cost is more than reasonable. *Gallery Hours:* 10:00am-5:00pm, Monday-Friday.

THE ATLANTA COLLEGE OF ART
1280 Peachtree Street, N.E
Atlanta, Georgia 30309 • 898-1164

The gallery displays faculty and student art and occasionally hosts travelling exhibitions of work by regional and international artists. The College offers a Saturday "Creative-Kids" arts class for school-age children, classes in the visual arts for preschoolers and a summer "Art and Theater Camp." *Gallery Hours:* 10:00am-5:00pm, Monday-Saturday; 2:00pm-6:00pm, Sunday.

ATLANTA INTERNATIONAL MUSEUM
Atlanta International Museum of Art & Design
285 Peachtree Center Avenue
Atlanta, Georgia 30303 • 688-2467

The Atlanta International Museum is located in downtown Atlanta in the Marquis Two Tower (adjacent to the Marriott-Marquis Hotel). This one-room museum exhibits work from around the world showcasing the arts and designs of the world's many cultures, past and present, such as recent exhibits of Turkistan art, Japanese tapestries, food containers and an American craft exhibit. When visiting the downtown area, be sure to take a quick look inside; the Museum will be quite enjoyable for the entire family. (A donation of $3.00 is welcome). *Hours*: 11:00am-5:00pm, Tuesday-Saturday; 2:00pm-5:00pm, Sunday.

CHASTAIN ARTS CENTER
135 W. Wieuca Road, N.W.
Atlanta, Georgia 30342 • 252-2927

Chastain Arts Center has a small art gallery which occassionally displays art that might be of interest to children. Year-round classes in the visual arts are offered for kids, including instruction in drawing and painting, weaving, clay and sculpture. A unique Saturday program has children and their parents working on art projects simultaneously in rooms next door to each other, with the hope that shared experiences will enhance parent/child communications. A summer camp program, "Artventures," offers children an opportunity to explore different art media.   *Gallery Hours*: 1:00pm-5:00pm, Wednesday-Saturday.

GWINNETT COUNCIL FOR THE ARTS, INC.
220 Crogan Street (Highway 29)
Lawrenceville, Georgia 30246 • 962-6642

The Gwinnett Council for the Arts sponsors a twice yearly "Arts Holiday" at the Holiday Inn in Suwanee, which is an exhibit of art created by Gwinnett County children. It also sponsors art shows at other locations in Gwinnett such as the Humana Hospital in Snellville and the Myrick Co. at Peachtree Corners. The Art Center's Gallery has changing exhibits which are sometimes of interest to children. The Council regularly offers courses for children in art and mixed media and is planning on expanding its offerings to include classes in the performing arts. *Gallery Hours*: 9:00am-5:00pm, Monday-Friday; 10:00am-2:00pm, Saturday.

HAMMONDS HOUSE
503 Peeples Street, S.W.
Atlanta, Georgia 30310 • 752-8730

The Hammonds House is a gallery and resource center of African-American art, housed in a restored 1857 Victorian home formerly the home of Otis T. Hammonds, a physician and arts patron. The Fulton County Board of Commissioners has acquired the home together with Dr. Hammond's vast art collection, and the Hammond House now serves as a cultural facility and resource center in historic West End. Although the educational programs, forums, lectures and workshops offered by the gallery are generally geared to adults, the permanent collection is delightful and can certainly be appreciated by children. There are also special traveling exhibits which change about six times a year and these, too, are usually quite appropriate for children.   There is a small but well-stocked African-American gift shop in the gallery. The gallery is spacious and the staff friendly. We recommend that you stop by the next time your family visits the Wren's Nest. *Hours*: 10:00am-6:00pm, Tuesday-Friday; 1:00pm-5:00pm, Saturday and Sunday.

KENNESAW COLLEGE ART GALLERY
I-75 and Chastain Road, Lower Level of Library
Marietta, Georgia 30061 • 423-6300

The Kennesaw College Art Gallery displays works primarily of importance to adults; however, they occassionally have more fun, hands-on exhibits, so keep an eye out for their special programs and exhibits. Throughout the year, studio art classes are offered for children age 7 years and older. During the summer months, the College offers a dazzling array of summer camp programs including instruction in the visual arts. *Gallery Hours*: 10:00am-4:00pm, Monday-Friday; 1:00pm-5:00pm, Saturday.

LE PRIMITIF GALLERIES
631 Miami Circle, Suite 25
Atlanta, Georgia 30324 • 240-0226

Le Primitif Galleries welcomes children to the gallery believing that if children are exposed to the arts early in life, then they will develop an appreciation for art. The Haitian exhibits at the gallery are colorful fun and interesting to children. *Hours:* 11:00am-5:00pm, Monday-Saturday.

MABLE HOUSE/
SOUTH COBB ARTS ALLIANCE
5239 Floyd Road, S.W.
Mableton, Georgia 30059 • 739-0189

The historical antebellum home which was taken over by federal troops during the Civil War is now the site of an art gallery with changing monthly exhibits and art classes for children and adults year-round. The South Cobb Arts Alliance also hosts festivals and special events at the Mable House, including visual, literary and performing artists from Cobb County and summer candelite concerts. *Hours:* 10:00am-5:00pm, Tuesdays-Saturdays; Sundays for special events.

MARIETTA/COBB MUSEUM OF ART
30 Atlanta Street
Marietta, Georgia 30060 • 424-8142

The gallery has a few exhibits each year which are appropriate for children, and "Kid's Place," a fun participatory exhibit. The Museum's afternoon and weekend classes for children are excellent and include instruction in pottery, painting and drawing, photography and creative expression. A summer art camp offers activities in drama, drawing, printmaking, painting, clay and papiér-mâche. *Public Hours:* 11:00am-5:00pm, Tuesday and Saturday.

JOHNNY MERCER EXHIBITION
Georgia State University, 8th Floor of the Pullen Library South
103 Decatur Street, Atlanta, Georgia 30303 • 651-2477

Georgia State University's Library has a small exhibit "I Remember You" honoring Georgia native, Johnny Mercer, writer of the hit songs "That Old Black Magic," "Moon River," and "Days of Wine and Roses." Posters, photographs and Oscar and Grammy awards are available for viewing while a tape recording of continuous Mercer hit songs plays. *Hours:* 8:30am-5:00pm, Monday-Friday.

NEXUS CONTEMPORARY ART CENTER
535 Means Street
Atlanta, Georgia 30308 • 688-2500 or 577-3579

Nexus' new gallery is located on Means Street in downtown Atlanta. We do not recommend that you make a special trip to the gallery, but we do suggest you keep your eye out for announcements about the Nexus Press Kids Club for children age 3-12 years. The club meetings are conducted by the Nexus Press Staff and offer children an opportunity to learn about fine art printing, paper construction and folding and the world of artist's books.

NORTH ARTS CENTER
5339 Chamblee-Dunwoody Road
Atlanta, Georgia 30338 • 394-3447

The gallery provides a diverse selection of works by local, national and international artists that are appropriate for children. Guided tours are FREE. Arrangements can be made for individuals with special vision and/or hearing needs. Year-round classes for children are offered in ceramics, literary arts, drama, music and cartooning. Summer camp programs include instruction in the visual and performing arts, a "Drama Camp," and an "Arts Honor Camp" for exceptional children providing advance classes in drawing, painting, clay and sculpture. *Gallery Hours:* 10:00am-5:00pm, Monday-Friday; 10:00am-1:00pm, Saturday.

PINCKNEYVILLE ARTS CENTER
4300 Holcomb Bridge Road
Norcross, Georgia 30092 • 417-2215

Located between Spaulding Drive and the Chattahoochee River, the Pinckneyville Arts Center is part of the Gwinnett County Parks and Recreation Department. The Arts Center offers a dazzling selection of classes and workshops for children in drawing and painting, sculpture, art explorations, music, movement, jewelry and cooking. "Friday Night Specials" have included puppet shows, family theater and family workshops. The Center has no gallery but it does hold open houses during the year showcasing the children's art work. Summer Art Camps are offered for preschoolers and school-age children and include a variety of classes in the visual and performing arts.

RAY'S INDIAN ORIGINALS
90 Avondale Road
Avondale Estates, Georgia 30002 • 292-4999

Ray's Indian Originals is part gallery, store and souvenir shop. There are permanent and touring museum-quality exhibits of Native-American pottery, clothing, baskets, jewelry, totems and artifacts; but, there are also general and souvenir quality items as well. Prices in the gallery are high, but for those children who are interested in Native-American history and culture, a visit would be worth your while. Also, the Gallery occasionally sponsors special storytelling sessions and other unusual events relating to Native American culture and traditions. *Hours*: 10:00am-6:00pm on Saturday or by appointment.

SOAPSTONE CENTER FOR THE ARTS
One South DeKalb Center, Suite 21
P.O. Box 370219
Decatur, Georgia   30037 • 241-2453

Funded largely through the Georgia and DeKalb Councils for the Arts, this burgeoning center for folk, ethnic and fine arts has children's workshops and classes in drawing and painting, cartooning, dance, acting, character development, piano and voice. The gallery often has exhibits appropriate for children. *Gallery Hours*: 10:00am-6:30pm, Monday-Thursday; 10:00am-5:00pm, Friday; 9:00am-5:00pm, Saturday.

STEEPLE HOUSE ARTS CENTER
(EAST COBB ARTS CENTER)
300 Village Place
Marietta, Georgia   30067 • 952-8661

The Arts Center's gallery often has exhibits appropriate for children, including shows of students' art work displayed at the end of each class session. Classes for preschoolers, families and children include drawing and painting, clay, ceramic, mobile making, print making and collage/assemblage. Special "Family Classes" are offered on Saturdays and early weekday evenings, where children and adult classes are held simultaneously, often on the same theme. Summer "Art Camp" involves activities in both the visual and performing arts. The Center will soon be moving to the intersection of Sandy Plains Road and Shallowford Road. *Gallery Hours*: 10:00am-5:00pm, Monday-Friday.

TULA ARTS COMPLEX
75 Bennett Street
Atlanta, Georgia 30309

The TULA Arts Complex, which is located at the end of Bennett Street (off Peachtree Road, behind Brookwood Shopping Center), is an attractive and airy complex of over 20 art galleries and artist's studios exhibiting, for the most part, contemporary art. All forms of media are represented, including paint, sculpture, photography, art glass, pottery, naive art, graphics and holography. The public is also welcome to watch the artists in their studios. Each of the galleries has its own hours of operation, although most are open from 11:00am-5:00pm, Mondays-Saturdays. One of the galleries in TULA especially worth mentioning is the **Atlanta Gallery of Holography** (352-3412). Holography is a fascinating art form and the exhibits in this gallery will amaze children of all ages. *Hours*: 11:00am-5:30pm, Tuesday-Saturday. Bennett Street itself houses numerous galleries, antique shops, and furniture stores, so if time and energy permit, plan on walking up the street to continue your adventure in art appreciation.

CATHERINE WADDELL ART GALLERY
Trevor Arnett Building
Clark Atlanta University
223 James P. Brawley Drive
Atlanta, Georgia 30314 • 651-3424

This magnificent collection of work by African-American artists was begun in the 1940's when Atlanta University started sponsoring one of the only black arts festivals in the country. Works of art shown during the annual festivals were acquired by the University over the next three decades. The festivals ended in the 1970s, but the collection has still grown thanks to the generosity of various donors. *Hours:* 11:00am-4:00pm, Tuesday-Friday. Group tours for elementary age children are available by appointment.

SHOPPING AND HOBBIES

Atlantans love to shop. Whether we're talking malls, strip shopping centers, super discount stores or small boutiques, there can be no doubt that the retail industry in this city has grown tremendously through the years. But shopping is not for every kid. In fact, my two-year-old has been known to scream "No, not again!" everytime I try to convince him to take a quick peek into a clothing store. But, that's only when it's a clothing store. Toy stores, hardware stores and even drug stores are quite a different story. In our home, during cold or rainy weather, a shopping excursion often takes the place of a trip to the neighborhood park.

SHOPPING CENTERS

Shopping centers abound in Atlanta. Spacious, modern and attractive, these malls have it all–glass bubble elevators, long escalators, food courts, game rooms, elaborate fountains, running space and, of course, shopping. The malls have recently become a common locale for year-round special events, such as **Art Festivals, Book Fairs, Fashion Shows, Musical Performances, Collector and Hobby Shows** and **Community Awareness Events.** During holidays, almost of the metro-Atlanta area malls have visits by **Santa Claus** and the **Easter Bunny** and provide **Safe Trick- or-Treat Halloween** events. During the summer months, the malls have been sponsoring special activities for younger children to help bring families into the air conditioned mall.

Our favorite mall for preschoolers is **Market Square Mall** located on Lawrenceville Highway in Decatur. The small "regional" mall has a small selection of stores that children enjoy, such as **The Early Learning Center** (a great toy store which has a play area for children), **The Aviarium** (a well-stocked fish and bird store), two other smaller toy stores and a store where everything for sale costs only $1.00. There is a diaper changing counter and nursing area in the restroom. But, the best thing about the mall is that it is filled with young children. Whether you are at the clock tower, the cookie stand or the food court fountain, there is always a good chance that you can find a temporary play partner for your sociable children!

157

Rio, the bright blue shopping center located at the corner of Piedmont Road and North Avenue in Midtown, has won national awards for its creative architecture and design. The focal point of the shopping center is a geodesic sphere and fountain area lying amid a multitude of gold frogs (statues, of course!). These frogs are guaranteed to make a lasting impression on young children. Although most of the retail space remains vacant, the shopping center is the home of the **Renaissance Book Store** which stocks a large selection of children's books, **Lettuce Souprise You,** a salad bar with scrumptious salads, soups, muffins, fruit and potatoes (children under 5 eat for free), and an **Interactive Video Wall** in the central court consisting of a 100-square foot screen broadcasting specially created work. Special events such as fashion shows and live entertainment can frequently be enjoyed on weekends at the fountain area.

For an unusual mix of stores, try **Ansley Mall Shopping Center** located on Monroe Drive and Piedmont in the midtown area. Although, the mall is not enclosed, the store selection, **Pickadilly Pet Shop** (fish, exotic birds, kittens, snakes, iguanas, lizards, and more), **The Toy Store** (an imaginative toy store having a large selection of imported, hard to find toys and crafts), the **Ansley Mall Bookstore** (with a children's section), and **The Royal Bagel** makes a visit here well worth your while.

TOY STORES

The trouble with visiting toy stores is that there is no way you are going to walk out empty-handed unless you have a heart of stone. So, if your budget allows for the purchase of another toy, puzzle, art supply or book, then a trip to a toy store can turn into a purposeful and fun filled excursion. The larger toy store chains, **Toys R Us** and **Lionel Playworld**, have not officially set aside a play area in the store where children can experiment and play. (Hint, hint!). Nevertheless, our children have managed to make themselves at home, and test ride the Big-Wheels, bicycles, play cars and spring horses. **The Early Learning Center,** which has stores at Market Square Mall and Perimeter Mall, encourages you to bring your children to the stores to play and enjoy a selection of the toys offered for sale in their mini-playground area. They have activities for children every month, such as storytimes, sing-a-longs, and new toy and game introductions you can play with in the store. And, almost all of the other toy stores in Atlanta have some products set out for temptation–Brio train sets, race car tracks, and erector sets are favorites. Even if your child doesn't get to pick out a toy at the end, the trip should be quite enjoyable.

A very popular toy store in north Atlanta is **The Toy School**, 5517 Chamblee Dunwoody Road (Dunwoody Village), Dunwoody, Georgia 30338 (399-5350). The Toy School's philosophy is "Every child deserves some success today." Immediately upon entering the store you will have no doubts that your child will be successful in finding hundreds of top quality toys, games, puzzles, art supplies, tapes, Brio sets and stuffed animals that she will want to take home with her. Or, perhaps she will be successful in convincing you to read to her one of the 4,000 plus children's book titles found in the store's roomy "library" area, or if she is older, in convincing you to buy quite a few of the carefully selected titles. Consider your child's success if she were to come on one of the days where a special workshop, concert, or storytelling session is in progress or when a renowned literary figure is visiting the store such as Lyle the Crocodile, Spot the Dog or Curious George! The Toy School also has two different party rooms and birthday celebrations may be customized to meet your child's wishes. *Hours:* 10:00am-5:50pm, Mondays-Saturdays; extended hours during the holiday season.

Some other popular toy stores are:
ABC Parent/Teacher Learning Center, Children's Book & Gift Mart, Children's Hour Toys, The DinoStore–"Gifts of Extinction," The Disney Store, Early Learning Centers, FAO Schwarz, Father Goose's International Toys, Kiddie City, Lenox Toys and Hobbies, My Storyhouse, Noah's Toy Shoppe, Sanrio Surprises, The Toy Store

HOBBIES

A hobby is something that can occupy and amuse an older child for long periods of time. Children are natural collectors. (I remind myself of that every time I go into my daughter's room and look at her shelves and closet!). Whether your child chooses collecting (rocks, baseball cards, coins, dolls, and so forth), model building, arts and crafts, reading, photography, comic books, computers or any other hobby, you can bet your life that these interests will become part of the entire family's life.

The excitement is contagious and trips to **Hobby Stores, Book Stores, Trade Shows** and **Collector Fairs** will become part of the regular routine for the family. When your child gets older, he or she may also want to join one of the many **Collector Clubs** thriving in Atlanta, a place where your child is sure to meet others with similar interests.

You can help your children find a hobby by exploring with them the various possibilities. First, try the **Atlanta All Hobby Show** held annually in July at the Exhibit Hall at the Atlanta Farmer's Market which features baseball cards, sports items, comic books, model cars, toys and just about anything else that is collected. Then look out for unusual hobby and collector shows. Almost every weekend, you can be sure to find a fair, whether it features antique automobiles, dolls, toys, flowers, baseball cards, comic books, railroad models, gems and minerals, radio control vehicles, coins, stamps and so on. Look in the *Weekend* section of the *Atlanta Journal and Constitution*, *Creative Loafing* and *Entertainment Atlanta* for listings.

Also, visit hobby shops. Atlanta hobby shops are listed in the *Yellow Pages* under headings which include **Hobby & Model Shops, Baseball Cards, Collectibles, Coin Dealers,** and **Stamps for Collectors**. Walk around the stores and see what appeals to your child. Perhaps, you will be rewarded by sparking an interest in your children that will lead to an adventure that will bring them enjoyment for the rest of their lives!

HARDWARE STORES

We know that going to a hardware store is one of the many chores frequently appearing on your "To Do" list. But, we cannot think of a better place to bring preschoolers and young children. Whether it's a mega-hardware store like **Home Depot**, a helpful **Ace Hardware**, or a small neighborhood shop, a child will be dazzled by the machinery, tools and gadgets on display. Sitting on a riding lawn mower, ringing door bells, hiding in display bathroom cabinets and picking favorite colors of paint are common activities on our trips. And, since we discovered this pastime, most of the repairs needed at our house actually do get done!

HOTEL HOPPING

We all know that Atlanta's number one industry is tourism and our city has the hotels to prove it. There are the ritzy downtown tourist hotels–the Hyatt Regency, Westin Peachtree Plaza, Ritz-Carlton, Atlanta Marriott Marquis, Atlanta Hilton Towers and Omni Hotel, with glass bubble elevators, revolving roof-top restaurants, elegant shopping malls, elaborate water fountain displays, exotic gardens and sun-filled space. There are also the magnificent hotels springing up in Buckhead and around the city's perimeter. The growth is phenomenal!

HOTEL HOP! Visit the hotels, and tour the architectural marvels. Spend some time in the bustling lobbies which are filled with tourists from around the world, business people and conventioneers. The people watching is fascinating. So, if it's a rainy day or you and your children just need to get out of the house for a while, stop in, ride some elevators, eat lunch, sit in a lobby and enjoy the people show at a nearby hotel!

SUNDAY BRUNCH. For those with children old enough to appreciate and enjoy elegant dining, try one of the gourment Sunday brunches offered by Atlanta hotels. These are always listed in the _Weekend_ section of the _Atlanta Journal and Constitution_.

SWIMMING. Recently, Atlanta hotels have begun realizing that hotels should not be for tourists only. For example, **The Atlanta Marriott Northwest** (952-7900) at Windy Hill Road, will allow a family to use the hotel's indoor pool facilities for a small fee ... a great idea for mid-winter doldrums. They also allow birthday parties at the pool with the hotel providing the ice cream cake, decorations, towels and lifeguard. Call around to other hotels in your area to see if they will allow you to use their facilities.

ON THE HORIZON

There are a few museums and attractions "On the Horizon" struggling to get enough money to become a reality. Their sponsors have a dream and we hope they will find enough financial support so that these new facilities will soon be available to the children of Atlanta.

CASCADE SPRINGS NATURE PRESERVE, Cascade Road, Atlanta (658-6385). This historical preserve is being developed by the City of Atlanta Park and Recreation Department and is scheduled to be open by the end of 1992. These 100 or so acres have a rich and varied history, originally probably belonging to Sandtown Indian Village. There are Civil War artifacts here such as rifle encasements, the ruins of the plantation of the first physician in the area, William Gilbert (father of Jeremiah for whom the Gilbert House is named), a quarry, and the natural spring water which once was sold to Atlanta residents. The first portion of the park will be handicapped accessible. Eventually trails will go all the way to the Cascade; there will be a conservatory and other facilities.

THE CHILDREN'S MUSEUM OF ATLANTA (875-KIDS). The Friends of the Children's Museum aspire to construct a 40,000-square-foot Museum to be open sometime in 1994. The program is still being developed, but will certainly include hands-on activities and other exhibits designed for educational, aesthetic, entertainment, and social purposes. By the summer of 1990 more than $200,000 had been raised for this worthy project.

FERNBANK MUSEUM OF NATURAL HISTORY, 1788 Ponce de Leon Avenue, N.E., Atlanta, Georgia 30307 (378-0127). Scheduled to open in 1992, amid the beautiful Fernbank Forest, The Fernbank Museum of Natural History promises to offer Atlanta a world-class showcase (over 150,000 square feet) of the natural sciences. This will be the first people-oriented natural history museum in the world to bring a new approach to learning about natural history using hands-on exhibits, interactive displays and the most modern communications and learning techniques available. The theme of the Museum will be "Our Changing Earth" using the State of Georgia as a springboard to understand the major stages of development of life on Earth. Visitors will take *A Walk Through Time in Georgia* from the mountains to the seacoast, and in a brief period of time travel from the beginning of time to today, and onto the future.

The highlight of the Museum for children will be a hands-on Discovery Room linked to a Fantasy Forest where your children will be given an explorer's backpack filled with tools to help them learn about nature, including how a cat sees at night, how a water strider walks on water and what it's like to pick up a persimmon with raccoon paws.

The Museum will also house an IMAX Theater (with a 3-story high screen!), conference and meeting facilities, an atrium for grand functions and a Naturalist Center where amateur biologists, geologists, archeologists and families can use scientific tools and methods under professional guidance to identify objects found in the field. Summer programs, lectures, classes, workshops and special events will abound. We cannot wait for this Museum to open! Keep your eyes open for further information.

GEORGIA SPORTS HALL OF FAME (875-8509). The facility will be located in the Georgia Dome if sufficient funds are raised.

MARGARET MITCHELL HOUSE, P.O. Box 7541, Atlanta, Georgia 30309 (233-7915). Many tour buses drive by the boarded-up and vacant Crescent Apartments on 10th Street and Crescent Avenue in midtown Atlanta to view the site where Margaret Mitchell lived with her husband while writing most of *Gone With the Wind.* Although there is not much to see right now, plans for this building include a complete rennovation, museum and library. Fund-raising is in process, but a completion date for the attraction is still unknown.

UNDERSEA WORLD is a proposed $22 million mega-aquarium boasting three one million-gallon tanks of sea life, a series of smaller tanks, an educational theater, a tidal pool, a laboratory, gift shop and snack bar. The attraction will make use of a technological breakthrough in plastics that permits not only gigantic tanks, but also an exciting acrylic tunnel to provide walk-through visitors with the sensation of being surrounded by an underwater environment. Undersea World will most likely be located near Underground Atlanta and be operated by a private company under City of Atlanta auspices.

4. Performing Arts for Children
(Music, Dance, Theatre and Puppetry)

P|eople of all ages are thrilled by the illusory world created through the various performing arts media. Young children in particular seem to become transfixed by stage performances which often blur the distinctions between fantasy and reality. Their imaginations are titillated, their emotional intensity ebbs and flows, the realm of the possible expands, and ultimately their knowledge of themselves and the world around them grows. Your child can experience the excitement, wonder and beauty of the performing arts by attending classes and by watching other children as well as adults perform in a variety of settings. Peruse the number of opportunities listed below, and then you may think as we did, "There are so many performances we'd like to go to with our kids, how can we possibly find the time?"

The *Atlanta Journal and Constitution* publishes an annual guide to the arts each September which lists the season schedule of many performing arts organizations in Atlanta; unfortunately, children's series are not listed. Also, the Saturday *Weekend* section of the *Atlanta Journal and Constitution* lists many performances, though it is not always possible to tell if they are appropriate for children. We suggest you phone the organizations listed below that interest you and your children and get on their mailing lists to receive periodic up-to-date information. It is the best way to plan ahead.

SERIES FOR CHILDREN

ALLIANCE CHILDREN'S THEATER, 1280 Peachtree Road, N.W., Atlanta, Georgia 30309 (892-2414) or (898-1132). The Alliance Theatre presents two full-scale productions each year in their Family Performance Series. The professional actors, the extravagant costumes and the elaborate sets have delighted Atlanta families for over twenty years. The plays are either original plays commissioned by the Alliance or are selections from the best adaptations of classic children's literature, such as "Merlin!" and "The Velveteen Rabbit." Tickets are $5.00 each. Call for program information. The Alliance offers after-school and Saturday classes year-round in creative dramatics, music play, storytelling and film. A selection of camp programs are offered during the summer months.

THE ATLANTA SYMPHONY ORCHESTRA, Woodruff Arts Center, 1293 Peachtree Road N.E., Suite 300, Atlanta, Georgia 30309 (898-1189 or 898-9556).

Family Concert Series–The Family Concert Series on Sunday afternoons features a unique combination of The Atlanta Symphony Orchestra, visual arts, dance and mime in programs lasting one hour each–perfect for young children. This three-concert series is very popular and has sold out in past years. Season tickets are made available to the general public in early May.

Street Symphony–About half of the Atlanta Symphony Orchestra periodically performs for preschoolers trough second grade in various locations throughout the Atlanta area. The Symphony believes that younger children can better enjoy the music in more relaxed atmospheres, as they are really too young to sit in the symphony hall for a lengthy performance. Call the Education Department (898-9572) for locations.

Youth Orchestra–The Symphony's Youth Orchestra is composed of high school musicians who perform three Sunday concerts each year in Symphony Hall.

CENTER FOR PUPPETRY ARTS, 1404 Spring Street, Atlanta, Georgia 30309 (874-0398). The Center for Puppetry Arts is the most comprehensive puppetry center in the United States featuring master puppeteers from all over the world. There are two performance series that will appeal to every child. The "Family Series" consists of three productions of classical children's tales such as Cinderella, Pinocchio or Peter Pan. Individual or season tickets may be purchased and reservations are required. The "Summer Festival" is a series of six shows that combine traditional tales, contemporary stories and fantasy. These stories, as well as the Family Series productions, are performed in different puppetry styles. You can purchase a Summer Festival season pass for the incredibly low price of $17.00 per person. See our chapter "Places To Go" for a comprehensive description of the Center.

PINCKNEYVILLE ARTS CENTER, 4300 Holcomb Bridge Road, Norcross, Georgia 30092 (417-2215). Throughout the fall, winter and spring seasons, the Pinckneyville Arts Center presents Friday Night Specials for children and families, featuring the Vik Chik Puppets, storytelling, CREATE Theatre and other special performances. During the summer months there are occasional outdoor performances for families, including storytelling and theatrical performances. Call for a schedule of upcoming events. The Center also offers a large selection of classes for children in the visual and performing arts, and a summer art camp for children age 4-14 years.

PERFORMANCES FOR CHILDREN

ACADEMY THEATRE FOR YOUTH TOUR (formerly the Phoenix Theatre Academy and formerly the Academy Theatre for Youth) (365-8088). The Academy Theatre has an "Artist-in-Schools" tour program which brings "issue-oriented" performances to the schools. Additionally, you can enjoy these programs during certain Saturdays at the Atlanta Historical Society.

AGNES SCOTT COLLEGE, Gaines Auditorium of Presser Hall, Agnes Scott College, Decatur, Georgia 30030 (371-6394). Agnes Scott College hosts a few special theater performances for children each year, including its annual December Christmas productions such as "The Littlest Christmas Tree" and "Bob Humbug the Christmas Gump." The College occasionally hosts special performances for families such as the world-famous Bao Dao Acrobats of the Republic of China whose exciting and unique performances include acrobatics, magic and dance.

A.R.T. STATION, INC., 5384 Manor Drive, Stone Mountain, Georgia 30086 (469-1105). A.R.T. Station's performing arts series consists of nine different musical, storytelling and theatrical productions, almost all of which are appropriate for families.

THE ARTS EXCHANGE, 750 Kalb Street, S.E., Atlanta, Georgia 30312 (624-4211). The Arts Exchange is a multi-cultural, multi-disciplinary arts resource center which offers special events for children throughout the year, including theCircus Arts Troupe's Animal Rights Circus and the Festival of Southern Performance.

THE ATLANTA BALLET, 477 Peachtree Road, N.E., Atlanta, Georgia 30308 (892-3303). The Atlanta Ballet performs eight ballets for families each year at the Atlanta Civic Center, including the December performance of Tchaikovsky's "Nutcracker Suite."

ATLANTA CHAMBER PLAYERS, 1447 Peachtree Street, Atlanta, Georgia 30309 (892-8681). The Atlanta Chamber Players performs its regular concert series at the High Museum of Art, at various art galleries, and at Sunday brunches at select restaurants in Atlanta. It also presents special programs for children at schools and recreational centers consisting of skits about musical instruments and "light" classical fare. What a great way to introduce your child to chamber music! Call to find out the schedule of their next performances.

THE ATLANTA CIVIC CENTER, 395 Piedmont Avenue, N.E., Atlanta, Georgia 30308 (523-6277). The Atlanta Civic Center is the site of a large variety of concerts, productions and events for adults and children throughout the year. An advance schedule for the Center is not available, so check for advertisements or call the above number for a recording about current and upcoming events.

ATLANTA DANCE WORKS –"A MOVING EXPERIENCE", 749 Main Street, Stone Mountain, Georgia 30083 (469-8503 or 978-3557). Atlanta Dance Works is a private dance school with studios located in Stone Mountain and Lawrenceville. Its dance company, called "A Moving Experience," performs at Center Stage Theater, at various other festivals and special events in Atlanta, and for school age children at schools and recreation centers. Every Christmas holiday season, the Company presents a special children's Christmas Ballet (but not the "Nutcracker Suite").

THE ATLANTA JEWISH COMMUNITY CENTER, 1745 Peachtree

Road, Atlanta, Georgia 30309 (875-7881). The J.C.C. presents a few plays and events each year which are geared to families and children. Check for performances in the *Atlanta Jewish Times* and other news papers. The Center regularly offers classes for 10-12 year olds in acting and improvisation as well as a summer camp program, "Midtown Experience in the Arts," instructed by professional artists, actors and directors. Call for more information.

THE ATLANTA OPERA, 1800 Peachtree Street, Atlanta, Georgia 30309 (355-3311). The Atlanta Opera has a special Studio program to bring a taste of opera to children in kindergarten through the twelfth grade. The Opera performs two hundred one-act operas a year in the public schools and at community centers. The productions are carefully tailored to the age group, yet professional quality is maintained as the "best singers in town" are hired to perform in English. To enhance the scene, the singers are dressed in ornate period costumes and perform on carefully designed stage sets. Find out if they are scheduled to perform at your child's school, and if they are not, be sure to inquire if arrangements can be made!

ATLANTA WORKSHOP PLAYERS (951-1956). The Atlanta Workshop Players offer quite a few children's productions during the year such as "You're a Good Man Charlie Brown." Most performances are at the Roswell Municipal Auditorium or the Village Center Playhouse, also in Roswell. Additionally, the group offers acting classes for children at a few locations in Atlanta and a summer camp drama program at Oglethorpe University.

BALLETETHNIC DANCE COMPANY (933-9050). Founded in 1990, this is Atlanta's premier African American ballet company whose performances appeal to children as well as adults. It is a resident dance company of Soapstone Center for the Arts.

BULLOCH HALL, 180 Bulloch Avenue, Roswell, Georgia 30077 (992-1731). Bulloch Hall is often the location for unusual performances for children and families, including programs starring young Russian violinists visiting the United States and storytelling sessions. Call for upcoming events.

CALLANWOLDE FINE ARTS CENTER, 980 Briarcliff Road, N.E., Atlanta, Georgia 30306 (872-5338). The Callanwolde Fine Arts Center presents a few children's theater and puppet performances each year. Regular theater, dance and musical performances may also be appropriate and enjoyable to older children. Callanwolde supports the Young Singers of Callanwolde, described in the next section "Performing Children." Callanwolde also has an annual storytelling festival in January. See our chapter on "Festivals and Special Events" for more information. Callanwolde has a large selection of classes and workshops for preschoolers through adults including offerings in dance, drama, improvisation, movement and the visual arts. The Summer Arts Camp, "Kaleidoscope," for children age 6-12 years, includes many activities in the performing arts.

CENTER STAGE THEATER, 1374 West Peachtree Road, Atlanta, Georgia 30309 (873-2500). The Center Stage Theater is the location for a large number of children's productions (approximately twenty per year) produced by local theater and dance groups, as well as national touring companies. (The National Theater for Children visits Atlanta at least once a year.) Advance schedules of performances at Center Stage are not available, so you will have to watch for advertisements or call the Theater for performance information.

CLAYTON STATE COLLEGE MUSIC THEATER ENSEMBLE, 5900 N. Lee Street, Morrow, Georgia 30260 (961-3510) This College performance troupe presents a musical at least once a year that is aimed at familes and young audiences such as "You're a Good Man Charlie Brown," a family musical.

COBB SYMPHONY ORCHESTRA, P.O. Box 452, Marietta, Georgia 30061 (424-5541). The Cobb Symphony Orchestra's regular subscription series consists of four concerts performed at the Cobb Civic Center. There is also a Summer Pops Series held at the The Galleria Amphitheatre and elsewhere in Cobb County. The Symphony has an active schedule during the Christmas holiday season and presents numerous concerts for children and families at Kennesaw College.

DEKALB MUSIC THEATRE AND DEKALB THEATRE COMPANY, DeKalb College, Central Campus, 555 N. Indian Creek Drive,

171

Clarkston, Georgia 30021 (299-4136). The Theatres present at least two musical performances for children every year such as "Cinderella" and "Oliver."

DEKALB SYMPHONY, DeKalb College, Central Campus, 555 N. Indian Creek Drive, Clarkston, Georgia 30021 (299-4270). The Orchestra's regular series consists of approximately seven performances throughout the year performed mainly at DeKalb College Central's theatre. In January they present a special Children's Concert at the College's gymnasium featuring Monica Kaufman as narrator and dance, magic and other special entertainment.

THE FOX THEATRE, 660 Peachtree Street, Atlanta, Georgia 30365 (881-2100). The Fox Theatre is a popular site for a wide variety of events for adults and children throughout the year. The Fox Family Film Festival features movies, cartoons and sing-alongs in June, July and August. Many groups schedule special performances for children at the Fox. An advance schedule for the Fox is not available, so look weekly in your local newspaper or call the above number for information about current and upcoming events.

GEORGIA BALLET, 999 Whitlock Avenue, S.W., Marietta, Georgia 30064 (425-0258). The Georgia Ballet presents three performances each year, all appropriate for children, including the holiday special, "The Nutcracker Suite." Occasionally, the Ballet will even present a musical such as "You're A Good Man Charlie Brown." Most performances are at the Cobb Civic Center.

GWINNETT BALLET THEATRE, 2296 Henry Clower Boulevard, Snellville, Georgia 30278 (921-7277). The Gwinnett Ballet Theater is a semi-professional dance company which presents two productions each year: the winter favorite, "The Nutcracker Suite" and a spring peformance. DeKalb Community College is the usual location for the productions.

HIGH MUSEUM OF ART, 1280 Peachtree Street, N.E., Atlanta, Georgia 30309 (892-4444). The High Museum sponsors special peformances and activities for children throughout the year, including storytelling hours, puppet shows and other theatrical, musical and dance events. Occasionally, it is the location for a summer Children's Film Festival featuring Saturday morning films appropriate for children of all ages.

INTERNATIONAL BALLET ROTARU (365-0488). This Ballet Company performs colorful and exciting ballets at the Fox Theatre. In additon to the evening performances, there are matinees for each program, making it easier for parents to bring children. The programs are approximately two hours long with an intermission, making Ballet Rotaru appropriate for the more sophisticated younger person. Recently, they have added the"Nutcracker" to their repertoire.

JOMANDI PRODUCTIONS (876-6346). Jomandi Productions' performances combine drama, dance and music to dramatize the African-American experience. Many of their performances are quite appropriate for children. Most productions are at the 14th Street Playhouse.

KENNESAW STATE COLLEGE PERFORMING ARTS THEATER (423-6151). The College often presents performances appropriate for families such as "A Midsummer Night's Dream," and the "Big River, The Adventures of Huckleberry Finn." Additionally, the College is the location for free professional storytelling sessions which include folktales and music for audiences age 12 through adult.

MUSIC SOUTH CORPORATION ORCHESTRA AND CHORALE (346-3417). Atlanta's first professional all-black orchestra performs works by black composers in pop, gospel, jazz and classical fields. The programs are appropriate for families, and groups such as the Boy Scouts often attend productions. In 1991, the Orchestra was able to work with the Fulton County School System to develop a special program to bring to the schools. As the Orchestra receives more funding, it will continue to develop special programs specifically tailored to young audiences.

THE NEIGHBORHOOD PLAYHOUSE, 430 W. Trinity Place, Decatur, Georgia 30030 (373-5311). The Neighborhood Playhouse is a family-oriented community theater. Expansion plans include a new theater to be primarily used for children's performances. Performing companies, such as Theatre Gael's Children's Theatre and Picadilly Puppets, use the

Playhouse for limited engagements. Call for a schedule of upcoming events.

OGLETHORPE UNIVERSITY THEATER–"THE PLAYMAKERS," 4484 Peachtree Road, N.E., Atlanta, Georgia (261-1441). The University Players perform mainly for adult audiences, although ocassionally, they will present a special children's performance such as "Snow White and the Seven Dwarfs." During the summer, the College co-hosts resident dance and drama camps with the Atlanta Workshop Players and "Camp Shakespear" with the Georgia Shakespeare Festival, a two hour program for children ages 5-12 years.

OMNI COLISEUM AT CNN CENTER, 100 Techwood Drive, Atlanta, Georgia 30303 (681-2100). The Omni Coliseum is the location for numerous special events for children and families throughout the year, including Ringling Brothers and Barnum and Bailey Circus which performs in late January and early February, and Disney's World on Ice which comes to Atlanta in early November. An advance schedule for the Omni is not available, so look for advertisements for special events in newspapers and magazines.

OPEN CITY THEATRE/CREATE, 673 Brownwood Avenue, Atlanta, Georgia 30316 (378-3539). CREATE has a repertoire of over twenty different productions available for audiences age kindergarten through high school. The programs use the arts to entertain, educate and excite the creative spirit of the children. Performances are participatory and allow children to interact with the actors. Workshops for smaller groups are also available. CREATE sponsors "Artsbusters," an excellent visual and performing arts summer camp program for children age 2-12 years old, which includes activities in the visual and performing arts.

THE PANDEAN PLAYERS, 30 Trammell Street, Marietta, Georgia 30064 (427-8196). The Pandean Players is a small professional chamber music group performing on reed and wind instruments. The Players have a wonderful selection of special performances for children, including "Pops Potpourri," "Winter Wonderland," and "Zoo Music," created in cooperation with Zoo Atlanta. All of their programs are exciting and educational, and we recommend that you call to find out the location of their next performance.

PICADILLY PUPPETS, 621 Densley Drive, Decatur, Georgia 30030 (636-0022). Picadilly Puppets is a touring company that performs for children at various theaters, festivals, schools and special events in the Atlanta area, including the Neighborhood Playhouse and Callanwolde Fine Arts Center. They have quite a large repertoire, so it is possible to see five different shows in the span of just a few weeks. Keep your eye out for them they're quite good!

SEVEN STAGES PERFORMING ARTS CENTER, 1105 Euclid Avenue, N.E., Atlanta, Georgia 30307 (523-7647) or (522-0911). Seven Stages' performances represent Atlanta's ethnic diversity through dance, music and the performing arts. Almost all are appropriate for families, and from time to time, certain performances are created especially for children.

SOAPSTONE CENTER FOR THE ARTS, One South DeKalb Center, P.O. Box 370219, Decatur, Georgia 30037 (241-2453). Numerous special events and festivals are help at Soapstone throughout the year such as the Festival of International Dance, the Caribbean Cultural Festival, and a Jazz Concert Series. The Center's touring ensemble is comprised of children age 12-16, who perform at schools, community theaters and shopping malls. The performances deal with serious "issue-oriented" topics such as drug prevention and teenage pregnancy. The Center also offers classes year-round for children in dance, acting, character development, piano and voice.

SOUTHEASTERN SAVOYARDS, 6840 Ramundo Drive, Doraville, Georgia 30360 (396-0620). For over 10 years, the Savoyards have been performing light operas, mostly Gilbert and Sullivan of course, to rave reviews. These operas are full-scale, lavish productions of about 30 performers supported by a 14-piece orchestra, which should be really exciting for families with elementary age children. Since much of the enjoyment of these operas is Gilbert's clever lyrics, the Savoyards thoughtfully provide the audiences with librettos in advance of the performances. Be sure to request one and sing at home ahead of time with your children! In addition to their regularly scheduled program, "Gilbert and Sullivan

Samplers" are offered to schools, churches, and other community and business groups at nominal cost. The Savoyard productions are presented at Center Stage Theatre, West Peachtree at 17th Street. Occasional diversions from the usual Gilbert an Sullivan repertory have included other productions such as "The Student Prince."

SOUTHSIDE THEATER GUILD, 200 West Campbelton Street, Fairburn, Georgia 30213 (969-0956). This theater company puts on one production each summer for children, such as "Charlotte's Web."

STAGE DOOR PLAYERS, North DeKalb Cultural Center, 5339 Chamblee-Dunwoody Road, Atlanta, Georgia 30338 (396-1726). The Stage Door Players has recently started a summer one-act children's festival held on three different weekends. Occasionally it presents a musical production performed by children such as "A Kids' Khorus Line." The groups usually performs at the North Arts Center in Dunwoody.

TELLTALE THEATRE, 30 Trammell Street, Marietta, Georgia 30064 (427-8206). Professional actors and actresses put on high energy, imaginative and educational performances for children. They have no theater of their own, but their performances can be found throughout metropolitan Atlanta. Call for their upcoming schedule. In June and July the Theater runs a summer theater camp for children age 7-17 years in conjunction with Theater on the Square, where professional actors invite children to explore the world of acting. The Theatre also has a "Safe Kids" program developed in conjunction with Egleston's Children's Hospital promoting the use of seat belts.

THEATER OF THE STARS (252-8960). Recently, Theater of the Stars has begun bringing performances to Atlanta which are appropriate for families such as "Annie," "Cats," and "A Chorus Line." Perforamnces are at the Fox Theater.

THEATRE GAEL, 776 N. Highland Avenue, N.E., Atlanta, Georgia 30306 (876-1138). Once a year, Theatre Gael's Children's Theatre performs at the Neighborhood Playhouse in Decatur. At the same location, you may attend Theatre Gael's regular performances which are often appropriate for families.

THEATRICAL OUTFIT, 1012 Peachtree Street, N.E., Atlanta, Georgia 30309 (872-0665). The Theatrical Outfit's performances are appropriate for children, such as their annual production of "Appalachian Christmas." Call for information about the suitability of their upcoming production.

THEATRE IN THE SQUARE, 11 Whitlock Avenue, Marietta Square, Marietta, Georgia 30064 (422-8369). Fall 1990 marked the beginning of the Young Audience's Theatre. Although there are no regularly scheduled perforamnces, occasionally a production will be geared to younger audiences. Keep an eye on this growing theatre.

VIK CHIK'S PUPPET THEATRE, The touring puppet theatre performs for children in locations throughout Atlanta such as the Wills Park Recreation Center and Pinckneyville Arts Center. Look for announcements in your local newspapers.

FOR MORE INFORMATION ABOUT TOURING COMPANIES that are eager to perform at your child's school, recreation centers, birthday parties or other special group events, you can call **Alternate ROOTS** (577-1079), **Young Audiences of Atlanta** (589-0644) and the **Atlanta Theatre Coalition** (873-1185). These service organizations have lists of theatre companies, puppeteers, storytellers, musicians, and dancers who have programs appropriate for elementary age children.

PERFORMING CHILDREN

THE ATLANTA BOY CHOIR, 1215 S. Ponce de Leon Avenue, Atlanta, Georgia 30306 (378-0064). Only boys, age 5-13 years are permitted to sing in this Choir. They perform classical concert repertoire at various locations throughout Atlanta, including churches, festivals, and parades, and with the Atlanta Symphony Orchestra as part of the Symphony's regular series. The Atlanta Boy Choir makes an annual international tour to Europe where it performs at many distinguished churches and institutions. Auditions are held yearly.

ATLANTA CHILDREN'S CHORALE, c/o The Church of the Atonement, 4945 High Point Road, N.E., Atlanta, Georgia 30342 (728-0643). Atlanta's newest children's choir presents an alternative for Atlanta's boys and girls. Children from kindergarten through 8th grade, who love to sing in a fun and relaxed atmosphere, are invited to audition for this group. The Choir takes an eclectic approach to their musical repertoire, offering songs in foreign languages, ensemble singing, musical games, musical movement as well as secular and sacred works. The Choir presently performs seasonal concerts and during special events throughout Atlanta.

THE ATLANTA JAZZ THEATER, Dan & Company Studios, 5544 Chamblee Dunwoody Road, Atlanta, Georgia 30338 (393-9519). The Atlanta Jazz Theater, the resident company of Dan & Company Studios, is the first dance company in Atlanta devoted entirely to the study and performance of jazz dance works. The Junior Company, comprised of children 9-13 years, presents a "History of Jazz Dance" and has appeared at elementary schools all over Atlanta, the Kingfest and at other special events.

THE ATLANTA MUSIC CLUB, 1900 The Exchange, Suite 160, Atlanta, Georgia 30339 (955-5416). The Atlanta Music Club is a non-profit association which supports young musical performers in Atlanta. One of its programs, the Young Performers of Atlanta, is a series of recital meetings held to provide young students with an opportunity to perform in professional settings. The Atlanta Music Club also provides scholarships for young performers and gives formal concerts at various locations.

CHILDREN'S TELEVISION WORKSHOP–Metro-Media Services (986-0644). Atlanta area kids are offered an opportunity to gain experience in acting, producing, directing and camera operation by participating in the production of TV shows to be aired on local television stations. Productions include, "Kid's Talk" for children age 12 and younger, and "Teen Talk" for children age 13 and older.

CLAYTON FESTIVAL BALLET, 2286 Lake Harbin Road, Morrow, Georgia 30260 (366-3494). The performers of the Clayton Festival Ballet are students who are training at the Clayton Festival Ballet School and a few others from outlying communities. The Ballet has an active performance schedule, as well as representing Clayton County during numerous festivals in Atlanta, including the Children's Festival and Festival of the Trees. A few of the performances have included "guest artists" from the Atlanta Ballet, International Ballet Rotaru and Joffrey Ballet.

COBB CHILDREN'S THEATER, 5195 Clark Street, S.W., Austell, Georgia 30001 (941-1391). Children performers, 7th grade through high school, present two performances each year at the Cobb Civic Center such as "Charlotte's Web." All of their performances are appropriate for the entire family. Call for audition and performance information.

COBB CIVIC BALLET, c/o Scarborough Academy, 3301 MacLand Road, S.W., Powder Springs, Georgia 30073 (943-7038). The Cobb Civic Ballet is comprised of children age 7-13 years who perform in at least two different productions each year, including a traditional "Nutcracker Suite" during the holiday season. Other productions have included "Hansel and Gretel" and "Alice in Wonderland." Most performances are held at the Cobb Civic Center, although there are sometimes FREE performances at different schools in the Cobb County area. Call for audition and performance information.

COBB YOUTH CHORUS OF GEORGIA, P.O. Box 316, Marietta, Georgia 30061 (425-2271). The Cobb Youth Chorus provides voice training and performance experience for children age 7 -14 years. The younger children are accepted without auditions. Selection for the older chorus is by audition only. The Chorus performs at special concerts given during the year, and at Cobb County area festivals. During the month of December, the children have an extensive performance schedule. All productions integrate singing with dancing and costumes.

DEKALB CENTER FOR THE PERFORMING ARTS AT AVONDALE HIGH SCHOOL, 1192 Clarendon Road, Avondale Estates, Georgia 30002 (289-ARTS) DeKalb County's Magnet School for the Performing Arts puts on numerous special theater and dance performances throughout the year, all appropriate for children and families. It also offers a Children's Theater for very young audiences which is available at no cost for school children on weekday mornings. The public may attend on

Saturdays for a small admission cost. The Center also has a musical touring group and ongoing gospel performances.

DORAVILLE ARTS THEATRE, Doraville Community Center, 3765 Park Avenue, Doraville, Georgia 30340 (451-0573). Throughout the year, children age 6 and up present musical revues and theatrical performances for children of all ages, including preschoolers. Look for audition advertisements in *Creative Loafing*, *The DeKalb Neighbor*, and the *DeKalb News/Sun*.

THE YOUNG SINGERS OF CALLANWOLDE, 315 West Ponce de Leon Avenue, Suite 915, Decatur, Georgia 30030 (377-6081). The Young Singers of Callanwolde is a choral group for boys and girls in the 3rd to the 9th grade. Children are instructed in voice and music, and have an opportunity to perform in special concerts throughout the year at Callanwolde Fine Arts Center, Emory University, with the Atlanta Symphony Orchestra and at festivals and concerts in the United States and Europe.

AND DON'T FORGET . . . There are numerous opportunities for children to perform with school-based orchestras throughout Atlanta and to attend concerts performed by these orchestras. One such orchestra in the metro-Atlanta area is the **DeKalb Youth Pops Orchestra**. Comprised of students in DeKalb County schools who are in the seventh grade and older, the repertoire includes calpyso, classical, country, jazz, gospel, reggae, spirituals and Top-40 hits. In the past the group has performed at the Civic Center, Six Flags Over Georgia, the Omni and many other civic and social functions locally and nationally.

ANNUAL PERFORMANCE FESTIVALS AND CONCERTS FOR FAMILIES

JANUARY

DeKalb Symphony Orchestra, DeKalb College Central Campus Gymnasium, Clarkston (299-4136). The Orchestra presents an annual

Children's Concert for an admission price of $2.00.

MARCH

Jazz on Tap, Georgia State University, Atlanta (971-1109). Over 15 area dance companies participate in this day-long jazz and tap festival sponsored by Georgia State University.

Peach Blossom Bluegrass Festival, Southern Tech Auditorium, Marietta (299-6400). An afternoon and evening of continuous bluegrass music performances with proceeds benefiting WRFG.

APRIL

Atlanta College Dance Festival, Agnes Scott College, Decatur (371-6360). Agnes Scott Studio Dance Theater, Emory Dance Company, Spelman College Dance Company and Georgia State Dance Company have all participatd in this annual festival of dance.

Glover Park's Concert on the Square (429-4212). Concerts on Glover Park Square are held in the evening on the last Friday of the month, as well as during the Atlanta Dogwood Festival.

MAY

Blue-Sky Concerts in Old Courthouse Square, Decatur (371-8386). Outdoor concerts Wednesdays at noon on the Courthouse Square lawn throughout the month of May. FREE.

Evening Concerts in Old Courthouse Square, Decatur (371-8386). Outdoor concerts on Saturday evenings on the Courthouse lawn throughout the month of May. FREE.

Brown Bag Spring Concert Series, Glover Park, Marietta Square, Marietta (429-4212). Live entertainment mid-day every Thursday in May. FREE.

Atlanta Film & Video Festival, High Museum of Art and Image Film

Video Center at TULA, Atlanta (352-4225). Some of the films screened during the week-long film festival are not appropriate for children but certain of the animation films and other works are. Call for a schedule and decide for yourself.

Spring Music Festival, West of Hiawassee (400/896-4191). Country singers and fiddlers perform Friday night and Saturday afternoon at the Georgia Mountain Fairgrounds.

Dahlonega Folk Festival, Blackburn Park, Dahlonega (404/864-4127). Traditional, contemporary and international folk music together with old-time square dancing and storytelling highlight this weekend festival.

SUMMER

Atlanta Symphony Orchestra's Free Concerts in the Parks, Atlanta (898-1189). Sunday evening concerts at various locations in Atlanta during June, July and August (Piedmont, Grant, Perkerson, Lakewood Ampitheater and The Galleria Ampitheater). FREE.

Atlanta Symphony Pops Series, Atlanta (898-1189). Ten concerts at Chastain Park Ampitheater which feature superstar entertainers. Concerts are at 8:30pm rain or shine. You may purchase individual tickets at a cost of $14.50-$32.50. Series prices range from $62.50-$162.50 for 5 shows to $125.00-$325.00 for 10. There is a special July 4th program.

Center for Puppetry Arts, Atlanta (873-3391). The Summer Festival consists of a full season of daily puppet show performances during the months of June, July and August.

Fox Family Film Festival, Atlanta (881-2000). Family movies, cartoons and sing-alongs are scheduled through June, July and August. Evenings only.

High Museum of Art Children's Film Festival, Atlanta (892-3600, Ext. 433). Children's films are sometimes offered on Saturday mornings at 10:00am in Hill Auditorium, Woodruff Arts Center. The show lasts less than two hours. Admission is FREE and children must be accompanied by an adult.

DeKalb International Choral Festival (378-2525). The largest festival of its kind brings world-class choral groups to perform at various venues throughout DeKalb County with a finale at Stone Mountain Park.

Atlanta Jazz Series, Atlanta (653-7160). A 10-day event in June, the Atlanta Jazz Series hosts concerts, workshops, dance peformances, gallery exhibitions and film videos featuring jazz performers. The outdoor concerts are FREE. Other events have varying charges.

Brown Bag Concerts Spring Series, Woodruff Park Amphitheatre, Atlanta (653-7120). Wednesday mid-day concerts are scheduled during the months of April, May and June. FREE.

One Atlantic Center Summer Concert Series, 10th and West Peachtree Streets, Atlanta (870-2140). Mid-day free concerts in the park adjacent to the One Atlantic Center building in June, July and August. FREE

Atlanta Botanical Garden - Garden Evening Concerts on the Great Lawn. (588-4888). Enjoy a three concert series amid the beautiful flowers of the Garden. Picnicking is allowed.

Six Flags Over Georgia Summer Series, Mableton (739-3400). Special children's concerts at the Park during the summer. Some are FREE with park admission, while others have a surcharge.

Candlelite Concert Series, Mable House, Mableton (739-0189). Saturday evening peformances on the grounds of the Mable House twice a month in May, June and July. FREE.

Jubilee Summer Concert Series, The Galleria Ampitheater, Atlanta (988-9641). Sunday evening concerts in June, July and August under the stars. FREE.

Marietta - Concerts on the Square, Glover Park, Marietta (429-4212). On the last Friday night in April, May, June, July and August there are free music concerts under the stars in the Square in Marietta.

Lakewood Ampitheatre, Lakewood Freeway, Atlanta (627-9704). A varied line-up of pop, rock, country and blues concerts are scheduled throughout the summer.

Georgia Shakespeare Festival - Oglethorpe University, Atlanta (264-0020). June-August, Oglethorpe University is the location for three classics in repertory of works by Shakespeare or other period playwrights.

Drums Across America, Varying Locations, Atlanta (973-1357). Premier drum and bugle corps from throughout North America come to perform in Atlanta each July, with performances that combine theater, music, dance and marching.

Dahlonega Bluegrass Festival, Dahlonega (400/864-3711). Four days of bluegrass music, camping and plenty of good things to eat in the Georgia mountains.

Alpharetta Bluegrass Festival, Wills Park Equestrian Center, Alpharetta (475-3470). Over 45 performing acts play in an open-air covered arena during this annual bluegrass and gospel festival.

Appalachian Music Festival, Unicoi State Park (404/878-2201, ext. 282/283). Enjoy the musical festival at Unicoi State Park in July with concerts, instrumental displays, dancing and workshops on Appalachian and gospel music.

The Reach of Song, An Appalachian Drama (800/262-SONG). The "Official State Drama," re-creates the flavor of the homeland of Pulitzer Prize nominee Byron Herbert Reece. June-early August.

SEPTEMBER

Montreux Atlanta International Music Festival, Different Locations, throughout Atlanta (653-7160). Listen to jazz, blues, zydeco, classical, folk, pop and opera at different locations all through Atlanta, including day long free concerts in Piedmont Park over the Labor Day Weekend.

Georgia Music Festival, Georgia Department of Industry, Trade and Tourism (656-3551). A ten-day show of appreciation for the musicians of Georgia with concerts, shows, performances and musical events scheduled throughout the State.

Blue-Sky Concerts in Old Courthouse Square, Decatur (371-8386). Outdoor concerts Wednesdays at noon on the Courthouse Square lawn throughout the month of September. FREE.

Evening Concerts in Old Courthouse Square, Decatur (371-8386). Outdoor concerts on Saturday evenings on the Courthouse lawn throughout the month of September. FREE.

Brown Bag Concerts Spring Series, Woodruff Park Amphitheatre, Atlanta (653-7120). Wednesday mid-day concerts are scheduled during the months of September, October and November. FREE.

Fall Brown Bag Concert Series, Glover Park, Marietta (429-4212). Live entertainment mid-day every Thursday in September. FREE.

OCTOBER

Brown Bag Concerts Spring Series, Woodruff Park Amphitheatre, Atlanta (653-7120). Wednesday mid-day concerts are scheduled during the months of September, October and November. FREE.

Festival of Southern Performance, c/o Alternate ROOTS (577-1079). Sponsored by Alternate ROOTS, an actor's service group, this festival has over twenty-five different theatrical, dance, music, puppetry and storytelling performances scheduled over a one-week period performed by artists from all over the Southeast. A whole day is reserved for children's performances. The festival is held every second or third year.

Fall Harvest Festival, West of Hiawassee (404/895-4191). Bands, pickers, singers, cloggers and gospel singers entertain at the Georgia Mountain Fairgrounds.

North Georgia Folk Festival, Sandy Creek Park, Athens (404/354-

2670). Georgia's rich musical heritage is celebrated with blues, bluegrass and string-band musicians. Also showcased are pioneer skills and games, farm animals and folk artists and crafters.

———————————————— **NOVEMBER** ————————————————

Brown Bag Concerts Spring Series, Woodruff Park Amphitheatre, Atlanta (653-7120). Wednesday mid-day concerts are scheduled during the months of September, October and November. FREE.

———————————————— **DECEMBER** ————————————————

Holiday Performances. Holiday performances abound. See the late November edition of the Saturday *Weekend* section of the *Atlanta Journal and Constitution* for a complete listing of holiday theater, dance and musical performances throughout the Atlanta area.

5. Sports and Recreation

U nfortunately, in our highly advanced technological society, the value of physical exercise has almost been lost. In elementary schools, former full-time Physical Education instructors have too often been replaced with part-time instructors and daily recess time has been considerably short-ened. This requires parents to be more actively involved in their children's athletic development.

If your family does not have a "family sport," we urge you to skim through this chapter. We are sure you can find something enjoyable. Remember, in family sports skill levels need not be important, for even the youngest member can fit in a backpack on a family hike.

SPECTATOR SPORTS

PROFESSIONAL SPORTS

Atlanta Attack (National Division, American Indoor Soccer Associa-tion). Games at the Omni Coliseum from November-March. For information call 431-6111 or 577-9600. Attend on your birthday and have an autographed soccer ball and birthday cake delivered to your seat! Listen to home and away games on WCHK-105.7 FM.

Atlanta Braves (National Baseball League). Games at the Atlanta-Fulton County Stadium from April-October. For game information call 577-9100 and for tickets phone 249-6400. Celebrate your child's birthday at the ballpark. The Braves and Colonial Baking Company will supply everything–cake, invitations, ice-cream, Coca-Cola and party favors! Par-ties are for children age 13 and younger. You must purchase a minimum of 10 tickets and make advance reservations. Call the Birthday Coordina-tor at the number above.

Atlanta Falcons (National Football League). Games are held at the Atlanta-Fulton County Stadium beginning in September. There are eight regularly scheduled home games, and pre-season games are held in

August. In 1992, the Falcons should be moving to the new Georgia Dome. For information, call 945-1111; for tickets call 261-5400; and the SEATS charge line is 577-9600. Falcon Football practice is at the Falcon Complex in Suwanee, Georgia. For information on attending practice games, call 261-5400.

Atlanta Hawks (National Basketball Association). Games are held at the Omni Coliseum from October through March. For general information phone 681-3605 and for tickets call 827-3865.

Atlanta Thunder. Team tennis features top ranked players, and the Atlanta Thunder is under the direction and ownership of Billie Jean King. Home games are at the DeKalb Tennis Center in Decatur. Season tickets may be purchased by calling 250-3428. For other information call 498-6060.

COLLEGIATE SPORTS

Georgia Tech Yellow Jackets Basketball. (ACC Division I). Games are at the Georgia Tech Coliseum from November through February. For information, phone 894-5447.

Georgia Tech Yellow Jackets Football. (ACC Division I). Games are at the Bobby Dodd Stadium from September through December. For information, phone 894-5447.

Georgia Tech–Other Sports. Call 894-5447 for schedules and information.

University of Georgia Bulldogs Football. (Southeastern Conference). Games are at Sanford Stadium, Athens, Georgia from September through December. For information, phone 404/542-1231.

University of Georgia Bulldogs Basketball. (Southeastern Conference). Games are at UGA Coliseum, Athens, Georgia from November through February. For information, phone 404/542-1231.

University of Georgia–Other Sports. Call 404/542-1231 for schedules and information.

Other College Sports. There are many other colleges and universities in the greater metropolitan area that have athletic games open to the public. Here are the phone numbers of just a few if you are interested in their schedules: Emory University, 727-6547; Clayton State, 961-3400 (ask for the Athletic Director); Georgia State University, 651-2772; Ogelthorpe University, 261-1441; and, Atlanta University, 880-8126.

AUTO RACING

Atlanta International Raceway. 20 miles south of Atlanta in Hampton, Georgia. Events include Grand National stock car races: the Coca-Cola 500 in March and the Atlanta Journal 500 in November. Regular events include NTPA tractor-pulls and Bobtail 200-truck races. For information, phone 946-4211.

New Atlanta Dragway. 1 hour northeast of Atlanta in Commerce, Georgia (Exit #53 off I-85 at US 441). Races include Jet Funny Cars, Top Fuel Dragsters, The AC Delco Southern Nationals, the annual Ingles/96 Rock Nite of Fire, the SCAA Pro Racing Spectacular, and the Coca-Cola Kudzu Nationals. For information, phone 404/335-2301.

Road Atlanta. 30 miles north of Atlanta in Braselton, Georgia. (I-85 at Highway 53, which is Exit #49) This 1,000 acre world class facility is home to many roadracing events including the International Motor Sports Association GT series, the annual SCCA National Championship Valvoline Runoffs and the American Motorcycle Association. Parking is $5.00. Fees for races vary. Camping is permitted on Saturday nights only–no fee. For this year's schedule of events, phone 404/881-8233. Road Atlanta Hotline: 404/967-6143. Children under age 12 are FREE.

BICYCLE RACING

Dick Lane Velodrome. Every Friday night, amateur and professional cyclists compete in a variety of races, including USCF track events, on the Southeast's only Velodrome. Races are $3/adults ($5 for Grand Prix Races-General Admission) and FREE for children 12 and under. For upcoming events, phone the *Talking Yellow Pages* at 329-4500 ext. 3158. For further information, call 765-1085.

Road Atlanta. Road Atlanta hosts USCF races such as the Circuit Course, a 2.52 mile loop on the Road Atlanta road course. It also hosts the **Southeast Cycling Festival** which has included the Coors Light NORBA National Point Series Circuit Race. For more information call 967-6143.

Outdoor Cycling Races. Races to benefit various charities are held all year long. Good sources for these events are *Entertainment Atlanta* and the *Weekend* section of the Saturday *Atlanta Journal and Constitution.* Sponsor a bicyclist for a worthy cause and have fun at the same time!

GEORGIA STATE GAMES COMMISSION

The **Georgia State Games Commission** (853-0250) holds state-wide competitions in 26 events ranging from archery to volleyball. The games are open to the public for a small fee and many are held each year in the Atlanta area. Children may enter certain events, such as archery, track and field and judo. Games Hotline: 877-7578.

GOLF

Golf is big in Atlanta and there are many tournaments throughout the year. One of the most important is the Bell South Atlanta Classic held every May to benefit Egleston Children's Hospital. A recent event raised over a half million dollars!

GYMNASTICS

Several major gymnastics meets are held in Atlanta throughout the year including the Peachtree Classic, an international gymnastics meet, held in February.

HORSE SHOWS AND RODEOS

Greater Atlanta is host to several riding events each year. Among the more popular are:

Atlanta Steeplechase. Seven Branches Farm, Cumming, Georgia. Held in the Spring to benefit the Atlanta Speech School. Tickets are available by mail order only on a first-come, first-served basis. There is a fee for parking. For information, call 237-7436.

DeKalb Sheriff's Posse Rodeo. The Posse hosts an annual 2-day Wild West event at the Stone Mountain Coliseum that features bucking broncos, barrel riding, calf roping and more. They also host the State High School Rodeo in September. Call 498-5600 or 243-7334 for information.

The Hunter-Jumper Classic. Wills Park Equestrian Center, 11915 Wills Road, Alpharetta, Georgia. Sponsored by the Georgia Hunter Jumper Association, this two-week event held in July benefits a charitable organization. For information, call 740-8714 or 664-8462.

Wills Park Equestrian Center. 11915 Wills Road, Alpharetta, Georgia. This beautiful 46 acre facility is operated by Fulton County. Horse shows for all breeds are held all year long in both covered and open show rings. Of special interest to youngsters is the Little Britches All Youth Open Show held in June. There are picnic and camper areas. Farm tours are available on the weekends. Open daily. Admission is FREE or nominal. For information, call 475-3470.

POLO FIELDS

The Polo Fields. 6325 Saddlebridge Court, Cumming, Georgia, Exit #8 off GA 400. The Polo Fields is the home of the Atlanta Polo Club. Every Sunday from the first Sunday in June through October, from 2:00pm-4:00pm, your family may enjoy watching polo in a picnic-like, fun atmosphere. You may tailgate it or purchase soft drinks and sandwiches from the concession stand. The stands are not covered, so bring a hat or sunglasses. Though it is rare for a match to be cancelled, if you are in doubt, tune your radio to WPCH (94.9 FM) from 12noon-1:00pm and they will announce if the fields are closed for the safety of the riders and horses. The fee is $10.00 per carload. Call 688-POLO.

TENNIS

Because Atlanta is an important tennis city, it is home to the **Atlanta**

Thunder (mentioned above). The **AT&T Challenge** which draws many of the top world-ranked players is held in Atlanta at Horseshoe Bend Country Club every year, and keep your eyes open for the location of the **Junior National Championships**, which has been held in Atlanta and may be again.

INDIVIDUAL, FAMILY, and TEAM SPORTS

ARCHERY

Archery clubs for children under 18 are located in almost every metro-Atlanta county. Kids as young as 4 years can enjoy archery! Many clubs offer lessons on Saturday and compete with other clubs in their area. Contact your local archery store listed in the *Yellow Pages* under **Archery Equipment & Supplies** and **Archery Ranges,** for information on clubs in your area.

BADMINTON

Not only is badminton great fun, but it also develops hand-eye coordination and speed. The equipment is not expensive and can be set up in your yard if you have the space. If not, the equipment can easily be transported to a park. Badminton can be played at almost any age level by adjusting the net, and injuries are almost non-existent because the playing surface is grass. The game can be easy-going, but for the more skilled, you will be surprised to discover how vigorous and competitive it can be.

BALLOONING

Hot air balloons are fascinatingly beautiful to the youngest child . . . and the oldest adult. See our chapter on "Festivals and Special Events" for regularly scheduled balloon races. If you are interested in a ride, you can gather information at the festivals, look under **Balloons - Manned** in the *Yellow Pages* or call the **Georgia Hot Air Balloon Association** at 288-1867.

BASEBALL and T-BALL

Contact your City or County Department of Parks and Recreation, your area religious organizations, YM/YWCAs, and other groups listed below in this chapter, to locate an association or youth group that has a team for your child to join. Some of these facilities also offer special summer camp programs.

BASEBALL BATTING PRACTICE

There are several **Baseball Batting Ranges** listed in the *Yellow Pages*, located in Marietta, Duluth, Decatur, and Scottdale. The **Stone Mountain Park Sports Complex** also has batting cages which are open daily March-December, and on weekends year-round. For 50¢ you get 12 practice balls.

BASKETBALL

Contact your City or County Department of Parks and Recreation, your area religious organizations, YM/YWCAs, and other groups listed below in this chapter, to locate an association or youth group that has a team for your child to join. Some of these facilities also offer special summer camp programs.

BICYCLING

Bicycling is not only great exercise in the beautiful out-of-doors, but an activity that a family can enjoy together. Some of the more beautiful and relaxing family bicycle rides are on designated trails in city and state parks. A few places are listed below to get you started. You can also contact the **Southern Bicycle League** at P.O. Box 29474, Atlanta, Georgia 30359 for information about the many programs, rides and tours available through the association, including in-school cycling safety programs for children. Also, keep in mind that more and more, children are participating in youth bicycle races. **The Children's Life Cycle** is an annual bicycle ride through the neighborhoods of North Atlanta, to raise money for UNICEF. Call 636-5597 for more information. Another popular event is the annual **Tour D' Town** in Buckhead for all levels of bicyclists and includes a fun Celebrity Challenge at noon. This benefits the American Cancer Society. Call 350-0294 for information. Also, look in our chapter "Festivals and Special Events" for information about other bicycle races for youth. For the more adventurous, contact the **Southern Off Road Bicycle Association** at P.O. Box 1191, Decatur, Georgia 30031.

Piedmont Park, Piedmont Avenue and 14th Street, Atlanta (658-7406). Bicycling is permitted on paved trails. Bicycle rentals are available at **Skate Escape,** 1086 Piedmont Avenue, N.E., Atlanta (892-1292).

Stone Mountain Park (469-9831). Bike rentals are available for every age child on weekends from March-November, and on a daily basis from June-August. Single speeds are $2.50/hr., 10-speeds are $4.00/hr. and tandems (for two) are $6.00/hr. Babysitters are also available.

Callaway Gardens. Beautiful scenery and 7 1/2 miles of level bike paths await you. They have bike rentals for children and adults. See our chapter on "Day Trips" for more information.

BOWLING

Bowling is one of those rare participant sports that the whole family can play together with everyone playing at his/her own skill level. In other words, it can be just as challenging and enjoyable for parents as for kids, or great non-competitive fun when family members only play against themselves. There are numerous bowling lanes in the metro Atlanta area that have leagues for children. Did you know children can join as young as age 3? (Bowling balls come as light as 6 lbs.) Saturday mornings are a popular time for kid's league practices and games. Also, during the summer months, there are daily bowling league activities. Call or go to your nearby lanes listed under **Bowling** in the *Yellow Pages* for more information.

CAMPING

Georgia is made for camping with its natural beauty of forests, streams, lakes, waterfalls and mountains. For the novice camping family there is

Stone Mountain Park which has about 400 campsites by the lake. Not too far away to the north are **Allatoona Campground and Beach** (974-3182), **Lake Lanier Islands** (945-6701), and **Unicoi State Park** (404/878-2201). Be sure to call ahead for reservations. A fun way to get youngsters used to camping is to let them sleep in a sleeping bag in the livingroom or pitch a tent in the backyard.

CAVING

The 400 or so caves in Georgia are not developed, so it is recommended that those interested in the sport of caving contact an organized group of cavers for information on locations, specific cave information and whether or not the type of cave is within the range of your family's interest and experience. Contact Dogwood City Grotto, 1865 Ridgewood Dr. NE, Atlanta, Georgia 30307. The not-so-brave may just wish to visit the **William Weinman Mineral Museum** (404/386-0576) in Cartersville which has a simulated cave, or head to **Cave Spring** (404/777-8439 or 748-9443) which has a natural limestone cave. Take a fun day trip to Chattanooga, Tennessee where even three-year-olds can hike down to the spectacular **Ruby Falls** at Lookout Mountain (615/821-2544).

FENCING

The Atlanta Fencer's Club, 40 7th Street, N.E., Atlanta, Georgia (892-0307) is a good place to begin for information on fencing instruction for young children. They have offered classes to children as young as 5 and 6 years of age, and private and group instruction are available depending upon the child's age. Older children have an opportunity to participate in fencing tournaments throughout the southeast

FISHING

- Georgia State law requires all boaters to wear Coast Guard approved life-jackets.

- A fishing license is required for fresh-water fishing in Georgia for everyone over the age of 16 years. Call 493-5770 for more information about licenses.

• Fishing is permitted in all streams, lakes and ponds unless otherwise designated. Check with your local city or county Department of Parks and Recreation for information about fishing in your neighborhood parks.

For the child or novice angler, the first fishing trips should be kept simple. You may want to purchase a cheap (about $15.00) pre-packaged spincast rod and reel outfit which has everything you will need except bait. Pick up some crickets, a box of worms, and maybe a few dozen minnows to add interest. Bank fishing is a safe way to introduce very young children to fishing, but most children would be thrilled to have an opportunity to go out in a boat and would probably be satisfied even if no fish were caught. We suggest you bring food and beverages, to ward off boredom as well as hunger, along with life vests, hats and sunscreen.

Stone Mountain Park has a special fishing store selling licenses, bait, snacks and boat rentals to fish on the large, stocked lake. Across the street from the store is an area for bank fishing with picnic tables. Fishing is seasonal from mid-March to the latter part of October. **Sweetwater Creek State Park** and the **Chattahoochee River** are spots for both bank fishing and boating. Look under **Fishing Lakes-Public** in the *Yellow Pages* for more fishing spots in the metro-Atlanta area. And, don't forget to venture to the many lakes surrounding Atlanta such as **Lake Allatoona, Lake Hartwell** and **Lake Lanier**. Call 656-3524 for information on these and other lakes around Georgia.

"**Kids's Fishing Day**," sponsored by the Upper Chattahoochee Chapter of Trout Unlimited, is held in March of each year at the **Chattahoochee River** Park (on Azalea Drive between Willeo Road and Roswell Road in Roswell). The event is FREE for kids under 16, but they must bring their own bait and tackle. The Chapter releases trout in the river one half hour before the event begins. For more information, call 266-0577 or 447-9772. **Lake Oconee**, at the Old Salem Recreation Area, holds fishing tournaments for kids ages 4-14 with trophies and prizes (404/467-2850). **Reynolds Nature Preserve**, on the south side of Atlanta, has a fishing tournament for children age 6-14 years (961-9257).

FOOTBALL

Contact your City or County Department of Parks and Recreation, your area religious organizations, YM/YWCAs, and other groups (listed below in this chapter) to locate an association or youth group that has a team for your child to join. Some of these facilities and high schools offer special summer camp programs. The **Atlanta Colt Youth Association** (551-8956), one of the largest youth football associations in the country, is an example of what is possible for kids interested in playing football in Atlanta. Kids ages 5-7 play flag football. Girls and boys ages 8-15 are assigned to teams based upon weight, age and football experience. The Colts have been in existence for over 25 years and have won nine national championships and produced 26 All-American scholar-athletes.

GOLF

Golf seems to be an increasingly popular sport among Atlanta's youth. There are many **Junior Tournaments** such as the DeKalb Junior Classic and Griffin Junior Golf Classic, and other competitive events for both boys and girls from about age seven on up. *The Participants Page* of the *Atlanta Journal and Constitution* in the Saturday Sports Section, lists upcoming golfing events. You can also make inquiries at the more than 30 public courses or the many private courses in metro-Atlanta, or call the **Atlanta Junior Golf Association** (355-9472). Please note that there are several upscale public courses such as Mystery Valley in Lithonia (469-6913, Stone Mountain Park (498-5715), The Metropolitan Club in east DeKalb (981-5325), River's Edge Plantation in Fayetteville (460-1098), River Pines in Alpharetta (442-5960) and North Fulton Golf Course (255-0723).

There are over fifteen **Golf Practice Ranges** listed in the *Yellow Pages,* some of which offer golfing lessons. There are over twelve **Golf Courses - Miniature** listed as well. Additionally, there is miniature golfing at **Red Top State Park**. At the **Stone Mountain Sports Complex,** you may play miniature golf daily from March-December, and weekends year-round on a very simple course. The cost is $2.00 for adults and $1.50 for children under 12. And good news! You can even golf in the rain at the new indoor miniature golf courses at **American Adventures** (see our chapter "Places To Go" for more information) and at **Pebble Beach** in Marietta (973-7828).

GYMNASTICS

Gymnastics is one of the best individual sports to help children build self-confidence, flexibility, agility, and body control. They can work and develop skills at their own pace in a fun, active environment. For those who are ready and interested, an array of events in competitive gymnastics is available at the more notable private gyms in Atlanta. Emory University's 6-week **Summer Sports Fitness Camp** includes daily tumbling and gymnastics instruction. Classes are also offered at Recreation Centers, YM/YWCAs and other youth organizations. *Youth View* newspaper and *Yellow Page* listings under **Gymnasiums** and **Gymnastic Instruction** are good resources. Some of these facilities are available for birthday parties, too!

HIKING and NATURE TRAILS

We are fortunate to live in an ideal geographic area for outdoor activities. And what kid doesn't like to be outdoors every day? Hiking is a year-round activity - only heavy rain or snow will keep enthusiastic hiking families indoors. Some people need only walk around their neighborhood for a good hike, but for those who are looking for something more, there are good trails nearby.

Al Burruss Nature Park and Wildwood Park, Marietta (429-4220)
Arabia Mountain, Lithonia (371-2631)
Atlanta Botanical Garden, Atlanta (876-5858)
Atlanta History Center, Atlanta (261-1837)
Bush Mountain Outdoor Activities Center, Atlanta (752-5385)
Chattahoochee River National Recreational Area
- Visitors Center, Dunwoody (952-4419 or 394-8335)
- Sope Creek Trail (952-4419)
- Island Ford Parkway Trail System (394-8324)
- Mulberry Creek Loop (952-4419)
- Vickery Creek Trail System (394-8324)
Chattahoochee Nature Center, Roswell (992-2055)
Cochran Mill Park, Atlanta (463-4706)
Fernbank Science Center–Nature Trails, Atlanta (378-4311)
Kennesaw Mountain National Battlefield, Marietta (427-4686)

Panola Mountain State Conservation Park, Stockbridge (474-2914)
Red Top Mountain State Park, Lake Allatoona (975-4203)
W.H. Reynolds Memorial Nature Preserve (961-9257)
Stone Mountain Park, Stone Mountain (498-5600)
Sweetwater Creek State Park, Lithia Springs (944-1700)

See other chapters in this book for in depth descriptions of many of these places . . . and don't forget the North Georgia Mountains! (See our chapter "Day Trips.")

HOCKEY, ICE

The Georgia Amateur Hockey Association has seasonal league play at **Stone Mountain Ice Chalet** and **Parkaire Olympic Ice Arena.** For children under age 10 there is an instructional program, and House League Play for boys begins at age 10. For more information, call the Association at 249-4836.

HORSEBACK RIDING

Most stables in the Atlanta area do not rent horses for young children to ride; you should have better luck outside the metro-area in the North Georgia Mountains. English and Western Lessons are available at many of the stables listed in the *Yellow Pages* under **Riding Academies** and **Stables** as wall as at private polo clubs in Atlanta.

If you are interested in **Summer Riding Camps, The Huntcliff Stables** (993-8448) located on River Run Road in Dunwoody has weekly sessions for children age 6 and up during the months of June, July, and August. **Pounds Stables** (394-8288) in Doraville has a horsemanship day camp for children age 5 and up during the summer months. For fun with horses on a real working farm, call **Jan Serafy's Riding Camp** (355-5519). Look in the *Yellow Pages* under **Riding Academies** or **Stables** for further information.

Another source of scheduled events is your local count's extension Services. They often sponsor equestrian events and will be happy to mail you information. You may also contact the following **Associations and**

Clubs: Georgia Pony Club (893-3751), Georgia Horse Foundation (261-0612), Atlanta Equestrian Society (475-5551), and the Quarter Horse Association (483-2818).

Pony Rides are a big hit at birthday parties and carnivals. There are several pony rental groups that cater specifically to parties and carnivals. Look for ads in *Youth View* newspapers as well as the *Yellow Pages* under **Carnivals** and **Party Planning Service.**

ICE SKATING

For the ice skating enthusiast or the neophyte, your best bet for skating is the few indoor facilities in Atlanta.

Parkaire Olympic Ice Arena, 4859 Lower Roswell Road, N.E., Marietta, Georgia (973-0753). Ice skating is available year-round. Call for exact hours. The cost for adults is $5.00 plus $1.00 skate rental. For children under 12 the cost is $4.50 plus $1.00 for skate rental.

Six Flags Over Georgia, Mableton, Georgia (739-3440). Ice skating is available during the winter holidays. Call for exact dates and times.

Stone Mountain Ice Chalet, Stone Mountain Park, Georgia (498-5600). Skating year-round. Hours are Mondays-Fridays, 1:00pm-4:00pm and 7:30pm-9:30pm; Saturdays and Sundays, 1:00pm-3:00pm, 3:30pm-5:30pm and 7:30pm-9:30pm. Admission is $5.00 per person which includes skate rental.

KARATE and OTHER MARTIAL ARTS

Karate is the development of the whole self, body and spirit. Discipline of the mind and emotions is as important as discipline of the body. Thus, martial arts develop, among other things, a child's self-confidence, his/her ability to focus and concentrate, and a respect for other people. Remember that good karate instructors emphasize the defensive nature of martial arts, and they make this very clear to the students at all times. For schools of martial arts in Atlanta, look in *Youth View* and *Creative Loafing* newspapers as well as the *Yellow Pages* under **Karate and Other**

Martial Arts Instruction. Be sure to observe a class before you enroll your child. Some recreation centers and art centers also offer Martial Arts classes.

RAFTING AND CANOEING

If you haven't already, you simply must **"Shoot the Hooch;"** it's an Atlanta tradition and great family fun! For first-timers or families with preschoolers we suggest the approximately two hour drift from Powers Island to Paces Mill. Along the way we paddled ashore to have a picnic and found places shallow enough to explore the river bottom. We took a hike up the mountain and made exciting discoveries along the river's edge. (Keep those sneakers on!) We were in awe as several people dove off a rock from a breathtaking height, but such diving is discouraged by the Park. There is a bathroom halfway along this rafting route. To get you

back from Paces Mill to your car, use the Outdoor Center's shuttle bus at a cost of $2.50 for adults and $1.25 for children.

If the river and all the in and out points are unfamiliar to you, don't worry. The folks at the Chattahoochee Outdoor Center (the official park concessioner) are very willing to explain it all. A family of four might consider a 6-man raft to have plenty of room for a cooler, camera, sunscreen, towels, etc.

Yes, children can learn to **Canoe** safely and easily in calm water. Contact the **Georgia Canoeing Association** (421-9729) for general information, training, races and trips for canoeing and kayaking. There are guided evening rides down the Chattahoochee in the summer through the **Chattahoochee Nature Center** (992-2055).

River Safety:

- Georgia State law requires all people aboard a watercraft (including inner tubes) wear Coast Guard approved life-jackets.
- The National Recreation Area recommends no swimming.
- Wear old sneakers to protect your feet from any sharp rocks, shells and broken glass.
- Do not dive or jump into the water, as it is difficult to see submerged objects and rocks. (But don't be surprised to see people diving from breathtaking heights on your rafting trip.)
- No glass is allowed on the Chattahoochee River.
- Take along a plastic bag for litter.
- Call 945-1466 or 329-1455 for up-to-the-minute river conditions, if you are planning to raft in a Class II or Class III section of the river.

Chattahoochee Outdoor Center. (395-6851) Rental and put-in sites are 311 Johnson Ferry Road and 285 Powers River (Powers Island). Take-out facilities are at Powers Island (I-285 at Northside Parkway) and Paces Mill (intersection of the river and Hwy. 41). Rental is seasonal–May (weekends only); June to mid-September (daily). Hours are Monday-Friday, 10:00am to 8:00pm. Saturday, Sunday and holiday hours are 9:00am to 8:00pm. The cost for canoe rental is $30/day. Raft rental is $32/day for a 4-man, $48/day for a 6-man, and $64/day for an 8-man. Life jackets and paddles are provided for both canoe and raft rentals at no extra charge. Food, beverages and sundries are available at all sites, and reservations using a major credit card are suggested for the weekends. To secure a rental, you will need a valid driver's license and make a refundable security deposit of $75-$100.

Chattahoochee Canoe & Raft Rental at Chattahoochee River Park, 199 Azalea Drive (between Roswell Road and Willeo Road), Roswell, Georgia (998-7778). Rental is seasonal - April to September, 9:00am to 7:00pm on Fridays, Saturdays and Sundays. There is no shuttle transportation until May 1. Canoe prices are $10 for 2 hours, $15 for 4 hours. Raft prices are $20/day for a 4-man, $25/day for a 6-man, $40/day for an 8-man craft.

Stone Mountain Park (498-5683) rents canoes, rowboats, pedalboats and pontoon boats. The cost for canoe rental is $4.50/hour; rowboats are $6/hour; pedalboats are $2.50/20 minutes; and pontoon boats range from $25/hour-$35/hour. The Park also permits private boating (limited to 10 HP), but not after 11:00am on weekends and holidays between April 1 and September 20.

Those of you who are experienced and adventurous might want to join the **Atlanta Whitewater Club** (299-3752). Be sure to check out our chapter on "Day Trips" for some other places to rent canoes, rafts or kayaks, including Lake Allatoona, Callaway Gardens and Lake Lanier Islands.

ROLLER and IN-LINE SKATING

There are about fifteen roller rinks, including the **Stone Mountain Park Roller Rink**, listed in the *Yellow Pages* under **Skating Rinks**. Don't forget that roller skating birthday parties are great fun for school age kids, boys and girls alike. Call your nearest rink for individual and group prices, skate rentals and availability.

Speed skating may soon be in the Olympics. For speed skating fun visit **Skate-A-Long USA** roller rink in Lilburn (921-0800).

In-line skating has become quite the craze. Contact **High Country Outfitters** (several locations in Atlanta) for demonstrations, skates, rentals, safety equipment, instruction and race information.

RUNNING

People of all ages run, and at all times of the day, in light rain, and up the steepest hills . . . in their neighboorhoods and in parks. Elementary schools have running clubs and sometimes a "run day" for the whole family. Atlanta-area festivals have begun including races as one of the activities of the day, and many non-profit organizations are holding "fun runs" as fund-raising events. **The Atlanta Track Club** has established a tradition of sorts in Atlanta with its annual children's race, **The Peachtree Junior** for 7-12 year olds. Held in June of each year at Piedmont Park, it's the children's version of *the* Peachtree Road Race. Almost 2,000 kids participate. For information, phone 231-9066. Look in the *Weekend* section of the Saturday *Atlanta Journal and Constitution* as well as *Youth View* newspaper for upcoming runs.

SCUBA DIVING

According to the P.A.D.I. (Professional Association of Diving Instructors) regulations, the minimum age for kids to begin scuba diving is 12 years of age. If you are interested in pursuing diving for your older child or anticipating instruction for your near-twelve year old, see the *Yellow Pages* under **Diving Instruction**. Be sure to look for aquatic centers that have P.A.D.I. certified instructors. Scuba equipment is expensive, but can be rented. For more information, contact the **Atlanta Scuba and Swim Academy** (973-3120) or the **Atlanta Reef Dwellers** (477-5176), a group that dives almost everywhere, including the Chattahoochee River. Take heed: lessons are absolutely vital.

SKATEBOARDS

If your kids are skateboard enthusiasts, remember that helmets and padding should be worn at all times. To try an actual skateboard rink, try **Surf's Up Street Waves** in Lithonia (482-7471) or **Skate Zone Skateboard Park** in Tucker (491-0656).

SKIING

The North Georgia Mountains provide fine **snow skiing** for families. Locally, the Atlanta Ski Club (255-4800), can help you with questions and other information. The Club offers ski instruction for school age children beginning in October.

Water skiing requires no lessons–just hold on to the rope, bend your knees and let the boat pull you up! Lake Allatoona is used by the **Atlanta Water Ski Club** (425-7166) which hosts the annual Atlanta Open ski tournament. Lake Lanier is great for skiing and is an easy drive. Just remember to adhere to the boating laws in Georgia.

SOCCER

According to the Soccer Industry Council of America, only basketball is more popular among kids under the age of 12. Soccer has mushroomed in popularity all across our country in recent years, and is available at recreation centers and churches. Many youth groups also have teams. For those children who want serious information about the sport, call the Georgia State Soccer Association at 452-0505, 8:00am-4:00pm, Mondays through Fridays. For information on private soccer clubs, see **Soccer Clubs** in the *Yellow Pages*. **Summer Soccer Camps** are held at colleges, such as Agnes Scott College and Emory University, and are hosted by the Atlanta Attack (431-6111 or 577-9600) at numerous metro-Atlanta locations.

SPECIAL OLYMPICS

For information on the very active Georgia **Special Olympics** organization and events, contact their main office at 3166 Chestnut Drive, Doraville 30340 (458-3838). They will put you in touch with an area coordinator.

SUMMER SPORTS CAMPS

Comprehensive summer sports camps are offered at many educational facilities throughout Atlanta such as Agnes Scott College (371-6491), DeKalb College (244-5050), Emory University (727-6547), Georgia Institute of Technology (894-5400), Kennesaw State College (423-6400) and Oglethorpe University (261-1441). Other unique camps are offered by the Atlanta Attack (431-6111) and the City of Atlanta's Outdoor Survival Camp (658-6381). Also, see our section, "Recreation Centers and Youth Organizations" for names and phone numbers of many facilities you can check into.

SWIMMING AND AQUATICS

Pools, Lessons and Teams. Whether you wish to swim for pleasure or take swimming or life saving lessons, your local Recreation Center and YM/YWCA's have good programs for children of all ages and abilities. Some residential areas have community clubs with pools as do apartment complexes and condominiums. Be creative. If your club or residential pool does not offer lessons by certified instructors, try to organize such a service through the governing board. If enough of your neighbors are interested, the cost might be acceptable, and it would certainly be convenient. Swimming instruction is available at larger facilites such as **Dynamo Swim Club** in Chamblee (451-3272), which has a **U.S.S. Swim Team** for ages 7 and up, and **SwimAtlanta**, located in Lilburn (381-7926), Roswell (992-7665) and Decatur (981-7946). See the *Yellow Pages* under **Swimming Instruction.**

Many community clubs have **Swim Teams** that all member children may join. The only requirement is that the child be able to make his or her way unassisted from one end of the pool to the other. Swim meets are organized with local clubs competing with one another, and the season usually ends with an awards dinner. Whether fun takes precedent over competition or vice versa depends upon the club, so find out if you are comfortable with the philosophy before you commit.

There are numerous outdoor summer only **Public Pools** in cities and counties in and around Atlanta, and a few indoor year-round public pools in the city of Atlanta. Admission varies from FREE for youngsters to $1.50 for adults depending upon the facility. Look in the *Blue Pages* under your county's or city's Parks and Recreation Department.

Beaches. There are manmade white sand beaches at **Stone Mountain Park** (469-9831), **Lake Lanier Islands** (945-6701), **Lake Allatoona** (974-5182) and **Sun Valley Beach** in Powder Springs (943-5900). See our chapters "Places To Go" and "Day Trips" for more information. Be alert for beaches that are closed because of unacceptable levels of pollution.

TENNIS

Atlanta is a mecca for tennis buffs with numerous public tennis centers as well as private courts available year-round. Many offer lessons as well as team play for children. There are many public courts managed by the city of Atlanta and surrounding counties. Call the numbers listed below for information on locations, children's lessons and teams. Some centers offer junior tennis camps, so be sure to inquire if you are interested.

Atlanta City Courts - 658-7277
Clayton County Courts - 477-3766
Cobb County Courts - 424-0204
DeKalb County Courts - 371-2548
Fulton County Courts - 572-2526
Gwinnett County Courts - 448-4464

Some recreation centers and YM/YWCAs have tennis facilities and offer lessons to children. **The Stone Mountain Sports Complex** (498-5728) has eight lighted courts available seasonally at a low per-hour fee. Ask about their free summer tennis lesson program.

Atlanta Lawn Tennis Association (399-5788) or **ALTA** is the "world's largest local tennis association." Juniors as well as adults can join and be involved in competitive play. Call for more information.

There is no dearth of private **Summer Tennis Camps** for juniors. *Net News*, a publication of ALTA free to all members, contains ads for camps as well as other pertinent information for the serious tennis player. Check out the summer programs offered at Agnes Scott College, Emory University and Georgia Tech.

RECREATION CENTERS

Recreation Centers, both city and county run, provide an incredible variety of programs and facilities for children and youth in metro-Atlanta. A sample of recent **Classes** included swimming, karate, basketball, gymnastics, tennis, baton twirling, chess, ballet and tap, doubledutch, drama, arts and crafts, horseshoes, guitar, cooking, scrabble, and roller skating. Some facilities have **Preschool Classes** all year long and **After School Programs** during the school year. In the summer time, most recreational facilities have **Summer Day Camp** programs for elementary age kids which may include arts and crafts, swimming and field trips. A few offer extended care after regular camp hours. The day camp programs vary from location to location; some have a series of one week programs, others offer only one weeklong program at a particular center, and yet others have developed a summer camp your child can attend all summer long, but inquire as early as March for these camps!

Non-profit **Youth Associations** provide competitive sports opportunities for children in football, baseball, softball, soccer, and even cheerleading. Many counties in Georgia require that all coaches be trained and certified annually through the National Youth Sports Coaches Association (NYSCA), a non-profit certification program begun in 1981 to improve the quality and safety of out-of-school sports. Coaches learn first aid and safety, teaching techniques, the psychology of coaching, how to make practices interesting and fun, and sports ethics. Youth Associations are independently run, but use county and city playing fields.

For information on the sports your children wish to play, contact your local County and/or Recreation Department. They will provide you with the name and phone number of the person you should contact.

City of Atlanta (653-7111)
City of Decatur (377-0494)
City of Lawrenceville (963-3510)
City of Marietta (429-4211)
Clayton County (477-3766)
Cobb County (427-7275 or 428-1300)
DeKalb County (371-2631)
Fulton County (730-6200)
Gwinnett County (822-8840)

Special populations should contact the following county offices: DeKalb (377-3616), Cobb (944-0868), Fulton (303-6181) Gwinnett (822-5150) and for the City of Atlanta (658-6381).

YOUTH ORGANIZATIONS

BOY SCOUTS OF AMERICA (577-4810). The scouts provide a broad range of activities in the arts, sciences, social skills and out-of-doors, while encouraging self-confidence, skill development and lots of fun! They perform various activities and earn badges upon completion of specific tasks. Boys can enter scouting as a Tiger cub at age 6; they move up through the ranks as they get older. Scouts normally meet once a week. Call for information on scouting in your area.

BOYS CLUBS OF METRO-ATLANTA (527-7100). Although the Boys Clubs are part of nationwide organization called Boys and Girls Clubs of America, each club operates autonomously. The metro-Atlanta clubs serve boys age 6 to 18 years. Programs and times may vary from club to club, but most are open from 2:30pm-9:00pm during the school year with transportation being provided from nearby schools for after school programs. There are summer programs for children and the clubs are usually open a full day during school vacations. Activities may include arts and crafts, drama and poetry clubs, T-ball, ping pong, pool, a sign language club and a newspaper club.

CAMPFIRE BOYS AND GIRLS (527-7125). Campfire offers programs for both boys and girls which include camping, community service and learning to take care of oneself. Campfire accepts children age 5 on up. For information on Campfire's Summer Camp Toccoa, call 800/822-9541.

4-H AND YOUTH. Operating through the Extension Service of the University of Georgia, this organization serves youth age 9-19 years. During the school year there are after-school programs, Saturday activities and on teacher workdays, they try to have some program for children. Summer programs and summer camps include field trips, talent shows, cooking, swimming, arts & crafts, woodworking and photography. Transportation is provided. Contact your nearest 4-H office for up-to-date information: **Clayton** (473-5450), **Cobb** (528-4076), **DeKalb** (371-2821),

Fulton - North (393-4670), **Fulton - South** (964-7854) and **Gwinnett** (822-7700).

GIRLS CLUBS OF METRO-ATLANTA. Girls Clubs are members of Girls Incorporated (formerly Girls Clubs of America). Girls Clubs provide essentially the same services as Boys Clubs and are staffed by paid professionals. Each individual club operates autonomously, and even admit boys. There is a new focus on developing a science and math project called Operation Smart, but the main focus of the organization is still on bolstering girls' self-esteem. Contact your nearest branch for more information: **Decatur Girls Club** (378-6683), **Grant Park Girls Club** (627-0677), **Grant Park Gym Center** (659-4441) and **Redan Girls Club** (469-2126).

GIRL SCOUTS OF AMERICA (527-7500). Girls may enter scouting at age 5 (Daisy's) and participate until they are 17 years old (Seniors). The primary goal of scouting is to help the girls develop self-esteem, appreciate nature, gain new friends, acquire social skills and have experiences in the arts and sciences. Troops usually meet once a week and girls earn badges by performing various activities. For information on Girl Scout Day and Overnight Camps, call the number above.

INDIAN GUIDES AND PRINCESSES. This is a very unique and little known organization whose primary purpose was originally to afford fathers and their children (ages 5 and up) a very special, fun-filled time together on a regular basis. However, more and more "tribes" are involving moms too. They operate through local YMCAs, so you will need to call your local "Y" to find out if one is available. Since the programs vary in size and in program offerings, we will describe one of the more comprehensive ones as an example of what is possible. In Cobb County, there are currently 38 tribes consisting of 8 pairs of parents and kids. Each tribe has its own special name. There are two meetings a month; the first is at alternating family homes and deals with any business that must be conducted, followed by activities such as crafts and singing. The second is an outing, such as to Stone Mountain Park, a bike rodeo, or a swimming and pizza party. Twice a year, in the Fall and Spring, all the tribes get together for a weekend campout! Call the **YMCA General Metropolitan Program Information** number 588-9622 for the location of your nearest

YMCA.

THE SALVATION ARMY BOYS AND GIRLS CLUBS. The Salvation Army's programs are essentially the same as the offerings at other boys' and girls' clubs in Atlanta, serving children in kindergarten-5th grade. Transportation is *not* provided from schools. For further information, **visit:** 3500 Sherrydale Lane, Decatur, Georgia 30032 (284-9671).

YMCAS AND YWCAS. Family memberships are available at a low cost and usually include reduced fees for programs and a newsletter with updates on special events and programs. Additional fees are charged for a wide range of programs that *may* include:

- Summer Day Camps
- After-school child care (on site or at public schools)
- Sports lessons (basketball, swimming, soccer, tennis, etc.)
- Programs for preschoolers
- Babysitting while parent is participating in a class
- Indian Guides and Princesses (see above)

We are fortunate to have numerous "Ys" all over the Atlanta metropolitan area; there is sure to be one near to you. For the exact location and telephone number of the YWCA or YMCA closest to you, call: YMCA-General Metropolitan Program Information (588-9622) or YWCA Of Greater Atlanta (527-7575).

6. Festivals and Special Events

W ith a few exceptions, the festivals, parades and special events listed below are annual events. (We have included some first year events as it seems likely that they will receive enough community and financial support to become annual affairs.) You may discover that the dates, locations and telephone numbers of the sponsors vary from year to year, but we have tried to provide you with enough information to plan ahead and keep your eyes open for announcements about those events which are of interest to you. Please be sure to check the last section of our chapter "Performing Arts," for additional listings of annual festivals and concerts which consist primarily of musical, theatrical, dance or puppetry performances.

JANUARY

Olde Christmas Storytelling Festival, Callanwolde Fine Arts Center, Atlanta (872-5338). Two days of storytelling seminars, special children's activities and evening storytelling concerts featuring well-known local and national storytellers.

Martin Luther King, Jr. Week, Martin Luther King, Jr. Center for Nonviolent Social Change, Atlanta (524-1956). A week of events at the Martin Luther King, Jr. Center dedicated to the memory of Martin Luther King, Jr., and reminding the nation to focus on his philosophy of nonviolence. The week's events end with the **Martin Luther King, Jr. National Parade and March of Celebration** (526-8940) which begins at Baker Street and Peachtree Street in Downtown Atlanta, proceeds to Auburn Avenue and ends at the Center. Black stars and sports figures appear in the parade, along with outstanding Georgia and out-of-state bands and specialty units.

Chinese New Year Celebration, Chinese Community Center, Chamblee (451-4456). Held in January or February on the Chinese lunar New Year. Chinese food booths, traditional dance, folk songs and children's activities highlight the New Year's celebration.

Ringling Brothers Barnum & Bailey Circus, Omni Coliseum, Atlanta (249-6400). The Greatest Show on Earth comes to Atlanta every year, late

218

January through early February, and dazzles children with the largest and most spectacular of circus shows.

Atlanta Sports Carnival, Omni Coliseum, Atlanta (248-0037). Held in January or February of every year. The Omni Coliseum is transformed into a giant carnival midway with rides and booths for children. Famous sports figures give autographs and delight children with demonstration games.

━━━━━━━━━━━━━━━━━ **FEBRUARY** ━━━━━━━━━━━━━━━

Groundhog Day Jugglers Festival, Virginia Highlands, Atlanta (451-4847). This weekend-long festival includes juggling, other forms of object manipulation, magic, balancing and unicycle riding. Special children's activities are always included.

Musical Marathon Family Fest, Woodruff Arts Center, Atlanta (659-0919). The Atlanta Symphony Orchestra sponsors music and other performing arts activities for the entire family. Special activities include a musical petting zoo (hands-on playing with musical instruments), clowns, jugglers, face-painting, balloons and many more activities for children.

Jungle Love, Zoo Atlanta (624-5600). Zoo Atlanta celebrates animal lover's day with special activities, puppet shows, mime performances, face painting and more.

Black History Month features month-long educational activities and performing arts events throughout the city honoring African-American accomplishments. Contact the APEX Center (521-2654) for more information, and the DeKalb and Atlanta-Fulton County Public Libraries.

Atlanta Flower Show, Location varies (Atlanta Apparel Mart/World Congress Center), Atlanta (220-2223) . Held in February or March. The premier gardening event in the Southeast, sponsored by the Atlanta Botanical Garden, features trees and flowers, landscaped gardens, photography, educational exhibits, lectures, demonstrations, retail booths and a special children's corner.

Arbor Day Celebrations, The third Friday in February. Look for outdoor activities throughout Atlanta celebrating trees. Call 752-5385 to find out Atlanta's Arbor Day activities. Call 429-4224 to find out Marietta's activities.

Mardi Gras Parade and Party begins at Harris and Peachtree Streets in downtown Atlanta and proceeds to Underground Atlanta for an evening of celebration. (355-0440).

Fireside Arts and Crafts Show, Unicoi State Park, Georgia (404/878-2201 ext. 282/283). A high quality arts and country crafts show exhibits at Unicoi State Park yearly.

MARCH

St. Patrick's Day Festival and Parade, Buckhead/Bureau of Cultural Affairs, Atlanta (231-6215). The parade begins at Frankie Allen Park and proceeds down Pharr Road to Bolling Way to East Paces Ferry Road and then back to the Park. There is also a family carnival at the corner of East Paces Ferry Road and Bolling Way with rides, games, amusements and food.

St Patrick's Day Parade, Hibernian Benevolent Society of Atlanta, Atlanta (392-1272). The parade proceeds down Peachtree Road to Underground Atlanta and ends up in Woodruff Park. Afterwards, participate in evening parties and festivities at Underground Atlanta.

St. Patrick's Day Celebration, Stone Mountain Village (296-8058). Celebrate St. Patrick's Day with Irish dances, Irish "specials" in the Village restaurants and other Irish traditions.

O'Zoo Day, St. Patrick's Day Celebration, Zoo Atlanta (624-5678). Zoo Atlanta presents a St. Patrick's Day party featuring live entertainment, costumed characters, puppet shows, green ice cream sodas and other family festivities.

St. Patrick's Day Celebration, Chateau Elan, Georgia (404/867-8200). Celebrate St. Patrick's Day at Chateau Elan and enjoy Irish performers, afternoon tea, craft demonstrations and an evening Medieval Feast.

Antebellum Jubilee (formerly the Old South Celebration), Stone Mountain Park (498-5702). Held late March and/or early April every year, the Park sets the stage to experience life as it was during the antebellum era. Living history demonstrations, musicians, storytellers, period dancers, old-time travelling shows, folk music and crafts, an authentic Civil War encampment, marches, drill and firing demonstrations bring the Civil War era to life.

Atlanta Fair, Across from the Atlanta-Fulton County Stadium, Atlanta (740-1962). This traveling amuseument park brings carnival rides, games, food, exhibits and shows to Atlanta each year, including the world's largest Ferris Wheel at 7–stories high.

Georgia Springtime Festival of Arts and Crafts, Cobb Civic Center, Marietta (429-3045). A high quality, indoor arts and crafts fair that has participating artists from 15 states.

Spirit of South DeKalb–Kidfest, South DeKalb Mall, Atlanta (241-2453). Soapstone Arts Center sponsors Kidsfest in conjunction with Spirit of South DeKalb Festival. The children's portion features interactive performances, hands-on visual arts projects and other children's activities.

Kaleidoscope Fine Arts Festival, Cobb Civic Center, Marietta (426-3404). Held late March or early April. Co-sponsored by the Cobb County Parks and Recreation, the Marietta City Schools and the Cobb Arts Council, this festival exhibits children's art work and features live entertainment, including performances by choral groups, bands, orchestras, cloggers, ballet dancers and more.

Tapestry-Arts Festival, Gwinnett County (962-6642). Held throughout the month of March, Gwinnett's Fine Arts Festival, co-sponsored by the Gwinnett Council for the Arts and the Gwinnett County School System, features art exhibits and performances by student, amateur and professional artists held at various locations in Gwinnett County.

Civil War Relic Show, Exhibit Hall and Stage at the State Farmers

221

Market, Forest Park (366-6910). Over 200 Civil War dealers and displays exhibit newspapers, books, clothing and war artifacts. Also, Civil War reenactment camps and costumes of the period.

Callaway Azalea Festival, Pine Mountain, Georgia (404/663-2281). The world's largest azalea gardens are in full bloom and storytellers, puppeteers, musicians, face painters, jugglers, magicians and other entertainers join children in this celebration of spring.

EASTER

Eggstravaganza, Zoo Atlanta (624-5600). A giant Easter bunny, real rabbits and bunny games highlight Zoo Atlanta's celebration of Easter.

Easter Egg Hunts, Old Courthouse Square, Decatur (371-8386); Laurel Park, Marietta (429-4212); Gwinnett County Parks and Recreation Department–four locations (882-8873); Atlanta Speech School (233-5332); and, Cobb County–four locations (528-5405).

Easter Sunrise Service, Stone Mountain Park (469-5856). The Park opens at 4:00am to allow families to attend two non-denominational sunrise services–one at the top of the mountain, the other on the bottom. Occassionally, Easter Egg Hunts follow later in the day.

Easter Egg Hunt, Lake Lanier Islands, Georgia (404/932-7202). A giant Easter Bunny presides over the Easter Egg hunts usually held at Presentation Point with live DJ's, carnival games and food.

Magical Eggstravaganza, Cleveland, Georgia (404/865-5356). Billed as one of the world's largest egg hunts, Cleveland puts on an arts and crafts show and Easter celebration which includes its famous egg hunt, games, contests, a parade and of course, a visit by the Easter Bunny.

APRIL

April Fool's Festival, Little Five Points, Atlanta (524-1931). Held at the end of March and/or beginning of April. Music, food and games highlight the April Fool's Day celebration at the corner of Moreland and Euclid Avenue.

Earth Day throughout Atlanta (352-4080). Earth Day is a month-long national celebration bringing to the public's attention the urgency of environmental problems. Exhibits, festivals, performances, lectures, tree-planting ceremonies and other activities are scheduled throughout the month. The last weekend in April features a day-long festival to bring all of Atlanta together in a demonstration of concern for the environment. Special children's activities are planned throughout the month at the Atlanta Botanical Garden, Fernbank Science Center, SciTrek, Zoo Atlanta, Chattahoochee Nature Center and at other nature centers, parks, neighborhoods and book stores throughout the metropolitan Atlanta area.

The Children's Festival, Woodruff Arts Center, 1280 Peachtree Street, Atlanta (898-1152). Sponsored by the Atlanta Symphony Orchestra, High Museum of Art, Alliance Theater Company and Atlanta College of Art, the Children's Festival is the premier children's festival in Atlanta. The festival introduces children to the visual and performing arts and features dance, music, art, storytelling, theater, puppets, songs, clowns, magic, clogging, acting and many other activities for children.

Atlanta Dogwood Festival (525-6145). Events take place throughout Atlanta in conjuction with **Earth Day**, including house and garden tours and neighborhood festivals. **Weekend in the Park**–Piedmont Park, the focal point of the festival, features an arts and crafts festival, environmental exhibits, a children's parade, hands-on art activities, carnival games, kite-flying contests, a Sunday concert and hot-air balloon races. The Midtown portion of the festival features children's state entertainment, arts and crafts, an international market, ethnic music and losts of other great activities.

Buckheadesque and Earth Parade, Buckhead, Georgia (525-6145). As part of the **Earth Day** celebrations, the Buckhead Chamber of Commerce presents arts and crafts booths and local, national and global exhibits saluting the cultural diversity of Atlanta. There is also a children's parade, races, games, contests, tree-planting ceremony and lots of good food.

International Cultural Festival, Emory University Campus, Atlanta

(727-3300). Students from more than 50 different countries share information about their homelands presenting dances, costumes, jewelry, crafts, food and other information about their native countries.

B.C. Fest!, Emory Museum of Art & Archaeology, Emory University, Atlanta (727-4280). Held in March, April or May of each year (rain or shine). The Emory University Quadrangle is transformed into ports-of-call of ancient civilizations, each having a selection of children's activities. Children enjoy hands-on archaeological and arts and crafts projects, storytelling, and theatrical, musical and dance performances as well as samples of food from the ancient civilizations.

For Kid's Sake Day, Zoo Atlanta (624-5600). A special day for children full of games and fun activities sponsored by 11-Alive Television.

Caribbean Cultural Festival, Soapstone Center for the Arts–South DeKalb Mall (241-2453). The annual Caribbean Festival presently features reggae music, steel bands, folk songs, calypso dances and crafts. Plans for the future include expanding the celebration into a large multicultural festival.

Atlanta Botanical Garden Spring Plant Sale and Festival (876-5859). The Garden's annual plant sale has been expanded into a family festival with free activities for children such as art projects, planting seeds to carry home and face painting. Families may also enjoy demonstrations, lectures about gardening, as well as live entertainment.

Chamblee Spring Festival (986-5010). The festival features arts and crafts, music, antiques, a parade, a helicopter to climb on, book sales, animals for adoption and lots of other kid's activities.

St. Joseph's Hospital Auxiliary and WINGS' Spring Carnival, St. Joseph's Hospital (851-7292). Music, games, arts and crafts, hot-air balloon rides, petting zoo, barbeque and lots more children's activities highlight this annual fundraiser for the hospital.

Atlanta Hunt & Steeplechase, Seven Branches Farm, Cumming, Georgia (237-7436). Held in March or April of each year. Distinguished horses and riders meet at this beautiful farm in Cummings and race to benefit the Atlanta Speech School. Spectators bring gourmet tailgate picnics and live bands play continuously. Tickets must be purchased in advance.

Sweet Auburn Good Time Summit Festival, Auburn Avenue, Atlanta (523-2020). Street vendors, a children's carnival, roller-skating in the streets, southern food, arts and crafts and celebrities join people together on historic Auburn Avenue to listen and dance to local and national performers in a celebration of black heritage.

Taste of Atlanta, CNN Center, Atlanta (248-1315). Fifty of Atlanta's leading restaurants sell samples of their gourmet specialties to benefit the National Kidney Foundation. Entertainers perform continuously for the hungry crowds. Also, cooking demonstrations, arts and crafts and fireworks.

T.V. Turn-Off Week (261-3442). For one week in April, families throughout the United States are encouraged to turn off the television and discover alternative evening activities. At the end of the week, neighborhoods sponsor local festivals honoring those families who survived the week without turning on the tube.

Inman Park Spring Festival and Tour of Homes, Inman Park, Atlanta (242-4895). Historic Inman Park opens the doors of its homes, while outside the neighborhood arts and crafts festival entertains families with an artist's market, live entertainment, pony rides and other children's activities.

TechFest, Southern Tech, Marietta (528-7222). Southern Tech holds an open-house where young people are given an opportunity to see, feel and touch exhibits, and have hands-on experiences in labs and workshops. Roving entertainers and food round-out this annual educational festival for the family.

Atlanta Celtic Festival, Oglethorpe University, Atlanta (429-0107). Oglethorpe University hosts a celebration of Celtic heritage, including exhibits, food, wares, music, dance, theater, folklore and workshops.

Indian Heritage Days, Stately Oaks Mansion, Jonesboro (478-4800). Jonesboro's spring festival is located at historical Stately Oaks Mansion and features living history activities, entertainment and other festivities.

Villa International Atlanta Festival of Nations, Emory University, Atlanta (633-6783). Enjoy an international food fair, with information booths, crafts, and entertainment from native countries. Children's activities include storytelling, face-painting and magic shows.

Pinckneyville Arts and Crafts Festival, Pinckneyville Arts Center, Norcross (417-2215). Arts and crafts, live entertainment, children's activities and food highlight this annual festival.

Jonquil City Spring Festival, Bellmont Hills Shopping Center, Smyrna (434-6600). A parade, arts and crafts booths, races, food and entertainment highlight this spring festival. An entire area is devoted to children's activities, including games, pony rides, petting farm, kiddie train, moon walk, face-painting, and clowns.

Kennesaw/Big Shanty Festival, Downtown Kennesaw –near Big Shanty Museum (423-1330). Reenactment of the Battle of Kennesaw, arts and crafts booths, a parade, local business booths, old-time village demonstrations, live entertainment and food highlight this festival. There is a special children's activity area which features a ride on a small train.

Yaarab Temple Shriners Circus and Carnival, Cobb County Central Park, Marietta (875-0318). For ten days, the Shriners present a medium-size circus and carnival with over 30 rides for younger children.

Georgia Renaissance Festival, Royal Festival Grounds, Fairburn, Georgia (964-8575). For six weekends (including Memorial Day) beginning late April and ending early June, your family can visit a 30-acre Renaissance Village reenacting the times, customs, crafts, characters and culinary habits of the Renaissance in authentic detail with jugglers, magicians, fire eaters, comedia troups and minstrels peforming continuously. Also, knightly games and activities, an authentic crafts village, and food and drink fit for a king and queen (or prince and princess).

Old Town Sharpsburg Festival, Sharpsburg (6 miles west of Peachtree City), Georgia (253-4934). This arts and crafts festival is housed in authentic rural buildings dating from the late 1800 s and early 1900 s. There are also antiques, entertainment, children's activities and great food.

Appalachian SprinGreen Festival, Blue Ridge, Georgia (404/632-5680). SprinGreen celebrates the greening of the mountains with traditional music and dance, regional crafts and country cooking.

Return to Long Swamp Creek Pow Wow and Indian Festival, Tate, Georgia (800/342-7515). The three-day celebration of Native American culture and spiritual traditions, features traditional dancers, food, crafts and athletic events featuring members of the Indian nations of the Cherokee, Chippewa and Sioux.

MAY

East Atlanta Festival, Brownwood Park, Atlanta (876-5220). The neighborhood festival includes folk singers, dance groups, an international food court, arts and crafts, flea market and more.

Wren's Nest and West End Festival, West End Park, Atlanta (752-9329 and 753-7735). During the first weekend in May, the West End puts on a two day neighborhood festival with a parade, arts and crafts, African jewelry and art, entertainment and a children's tent. Nearby, the Wren's Nest, home of the famous children's book writer Joel Chandler Harris, has its own festival with storytelling, musical entertainment, jugglers, clowns, pony rides and many more children's activities.

Children's Art Festival, Glover Park, Marietta (424-8142). Sponsored by the Marietta/Cobb Museum of Art, this children's arts festival features hands-on arts and crafts activities, demonstrations, clowns, theater and dance performances, jugglers, musicians, puppets, balloons, food and more fun.

Historic Marietta Arts and Crafts Festival, Glover Park, Marietta (429-4424). This festival features arts and crafts in Marietta Square with live entertainment and food.

Spring Festival in Candler Park, Candler Park, Atlanta (378-8648). Along with arts and crafts and live entertainment, this neighborhood spring festival provides lots of unusual games, dog trick contests and special activities for children and families.

Children's Festival, Gilbert House, 2238 Perkerson Road, SW, Atlanta (766-9049). Join the parade of costumed children, or enjoy food, games and lots of family fun.

Very Special Arts Festival, Georgia Retardation Center, Dunwoody (551-7000). The festival provides a very special chance for people with disabilities to have fun and show others they are capable of enjoying and producing art. Besides arts and crafts activities, there are many other fun activities.

Mother's Day Festival, Lenox Park (between Roxboro and North Druid Hills Road) (669-0138). The festival benefits Village Atlanta, a shelter for homeless women and children. Activities for moms and their kids include music, mime, magic, storytelling, games, crafts, workshops for moms and more!

Springfest, Stone Mountain Park (498-5702). This springtime celebration at Stone Mountain Park features cooks from all over the South dishing up samples as they compete in barbeque cookoffs, along with arts and crafts booths, fireworks, clogging and other live entertainment. It also marks the debut of the summer laser show.

Atlanta Peach Caribbean Carnival, Downtown, Atlanta (525-7831 ext. 171). Three days of celebration throughout Atlanta, highlighted by a parade down Peachtree Street to Woodruff Park which is tranformed into a Caribbean marketplace with arts and crafts, retail vendors, folklife demonstrations, food, dance and literary, visual and performing arts. A whole afternoon of the festival is set aside for a special Children's Carnival.

Armed Forces Festival and Open House (752-3392). Each year, the armed services (Army, Navy and/or Air Force) have an open house and invite the public to view flying demonstrations, military displays, hand combat demonstrations, parachute jumping and band concerts. There are also refreshments. Watch for this year's location.

Georgia State Championship Chili Cook-Off, Lakewood Ampitheater, Atlanta (248-1315). Amateur and professional chefs compete for the right to represent Georgia in the National Chili Cook-Off while the public gets to sample the recipes and enjoy live entertainment. Proceeds benefit the National Kidney Foundation.

Atlanta Storytelling Festival, Atlanta Historical Society, Buckhead, Atlanta (261-1837). This annual festival features the best storytellers from the Southeast as well as musicians, entertainers and special guest celebrities who, for two days, bedazzle children with tall tales, folk stories, lying contests and more. Presented by the Southern Order of Storytellers.

Kingfest, Martin Luther King, Jr. Center for Nonviolent Social Change, Auburn Avenue, Atlanta (524-1956). Beginning in May, and continuing every other Saturday through mid-August, the Center hosts numerous afternoon and evening arts and performance festivals for the public. Song, dance, poetry, storytelling, theater, comedy and juggling are some of the performing arts that can be enjoyed all summer long. There is a special International Day, Gospel Day and Kid's Day with hands-on arts and crafts activities and performances especially for children.

Memorial Day Celebration, Stone Mountain Park (498-5702). The holiday marks the opening of the beach and water sports at Stone Mountain Park and the highlight of the evening is a special **Lasershow.**

Georgia Renaissance Festival, Royal Festival Grounds, Fairburn, Georgia (964-8575). _See_ April Festival listings.

Decatur Arts Festival, Old Courthouse, Decatur (371-8386). During Memorial Day weekend, the square in downtown Decatur comes to life with a three day arts festival celebrating the visual and performing arts. There is a whole day of children's activities with lots of hands-on arts and crafts projects, pony rides, moonwalk and more. Also, artist markets, live performances, an international village, food court, a street party and a

Sunday night concert on the square.

Sheriff's Posse of DeKalb County, Stone Mountain Coliseum Park (498-5600). A two-day Wild West event that features bucking broncos, barrel riding, calf roping, cowboys, cowgirls and more.

Sweetwater Fever Fine Arts Festival, Mable House, Mableton (739-0189). A fine arts and crafts market, country crafts, demonstrations, children's activities,performing arts and food can be found at Mableton's annual celebration.

Sugar Hill Maple Festival, E.E. Robinson Park, Sugar Hill (945-6716). Arts and crafts festival with children's activities, food and entertainment.

Snellville Days Arts and Crafts Festival, T. W. Briscoe Park, Snellville (932-2917). Arts and crafts, children's activities, country and western music, magic shows, food, and more.

Grayson Day Festival, State Highway 84 and Rosebud Road, Grayson, Georgia (985-3535). Arts and crafts, clogging and other live entertainment, food, pony rides and other children's activities can be found at this annual festival.

Suwanee Day, City Hall, Suwanee, Georgia (932-2917). Usually held during the third weekend in May (but every once in a while in the fall), Suwanee holds its arts and crafts festival with entertainment, children's activities and evening fireworks.

SpringFest at Lake Lanier, Gainesville (945-7201). Boat shows, exhibits, free boat and jet ski rides, fishing clinics and highlight this annual festival which is usually a real "splash" with families.

May Fest in the Mountains, Helen, Georgia (404/878-2181). Bavarian food, music and dancing festival during two weekends in May.

Helen to the Atlantic Hot-Air Balloon Race and Balloon Festival, Helen, Georgia (404/878-2271). Over 75 hot-air balloons participate in Helen's famous hot-air balloon race and festival which includes balloon rides, hay rides and music.

The Spring Art Festival, Dahlonega, Georgia (404/864-3711). Held the first weekend in May, this arts and crafts festival features work by juried exhibitors.

Dahlonega's Wildflower Festival of the Arts, Dahlonega, Georgia. (404/864-3711). Held during the third weekend in May. A visual and performing arts festival in Dahlonega's square featuring programs and exhibits on wildflowers of the area, and an area with hands-on art activities for children.

Prater's Mill Country Fair, Dalton, Georgia (404/259-5765). A quality arts and crafts show held in the atmosphere of an old fashioned country fair with entertainment of the 1800's period, country cooking, canoeing on Coahulla Creek, pony rides and other children's activities. There is also an operating grist mill which completes the country fair atmosphere.

Cherokee Fields Country Festival, Ball Ground, Georgia (404/973-6999). Paintings, woodworking, stained glass, jewelry, folk art, sewing, craft demonstrations and much more highlight this arts and crafts festival held on Memorial Day weekend.

Cherokee County Indian Festival and Powwow, Highway 5 on the Etowah River, Bolling Park, Canton (404/735-4930). This celebration of Native American culture with traditional dances, foods, crafts, and athletic events brings together members of several Indian nations including the Cherokee, Chippewa and Sioux.

Cotton Pickin' Country Fair, Gay, Georgia (404/538-6814). The fair is located on an old cotton-ginning complex which includes an 1890s vintage plantation home and features arts and crafts, antiques, continuous entertainment, activities for children and southern cooking.

JUNE

Log Cabin Story Hours, DeKalb Historical Complex in Adair Park, Decatur (373-1088). Wednesday mornings, June-August, the DeKalb Historical Society presents story hours and pioneer demonstrations for children at the restored log cabins located at the DeKalb Historical Complex. Reservations are required.

Cabbagetown Reunion Festival, Carroll Street, Cabbagetown (521-0815). The annual festival features an arts and crafts festival, flea market and barbeque with music and a few children's activities.

Virginia Highlands Summerfest, Virginia Highlands, Atlanta (892-3613). A juried art show, hot-air balloon rides, family races, mini-circus, performances, street vendors, face-painting, clowns, magicians and lots of children's activities highlight this summer festival.

Neighbor Day, DeKalb-Peachtree Airport, Clairmont Road, Atlanta (457-7236). Held in May or June. Families have the opportunity to see the airport up close and learn about aviation. Antique airplanes, corporate jets, helicopters and ultralight aircraft are exhibited to the public together with displays, exhibits and booths providing information about everything from whirly birds to emergency medical care. Aerial demonstrations and inexpensive airplane and helicopter rides over Atlanta are a very special treat for children.

Arts and Crafts Festival Stone Mountain Village, Downtown Stone Mountain (296-8058). Over 250 exhibitors from throughout the Southeast show off their arts, crafts, antiques and collectibles with lots of clogging, storytellers, singers, bands and food.

Stay and See Georgia Week at Underground Atlanta, Atlanta (458-0784). The Georgia Chamber of Commerce hosts this travel show highlighting the different attractions and vacation spots around the State of Georgia. Some booths have dioramas, others have people dressed in costume and all have information packets and lots of brochures. Learn about the different Georgia cities and enjoy the usual activities of Underground Atlanta, plus street entertainers, animal balloons, face-painting, special promotions and vacation give-aways.

Underground Atlanta, Anniversary Celebration, Downtown, Atlanta (523-2311). Underground Atlanta celebrates its anniversary with a big celebration, including special concerts, street performers and evening fireworks.

Taste of Chocolate, National Kidney Foundation of Georiga, Swissotel, Atlanta (365-0065). Atlanta's annual celebration of chocolate has over 30 chocolate exhibitors tempting the public with samples of their candy. Also, cooking demonstrations, live entertainment and special children's contests and activities benefit the National Kidney Foundation.

Beach Party, Old Courthouse Square, Decatur (371-8386). The Decatur Business Association creates a beach area for the entire family to enjoy, complete with sand, wading pools, beach music, dancing, volleyball and dunking machines.

Celebrate Israel, Zaban Park, Dunwoody (876-1554). An Israeli marketplace, hands-on arts and crafts, a Sesame Street theater, a petting zoo, pony rides, singing, dancing, Maccabian games and ethnic food mark this annual celebration of Israel.

Atlanta Downs Duck Derby, Chattahoochee River at Paces Mill at U.S. 41, Atlanta (892-0026). Thousands of yellow rubber duckies float down the Chattahoochee River for 500 yards in an event Ernie of Sesame Street would love. Though anyone can sponsor a duck at no charge, this event is a benefit for the American Cancer Society, so contributions are strongly encouraged. There are prizes and saving bonds available for winning duck sponsors. Also, enjoy a duck costume contest for children and adults, sack races and other games, a parade, refreshments and T-shirts for sale.

Renaissance Festival, Royal Festival Ground, Fairburn, Georgia (964-8575). *See* April Festival listings.

Kingfest, Martin Luther King Jr. Center for Nonviolent Social Change, Auburn Avenue, Atlanta (528-8947). *See* May Festival listings.

————————————— **JULY** —————————————

Peachtree Road Race, Peachtree Road, Atlanta (231-9064). July 4th officially starts with the running of the Peachtree Road Race, sponsored by the Atlanta Track Club. Over 40,000 Atlantans, together with world class runners, race down Peachtree Road to Piedmont Park. Spectators line Peachtree Road and gather in Piedmont Park to cheer on the runners and celebrate the start of the Independence Day holiday.

Salute 2 America July 4th Parade–WSB-TV, Downtown, Atlanta (897-7452). The largest Independence Day Parade in the USA starts early afternoon at the CNN Center, proceeds up Marietta Street and then north up Peachtree Street. Each year floats, bands, clowns, unicycles and other specialty units participate in this Atlanta tradition.

July 4th Fireworks, Decatur Square, Lenox Square Shopping Mall, Six Flags Over Georgia, Stone Mountain Park, Underground Atlanta, Atlanta-Fulton County Stadium, Marietta Square, Chastain Park Ampitheatre, Lake Lanier Islands, Wills Park Recreation Center, Peachtree City's Drake Field, Smryna's Tolleson Park, Marketplace Shopping Center in Lilburn, New Courthouse in Lawrenceville, Adams Park in Kennesaw and Lillian Webb Field in Norcross are the usual locations for evening fireworks displays.

Fantastic Fourth Celebration, Stone Mountain Park (498-5702). Major concerts, patriotic music, clogging and beach activities entertain the daytime crowds, while the Lasershow and fireworks atop the mountain entertain spectators at dusk.

4th of July Parade, Stone Mountain Village (296-8058). A traditional July 4th parade celebration with floats, bands and a bicycle contest for children.

July 4th Celebration, Courthouse Square, Decatur (371-8386). Decatur celebrates the 4th of July with a pied-piper parade (children allowed to join in on foot and bicycles), concert, picnics and evening fireworks.

The Let Freedom Ring Parade, Marietta (429-4212). Marietta's July 4th parade starts at the Roswell Street Baptist Church and proceeds to Marietta Square. Families enjoy live entertainment, games and contests and barbeque, as well as the evening fireworks.

South DeKalb Fourth of July Celebration, South DeKalb Mall, Candler Road, Panthersville Stadium (681-1847). A parade, family picnics and a free concert highlight the July 4th celebration.

Float the Fourth Tube Parade & Fireworks, Helen, Georgia (404/878-2181). The July 4th celebration in the Georgia mountains includes an old-fashioned barbeque and an annual tube parade down the Chattahoochee.

July 4th Family Day Celebration, Dahlonega, Georgia (404/864-3711). Fourth of July events includes dance, music, arts and crafts, colonial demonstrations and musical programs for the entire family.

National Black Arts Festival, throughout Atlanta (730-7315). Held biennially during the last week in July and first week in August. This arts festival, the only one of its kind, celebrates the accomplishments of African-American artists, and presents over 75 concerts, plays, films, dance performances, storytelling sessions, bookfairs, workshops, and art exhibits at over 40 different locations in Atlanta. The festival is attended by over one million people! There are specially scheduled storytelling and puppetry performances during the ten festival days, a large parade, an outdoor arts and crafts market and many other activities that the whole family can enjoy.

Old Town Lilburn Birthday Celebration, Old Town Lilburn (925-1870). Old Town Lilburn celebrates its birthday with a festival which includes arts and crafts, street vendors, live entertainment and more.

Atlanta Encampment, Atlanta History Center, Buckhead, Atlanta (261-

1837). Over 200 reenactors in authentic costumes stage a living history demonstration of Civil War camp life.

Kingfest, Martin Luther King Jr. Center for Nonviolent Social Change, Auburn Avenue, Atlanta (524-1956). *See* May Festival Listings.

Steam Engine Festival, Cumming, Georgia (404/889-0309). Twenty operating steam engines are the focus of this arts and crafts festival at the Courthouse Square in Cumming. Also featured are a parade, clogging, barbeque and other festivities for children.

Spirit of France Festival, Chateau Elan, Braselton, Georgia (404/867-8200). Chateau Elan Winery presents a celebration of Bastille Day with French artists, music, gourmet luncheons, wines, breads, pastries and chocolates.

Indian Games Festival, Etowah Indian Mounds Historic Site, Cartersville, Georgia. This annual festival features demonstrations of games played by Southeastern Native American cultures, including chunkey, stick ball and games of chance.

Children's Art Festival, Henderson Indoor Arena, College Park (729-3673). Hands-on arts and crafts, face-painting, and performance groups highlight this South Fulton festival.

AUGUST

Grant Park Festival and Tour of Homes, Grant Park, Atlanta (622-2015). A two-day tour of homes and neighborhood festival which includes arts and crafts booths, live entertainment, food, pet parades, a moonwalk and lots of other children's activities.

Tucker Days, Main Street, Tucker (255-8641). Continuous live entertainment, arts and crafts markets, road races, children's games and entertainment highlight Tucker's annual celebration.

Festival of the Painted Rock, Chattahoochee Nature Center, Roswell (992-2055). Held the third weekend in August. The Nature Center sponsors a fine arts and crafts festival for families which includes plenty of food, live entertainment and lots of children's activities.

Kingfest, Martin Luther King Jr. Center for Nonviolent Social Change, Auburn Avenue (528-8947). *See* May Festival listings.

Mountain Do Arts & Crafts Show, Lake Lanier Islands, Georgia (404/945-6701). Lake Lanier hosts a huge arts and crafts festival for the entire family complete with entertainment, food and other family activities.

Georgia Mountain Fair, West of Hiawassee, Georgia (404/896-4191). For twelve days, Lake Chatuga is the site of one of the largest of Georgia's State Fairs featuring farm, home and crafts exhibits, music, dancing, parades, rides, shows and lots more "mountain fun" for the whole family.

SEPTEMBER

Labor Day Celebration, Stone Mountain Park (498-5702). Celebrate the Labor Day holiday at Stone Mountain Park with continuous entertainment and other special events. The evening **Lasershow** is the last of the season.

Art in the Park, Glover Park, Marietta (429-1115). Marietta's Labor Day festival, formerly known as Founder's Day, features an arts and crafts show featuring paintings, photographs, pottery and other crafts as well as horse and buggy rides and live entertainment.

Yellow Daisy Festival, Stone Mountain Park (498-5702). Named after the annual blooming of the rare Confederate Yellow Daisy flower, Stone Mountain Park's annual arts and crafts show is huge featuring about 475 exhibitors. There is also a flower show, live entertainment and lots of southern cooking.

Acworth Pioneer Days, Lake Acworth Beach, Acworth (974-4221). This Labor Day weekend festival features arts and crafts, food, carnival rides, music and entertainment and an opening parade and closing fireworks show.

Arts Festival of Atlanta, Piedmont Park, Atlanta (885-1125). Atlanta's most famous outdoor arts and crafts festival features arts and crafts in every possible media, Atlanta's finest performing artists, street performers and a large selection of ethnic and southern foods. There are also exhibits of children's art, hands-on arts and crafts activities, musical, dance, puppetry and storytelling performances, face painting, sand-art, balloons, mimes, jugglers, acrobats and more.

Duluth Fall Festival and Parade, Duluth (476-1200). The city of Duluth puts on an arts and crafts show that includes artist booths, a parade, retail vendors, entertainment and lots more activities.

Gwinnett County Fair, Gwinnett County Fair Grounds, Lawerenceville (882-7700). This is a real State Fair with farm animals, home and craft exhibits, clogging and other live entertainment, rides, games, barbeque and more county fair festivities.

Steeple House Fall Festival, Steeple House Arts Center, Marietta (952-8661). The fine arts center's annual fair features an artist's market, live performances, children's art activities, artist's demonstrations and food.

Atlanta Greek Festival. Greek Orthodox Cathedral of the Annunciation, Atlanta (633-5870). Atlanta's Greek community puts on a three day festival celebrating Greek culture and tradition that includes dance, music, Greek food and pastries, crafts, storytelling, travel films, tours of the Cathedral.

Cobb's Best Taste, Glover Park, Marietta (429-4212). The Square in Marietta is filled with food samples from local restaurants, continuous entertainment and other food-related contests and activities.

Blue Ribbon Affair, Cobb County's Central Park, Callaway Road, Marietta (423-1330). An authenic country fair featuring a mix of traditional arts and crafts and decorating trends, including a special children's area. This precedes the North Georgia State Fair.

North Georgia State Fair, Cobb County's Central Park, Marietta (423-1330). Metro- Atlanta's largest fall State Fair features country crafts, amusement rides, games, agricultural exhibits, live entertainment and country cooking.

238

Smyrna Fall Festival, Community Center, Smyrna (434-6600). Arts and crafts, live entertainment, children's activities and food highlight the Jonquil City's annual fall festival.

Sweetwater Valley Festival, Mable House, Mableton (739-0189). Look for an artist's market, Civil War reenactments, children's activities, live entertainment and great food at this outdoor festival.

Heritage Days Festival, Bulloch Hall, Roswell (992-1731). The Roswell Historical Society presents an old-fashioned country fair with Civil War weapons exhibits and encampment, antiques, storytelling, crafts, music, pony rides and more.

Folklife Festival, Atlanta History Center, Buckhead, Atlanta (261-1837). Held in late September or early October. The festival is held at the Tullie Smith House on the Atlanta History Center's grounds and features demonstrations of traditional arts and crafts of the 1800's, folk music, storytelling and other period entertainment.

Roswell Arts and Crafts Festival, Roswell (889-0309). The Square in Roswell is filled with arts and crafts booths, children's activity areas, the sounds of live entertainment and other festival activities.

Sesame Street Live, Omni Coliseum, Atlanta (577-2626). Every September, the Sesame Street Muppets' Stage Show visits Atlanta and presents a musical show for children loaded with familiar songs, dancing and lots of audience participation.

Sandy Springs Festival, Sandy Springs Circle (257-1579). Folk craft demonstrations, needlework, jewelry, music, cloggers, car shows, races and tours of the historical Williams-Payne House highlight this outdoor feastival at the Sandy Springs Historical Site.

Ye Olde English Festival. St. Bartholomew's Church, Atlanta (634-3336). A re-creation of Merry Old England, complete with costumes, decorations, food, games, art, Rennaisance, Baroque and folk music, jugglers, handicrafters, and other period activities.

Heritage Week, Various locations throughout East Point (221-3169). Arts and crafts, family theatre offerings and a medieval village are featured during this week-long event sponsored by the East Point Chamber of Commerce.

Garden Hills Ice Cream Social, Sunnybrook Park, Atlanta (264-0867). Ice cream, hot dogs, arts and crafts, games, rides and contests for children highlight this neighborhood fall festival.

Historic Marietta Arts and Crafts Festival, Glover Park, Marietta (429-4212). The City of Marietta sponsors a fall arts and crafts festival which includes special children's activities, entertainment and food.

Apple Chill Arts and Crafts Festival, Wills Park, Alpharetta (475-7474). A variety of arts and crafts and performing arts may be enjoyed at this covered center, including a few children's activities.

Peachtree Crossings Country Fair, Fairgrounds (Exit 12 off I-85), Peachtree City, Georgia (434-3661). Artists and craftpersons, a pre-1840 camp, folk crafters, muzzle loaded rifle demonstrations, blue grass and Army brass music, cloggers and buggy rides highlight this annual festival which benefits Scottish Rite Children's Hospital.

Powers Crossroads Country Fair and Art Festival, Newnan, Georgia (404/253-2011). Held Labor Day weekend. This nationally recognized southern arts festival features over 300 artists and craftspeople, bluegrass music, barbeque, clogging and other country fair activities. There is a very large children's area filled with hands-on activities, rides and lots of other fun things to do.

Moss Oak Plantation Arts and Crafts Festival, Adjacent to the Powers Crossroads Country Fair, Newnan, Georgia (404/433-8395). This small country arts and crafts festival features a tour of the historic 1790 Moss Oak Plantation Home and about 100 arts and crafts exhibitors.

Riverfest, Boling Park, Canton, Georgia (404/479-1994). This festival features over one hundred artists and craftspeople as well as demonstrations of blacksmithing, stained glass, pottery and quilting. There is also a children's activity area, food and live entertainment.

Oktoberfest, Helen, Georgia (404/878-2181). Every Thursday, Friday and Saturday in September. The mountain village of Helen celebrates the fall harvest with Bavarian food, a parade, music and dancing.

Cumming Falling Leaves Festival, Downtown Cumming (404/889-9977). Arts and crafts exhibitors, an auction, Native American dances, dulcimer music, bluegrass, country and western music and lots more activities highlight this fall festival.

Annual Cherokee Indian Homecoming Festival, New Echota Historic Site, Calhoun (404/629-8151). Cherokee Indians return to their former national capital to demonstrate traditional songs and dances, skills, games and crafts.

OCTOBER

Ormewood Park Fall Festival, Ormewood Park, Atlanta (627-4313). A neighborhood street festival which includes a flea market, arts and crafts booths, a food court and live entertainment throughout the day.

Red Bandana Evening, Old Courthouse Square, Decatur (371-8386). Country barbeque, bluegrass music, square dancing and other fall festivities highlight this evening event in downtown Decatur.

Festival by the River, Pinckneyville Arts Center, Norcross (417-2215). This annual fall festival specializes in children's activities, including an appearance by the Zoomobile, arts and crafts activities, pony rides, entertainment and lots more.

Octoberfest Arts and Crafts Festival, 6701 Roswell Road, Sandy Springs (573-7050). This large arts and crafts festival also features entertainment, food, amusement rides, pony rides, mid-way games and lots of other fun activities for children.

Great Miller Lite Chili Cookoff, Stone Mountain Park (872-4731). Cooking teams from all over the Southeast compete in a chili-cooking championship. Samples are available for families to eat while they enjoy live entertainment throughout the event.

Scottish Festival & Highland Games, Stone Mountain Park (498-5702). The Park is the location for the International Gathering of Scots celebrating Scottish tradition with Highland athletic events, pipe bands, folk dancing, drumming competitions and parades. Over 100 different clans and societies participate in this unusual event.

Zoofest, Zoo Atlanta (624-5600). Zoo Atlanta presents two days of musical entertainment for children, featuring local bands and talent. Musical storytimes, face painting, clowns and special exhibits also highlight this event.

Gwinnett County–Festival of Nations, throughout Gwinnett County (962-6642). October is International Month in Gwinnett County and the Gwinnett Council for the Arts sponsors international art exhibits throughout the County as well as an international bazaar filled with craft exhibitors, international performers and international food. The location of the bazaar varies from year to year.

Lithonia PAL Festival, Lithonia (593-5464). Lithonia's fall festival features clogging, arts and crafts, music and lots of food.

Fernbank Science Center Fall Festival, Atlanta (378-4311). Bird walks, road races, special nature exhibits, games and other children's activities highlight the nature center's annual fall festival for children.

Youth Days and Festival, Roswell (641-3760). The City of Roswell honors its youth with week-long activities, culminating in a weekend parade and luncheon on the Roswell Square.

World Fest '90, Galleria Complex, Atlanta (980-2000). An international festival featuring world-class entertainment, cultural and educational events and exhibits, an international crafts market and international food. Children's activities include clowns, jugglers, circus performers, face painters, interactive international learning centers, a petting zoo comprised of animals from all over the world and educational displays.

Fall Festival of the Arts, Paideia School and Oakgrove Park, Atlanta (377-3491). Held at the end of October or early November. This children's festival features an artist's market, lots of hands-on art activities, games, entertainment and festival food.

Decatur's Heritage Festival, Old Courthouse, Decatur (371-8386). The Heritage festival includes participating demonstrations of country crafts such as candle-dipping, soap-making, spinning and pottery as well as demonstrations by bee keepers and blacksmiths. Storytelling, a petting zoo, live entertainment, hay rides and lots of food round off this fall festival.

Historic Vinings' Fall Festival, Vinings (436-9316). Antiques, crafts, family entertainment, clowns, music and storytelling can all be found during the historic village's annual festival.

Fall Festival and Annual Reenactment of the Battle of Jonesboro, Stately Oaks Mansion, Jonesboro (447-7949). Jonesboro's fall festival includes a reenactment of the famous Battle of Jonesboro, a tour of the plantation, and other fall festival activities.

Elisha Winn Fair, Elisha Winn House, Dacula (404/822-5174). Held during the first weekend in October. The Gwinnett Historical Society opens the doors of the historical Elisha Winn House and provides historical and Native American craft demonstrations, exhibits and living-history activities.

Lilburn Daze, Old Town Lilburn, Lilburn City Park (972-1662). Lilburn hosts an arts and crafts fair complete with community and educational exhibits and lots of children's activities. Included are pumpkin decorating contests, hands-on art activities, balloons, live entertainment and festival food.

Italian Festival, Hellenic Center, Atlanta (434-1459). This annual festival is held in honor of Christopher Columbus and features Italian crafts and cultural items and traditional Italian food. Mark your calendar for the 1992 celebration which will be the Quincentennial celebration of Columbus' discovery of America!

Arts Fest, Steeple House Arts Center, Marietta (952-8661). Children's activities include mask-making, button-making, Halloween gags, tie-dying and Native American headdresses. An arts and crafts festival and live performers also highlight this annual festival.

Arts in the Park, Briscoe Park, Snellville (972-0200). Over 150 arts and crafts booths, antiques and food make this a fun event for the entire family.

Oktoberfest, Helen, Georgia (404/878-2181). Held every day of the week in October, except Sunday. Helen celebrates the fall harvest with Bavarian food, music and dancing.

Gold Rush Days, Dahlonega, Georgia (404/864-3711). On the third weekend in October, Dahlonega becomes an open-air stage for special performances and activities celebrating Dahlonega's gold mining history.

Fall Prater's Mill Country Fair, Dalton, Georgia (404/259-5765). This quality arts and crafts fair show is held in the atmosphere of an old fashioned country fair with entertainment of the 1800's period, country cooking, pony rides and other children's activities.

Georgia Apple Festival Arts and Crafts Fair, Ellijay, Georgia (404/635-7400). Besides sampling apples of all kinds, this festival includes arts and crafts, square dancing, clogging, singing, pony rides, moonwalks and southern cooking.

Heritage Holidays, Rome, Georgia (404/291-3819). Fall in the mountains is the theme for Rome's annual festival which features concerts, boat rides, wagon train and trail rides, living history demonstrations, a parade, dancing, concerts and lots more activities.

Corn Tassel Festival, Gainesville, Georgia (404/532-5209). Arts and crafts, puppet shows, bluegrass and Appalachian music shows, storytelling, quilt exhibits and plenty of country cooking highlight this well known mountain festival.

Fall Festival, Callaway Gardens, Pine Mountain, Georgia (404/663-5186). Celebrate fall among the splendor of the Callaway Gardens, including food, storytelling, entertainment and gardening demonstrations.

Cotton Pickin' Country Fair, Gay, Georgia (404/538-6814). The fair is located on an old cotton-ginning complex which includes an 1890s vintage plantation home and features arts and crafts, antiques, continuous entertainment, activities for children and southern cooking.

Georgia Marble Festival, Jasper (404/692-5600). Guided tours of the Georgia Marble Company's quarries in Tate, a marble sculpture competition, historical tours and exhibits, arts and crafts, food and live entertainment highlight this North Georgia festival.

Heritage Days, Lanier Museum of Natural History, Buford (945-3543). The festival includs arts and crafts, storytelling, a Civil War encampment and games.

Fall in Festival, State Botanical Garden, Athens (404/542-1244). The Garden celebrates the fall with arts and crafts, live entertainment and lots of special activities for families.

HALLOWEEN

Little Five Points Halloween Festival, Little Five Points, Atlanta (524-1931). Live entertainment, costume fashion shows, food and a moonwalk highlight this October festival.

Great Halloween Caper, Zoo Atlanta (624-5600). A haunted house, a costume contest and lots of real bats, spiders and snakes highlight Zoo Atlanta's Halloween celebration.

Annual Haunted Castle at Rhodes Hall, Peachtree Road, Atlanta (881-9980). Historic Rhodes Hall is transformed into a haunted house and open to the public during the weeks prior to Halloween. More subdued children's tours are given on weekends followed by costume contests and other special Halloween activities.

Tour of Southern Ghosts, Stone Mountain Park–Antebellum Plantation complex, Stone Mountain (498-5600). The A.R.T. Station presents Halloween storytelling at the Park, including candle lit walkways, fortune tellers and refreshments.

Halloween Carnival and Haunted Forest, Laurel Park, Marietta (429-4215). Elementary age children can visit the Land of Make Believe, a Haunted Forest and participate in lots of games and fun during early evenings in late October.

Fright Nights, Six Flags Over Georgia (739-3400). Six Flags reopens during October weekends to help children celebrate the Halloween holiday. Enjoy some of the amusement park's rides, a Haunted House and other special Halloween activities.

Underground Atlanta/UNICEF Halloween Celebration, Downtown, Atlanta (523-2311). Underground Atlanta and UNICEF host a day of special Halloween activities for children, including a carnival, costume parades, coloring contests, balloons, face-painting and more.

Halloween Activities for Children, Glover Park, Marietta (429-4212). Look for costume contests and other special Halloween activities on the Square during the Halloween holiday.

Safe Trick or Treat–Cobb Center Mall, Cumberland Mall, Market Square Mall, Perimeter Mall, Greenbriar Mall, Southlake Mall, Northlake Mall, South DeKalb Mall, Town Center Mall and Gwinnett Place Mall. The malls offer special Halloween activities for children and allow children to go from store to store gathering special AND SAFE Halloween treats.

The Great Pumpkin Arts and Crafts Festival, Lake Lanier Islands (945-6701). Jack-o-lantern contests, arts and crafts live entertainment, food, pony rides, a petting zoo and jugglers are just some of the special activities for children that can be found at this special festival.

NOVEMBER

Head of the Chattahoochee Regatta, Chattahoochee River Park, Roswell (641-3100). The Regatta is an all-day rowing event held in the three mile stretch on the Chattahoochee between the dam at Azalea Drive and River Park. There are plenty of rowing events to watch and lots of other activities for spectators to enjoy.

Veteran's Day Parade, Downtown, Atlanta (321-6111, ext. 6256). The second largest Veteran's Day Parade in the United States proceeds down Peachtree Street with military and veteran units, high school bands, clowns, floats and other parade participants.

Holiday in the Park, Six Flags Over Georgia, Atlanta (739-3440). Six Flags is decorated for the holidays and open evenings during the months of November and December. The Park presents special entertainment, holiday crafts, a man-made snow hill for sledding, and ice skating activities. Amuseument park rides generally do not operate during these months.

Holiday Open House, Stone Mountain Village (296-8058). During Sundays in November and December through Christmas, Stone Mountain Village dresses up for the holidays and opens its doors to the public. There are holiday performances, refreshments, and storytelling scheduled throughout the open house.

The Holiday Celebration, Stone Mountain Park (498-5600). Held late November through December. To help celebrate the holiday season, Stone Mountain Park and Santa Claus present the South's largest "Tree of Lights." Also, horse-drawn carriage rides, ice skating shows, holiday entertainment and a traditionally decorated Antebellum Plantation mark this holiday celebration.

Walt Disney's World on Ice, Omni Coliseum, Atlanta (681-2100). Walt Disneys's Ice Capades come annually to the Omni to dazzle families with an exciting ice show.

Indian Heritage Week, Georgia State Capitol, Atlanta (656-2844). The

State Capitol Building is the location for lectures, demonstrations and special exhibits celebrating Native American history and culture.

Lighting of the Great Tree–Underground Atlanta (586-2488). Each Thanksgiving evening, Atlantans gather in a new location–Underground Atlanta–to watch the night-time lighting of the huge Christmas Tree. Atlanta school choirs sing Christmas carols.

Decatur Fidelity Family Tree Lighting and Concert, Fidelity Bank Building, Decatur (371-8386). The sixty-five foot tree atop the Fidelity Bank Building in downtown Decatur is lit the last Friday evening in November. Choirs and carolers sing and the crowd celebrates the start of the Christmas season.

Lawrenceville Christmas on the Square, Lawrenceville (963-5128). Thanksgiving evening, the Christmas celebration begins in the Square as carolers sing and the crowd watches the lighting of the great Christmas tree signifying the start of the holiday season.

Christmas on the Square, Glover Park, Marietta (429-4212). Held during an evening in late November or early December, Marietta starts the Christmas holiday with community group carolers, storytellers, the lighting of the Christmas tree and a visit by Santa Claus.

Grayson Christmas Tree Lighting, Grayson (963-8017). Held in late November or early December. The city of Grayson officially starts the holidays with Christmas caroling, the lighting of the Christmas tree and a visit from Santa Claus.

Underground Atlanta, Atlanta (523-2311). Held in November and December. Underground Atlanta celebrates the Christmas season with street performers, carolers, a strolling Santa Claus and a talking Christmas Tree.

Magical Alpine Christmas in Helen, Helen, Georgia (404/878-2181). Held in late November and throughout December. Helen celebrates a Bavarian Christmas in the mountains.

Cabbage Patch Kids Appalachian Christmas Celebration at Babyland General, Cleveland, Georgia (404/865-2171). Usually held on Thanksgiving evening, Babyland General provides special holiday entertainment for children of all ages. Also, the Great Christmas Tree is lit and Santa Claus makes an appearance.

DECEMBER

Holiday in the Park, Six Flags Over Georgia, Atlanta (739-3440). *See* November Festival listings. Also open daily for the last two weeks in December except Christmas Eve and Day.

Holiday Open House, Stone Mountain Village (296-8058). *See* November Festival listings.

The Holiday Celebration, Stone Mountain Park (498-5600). *See* November Festival listings.

Christmas at Callanwolde, Callanwolde Fine Arts Center, Atlanta (872-5338). Callanwolde Fine Arts Center's seasonal fundraiser showcases the talents of Atlanta's interior designers. The rooms of the mansion are decorated in Christmas splendor and there is a collectibles shop, a toy and gift boutique, an art shop and gallery, courtyard cafe and garden center to visit, plus daily holiday performances. This festival is for older children only.

Christmas on the Square, Glover Park, Marietta (429-4212). *See* November Festival listings.

Underground Atlanta, Atlanta (523-2311). *See* November Festival listings.

Atlanta Christkindlemart, Atlanta (266-8245). The benefit for Scottish Rite Children's Hospital features the sights, sounds and smells of an authentic outdoor German Christmas market with food, toys, ornaments and music as well as a special visit by St. Nikolaus.

Holiday Festival for Children, High Museum of Art, Atlanta (892-3600).

The day of family entertainment includes a play, singing, food, games and arts and crafts.

Country Christmas, Atlanta Botanical Garden, Atlanta (876-5859). The Atlanta Botanical Garden hosts a traditional holiday celebration with carolers,chestnuts roasting on an open fire, horse-drawn carriage rides, entertainment, arts and crafts and lots of activities for children.

Sugar Plum Festival, Stone Mountain Village (296-8058). Strolling carolers and seasonal entertainment in the gazebo in the Village are the highlights of this Christmas season festival.

Egleston Hospital Festival of Trees, (Atlanta Apparel Mart or World Congress Center), Atlanta (264-9348). The Festival of Trees showcases hundreds of elaborate christmas trees, wreaths, vignettes and ginger-bread houses. The Festival also features center-stage entertainment, botanical exhibits and a southern fair carousel, plus a large children's section has hands-on art activities, face-painting, play areas and other special activities for children.

Macy's Egleston Christmas Parade, Downtown Atlanta (222-2127). The star of the parade, Santa Claus, leads celebrity guests, clowns, award-winning bands, holiday floats, giant helium balloons, costumed story book and cartoon characters up Peachtree Street as part of Atlanta's famous Christmas parade.

Lighting of State Christmas Tree at the Governor's Mansion, Buckhead, Atlanta (261-1776). The public is invited to the the Georgia Governor's Mansion for an evening lighting of the official Christmas Tree of the State of Georgia. The ceremony includes caroling, tours of the first floor of the Governor's Mansion and refreshments served in the down-stairs ballroom.

Christmas Festival and Christmas Open House–Wren's Nest, Atlanta (753-7735). The annual open-house is held on the Sunday in December closest to Joel Chandler Harris' birthday. The Wren's Nest is decorated in Victorian Christmas finery and hosts a special Christmas storytelling festival for children.

Merry Market, Old Courthouse, Decatur (371-8386). The Old Courthouse in Decatur becomes a holiday market filled with handmade crafts, gifts and holiday decorations.

Roswell–Bulloch Hall and Allenbrook, Roswell (992-1731). The two historical homes in Roswell are decorated with seasonal greenery and are the sites for special musical and holiday events throughout the month.

Christmas in the Woods, Laurel Park, Marietta (429-4215). Christmas caroling and storytelling, hay rides and a visit with Santa Claus help children celebrate the holiday season.

Old Fashioned Christmas, Atlanta History Center, Atlanta (261-1837). Special Sunday afternoon performances and activities throughout the month of December include craft workshops and other holiday programs for children and adults.

Fernbank Planetarium, Atlanta (378-4311). "The Christmas Express," a planetarium show where a little green engine named Casey saves the day for the children of a small mountain village is held annually.

Peach Bowl Parade and Game, Downtown, Atlanta (586-8500). Atlanta hosts the post-season college championship Peach Bowl every year at Atlanta Fulton County Stadium. Prior to the game, downtown Atlanta is the site of the **Peach Bowl Parade**, featuring floats, bands and usual parade excitement.

The Twelve Days of Christmas at Callaway Gardens, Pine Mountain, Georgia (800/282-8181). The Gardens are bedecked with beautiful displays of holiday greenery and special holiday activities, including a breakfast with Santa Claus may be enjoyed by the entire family.

Magical Alpine Christmas in Helen, Helen, Georgia (404/878-2181). *See* November festival listings.

Dahlonega's Old Fashioned Christmas, Dahlonega, Georgia (404/864-3711). During the first weekend in December, Santa Claus visits Dahlonega and enjoys the caroling, a winter parade and other holiday entertainment.

251

7. Day Trips

S ometimes you just need to get away from it all, but it's not time for the family vacation, or you're not up to a long drive and don't have time for an overnight stay anyway. A day trip that won't require much more than an hour's drive is the perfect solution! We have described many of our favorite day trip activities and organized them into eight areas, each one being chock full of things to do and see.

We have placed symbols at the top of each listing to designaate the general categories that the day trip fits into. These symbols will help you recognize the essence of each "Day Trip" at a glance.

 NATURE

 SCIENCE

 UNIQUE ATTRACTIONS

 HISTORY AND GOVERNMENT

 PERFORMING ARTS

 FINE ARTS

ATHENS

Fondly known to many Atlantans as the home of the University of Georgia Bulldogs, Athens also is home to The State Botanical Garden of Georgia, the Georgia State Museum of Art, Sandy Creek Park and Nature Center and Bear Hollow Wildlife Trail all of which are appealing to youngsters . . . and even some die-hard Dogs fans.

If you are unfamiliar with Athens, you might want to stop by the Welcome Center located in the Church-Waddel-Brumby House, 280 E. Dougherty Street (404/353-1820). Built in 1820, it is the oldest residence in Athens and also serves as a house museum. It is open Mondays-Saturdays from 9:00am-5:00pm and Sundays from 2:00pm-5:00pm.

THE STATE BOTANICAL GARDEN OF GEORGIA

The State Botanical Garden of Georgia, 2450 South Milledge Avenue, Athens, 2 miles south of the University's main campus (404/542-1244). The Garden is located on over 300-acres of land, much of which is in its natural state with streams, woods, ravines and frontage on the Oconee River. It displays ordinary as well as rare and unusual plants, and is a natural habitat for numerous wildlife, with 5 miles of nature trails which are really fun to explore! In addition, the Garden has special collections such as the Rose Garden, Herb Garden and Dahlia Garden to complement the azaleas, rhododendrons, dogwoods and other indigenous plants.

The strikingly modern and magnificent glass-enclosed Visitor Center/ Conservatory Complex is the reception area for the Garden with a continuous slide show providing Garden information and housing a gift shop, offices and the Garden Cafe. It is home to many tropical and semi-tropical plants, a stream and a wishing pool, and features the work of various regional artists. The Callaway Building nearby is a center for teaching and research and includes a reading room, library, and art exhibits.

Conservatory and Visitor Center: Open Mondays- Saturdays from 9:00am-4:30pm and Sundays from 11:30am-4:30pm. **Cafe:** Open for lunch Mondays-Saturdays from 8:00am-Dusk, and Sundays from 12:00pm-3:00pm. **Garden:** Open daily from 8:00am-Dusk. **Callaway Building:** Open Mondays-Fridays from 8:00am-5:00pm and by appointment. FREE.

GEORGIA MUSEUM OF ART

Georgia Museum of Art, Jackson Street, North University Campus, Athens (404/542-3255). This is the official State of Georgia Art Museum and contains a permanent collection of over 5,000 works including 19th

255

and 20th century American paintings, as well as European and Oriental art. A visit here would only be of interest to the more sophisticated child. **Hours**: 9:00am-5:00pm, Mondays-Saturdays;1:00pm-5:00pm, Sunday. Closed on major holidays. FREE.

SANDY CREEK NATURE CENTER AND PARK

Sandy Creek Nature Center and Park, Old Commerce Road (404/354-2930). This Nature Center, a division of the Clarke County Department of Parks, is similar in concept to Fulton County's Chattahoochee Nature Center. The setting is 200-acres of woods, marshes and fields with nature trails weaving throughout. There are exhibits and numerous exciting educational programs offered throughout the year for people of all ages. There is also a gift shop. **Trail Hours**: Daily from sun-up to sun-down. **Center Hours**: 8:00am-5:00pm, Mondays-Fridays; 12:00pm-5:00pm, Saturday. The Center is closed on the weekends from Thanksgiving to March. FREE.

About 1 1/2-miles down the road from the Center is the 700-acre **Sandy Creek Park**. There are many recreational facilities including tennis courts, volleyball nets, picnicking, and a primitive campground that is available for Friday and Saturday nights. There is a 260-acre lake for boating (though motors are restricted to trawling) and swimming is permitted at a designated beach. **Park Hours**: 7:00am-7:00pm, Thursdays-Tuesdays (closed Wednesdays). **Admission**: Unlimited daily park use is $1.00/adults, 50¢/children 7-12 years, and children 6 years and under and seniors over 65 years are FREE.

BEAR HOLLOW WILDLIFE TRAIL

Bear Hollow Wildlife Trail, 293 Gran Ellen Drive, Athens (404/357-6060). Located in Memorial Park, this wildlife trail features animals native to Georgia such as deer, skunk, owls and river otters. The trail is paved and comfortably accommodates strollers. The trail takes about 20 minutes to traverse and is open daily from 7:00am to dark. FREE.

Directions to Athens: Athens is about an hour's drive from Atlanta on the Stone Mountain Freeway (US 78).

CALLAWAY GARDENS
AND
THE LITTLE WHITE HOUSE

CALLAWAY GARDENS

Callaway Gardens, Pine Mountain, Georgia 31822 (800/282-8181). An easy ninety minute drive south of Atlanta, lies the beautiful 12,000-acre world class resort of Callaway Gardens. But don't let the reputation of this facility daunt you; it is a place for everyone to enjoy, over and over again.

The Gardens feature **Robin Lake Beach,** a mile-long white sand beach for digging and building sand castles, swimming and watching water skiing spectaculars. You may ride on the riverboat Robin E. Lee and the miniature train Whistlin' Dixie. Miniature golf, ping-pong and the usual beach sports such as volleyball are available, and there are picnic areas and terrific playgrounds. Open daily 8:00am-6:00pm from Memorial Day to Labor Day. The cost is $12.00/adults, $6.00/children 6-11 years, and children under 6 are FREE.

Your family may **Bicycle** on over seven miles of paths that wind through beautiful woods, azalea gardens and along the lake. Bring your own bikes or rent them at Callaway. They actually rent small bikes for children! Rental prices are $3.00/hour or $9.00/half a day.

There are many **Walking Trails** through Callaway Gardens, but three of them are particularly suited to families. The Azalea Trail, which of course you would want to traverse in the spring, can take as little as 15 minutes or as much as 90, depending upon your pace. There is a Wildflower Trail which might take 25 or more minutes which features ferns and wildflowers. The Rhododendron Trail is at its peak of beauty in late spring and would take a family around 30 minutes to enjoy. Remember, children do love nature walks, especially if you point out the varieties of plant life, discuss who lives in the animal holes, examine insects up close, and guess what makes the various sounds you hear.

Mr. Cason's Vegetable Garden is a 7 1/2-acre demonstration garden that is featured on the television series "Victory Garden South." A wide variety of crops and flowers are grown, such as berries and grapes in the Upper Terrace, and corn, beans, broccoli, lettuce, and collards in the Middle Terrace. The Lower Terrace is the site of the Herb Garden which has medicinal and fragrant herbs as well as culinary herbs. A recent addition is the water garden which is home to many water plants and goldfish.

The **Pioneer Log Cabin** is an authentic 1800's log cabin which may be toured for a better understanding of daily life in early Georgia.

The **Cecil B. Day Butterfly Center**, the largest free-flight conservatory in North America, is home to about 50 species of tropical butterflies. This is truly a wondrous experience for young and old alike you should not miss. But before you enter the free-flight area, try to convince your kids to visit the theatre and gallery that explain the life-cycle of butterflies and provide other information to help orient you. Now, full of anticipation, enter the breathtaking conservatory. You will find the butterflies to be stunningly beautiful and very cooperative; they gracefully rest on leaves while you stare at them. One even landed on a friend of mine and stayed on her shoulder throughout her visit! After you exit, you may want to visit the gift shop that sells lots of butterfly-related items.

Walk through the **John A. Sibley Horticultural Center** on a curving footpath where each bend brings a whole new landscape of flowering plants in view. The greenhouse garden is meticulously maintained and boasts a beautiful 2-story waterfall surrounded by a flower display. There is also an outdoor garden of labeled plants and trees, and there are changing exhibitions.

- **Azalea Festival Weekends** in March and April, **Fall Festival Weekends** in October and **The Twelve Days of Christmas Festival** in December have storytelling, puppetry, magicians, music and other family-oriented activities and entertainment. See our chapter on "Festivals and Special Events" for more information.

• **The Summer Recreation Program** includes Florida State University Flying High Circus, water skiing, swimming, hiking, sailing, tennis, puppet shows and more.

• If you have ventured to Callaway via the Little White House, chances are you have some hungry children. We suggest you stop at the Country Kitchen and Store (intersection of GA 190 and GA 27) for delicious southern cooking you can eat on a veranda with a panoramic view of the valley. The Country Store has jarred jams, candy, souvenirs, arts and crafts and more for sale.

Hours: Open daily 7:00am-7:00pm during the summer and 9:00am-5:00pm during the winter.

Admission: $7.00/adult, $1.00/children 6-11 years, and children under 6 are FREE.

Directions: **From Atlanta:** I-85 South to I-185 South, exit on GA Hwy. 27 South. **From The Little White House:** Go right on Hwy. 85 West, right on GA 190 West and right on GA 27.

THE LITTLE WHITE HOUSE

The Little White House, Warm Springs, Georgia 31830 (404/655-3511). Franklin Delano Roosevelt, four times President of the United States, used to visit the warm springs in the area, because they were of therapeutic value to his polio-stricken body. Nestled in the beautiful Georgia woods near the natural spring waters, FDR built his "country home" which has been left exactly as it was on the day he died here, April 12, 1945.

The grounds of the Little White House have been more extensively landscaped since his death, and a Museum, shop and picnic area have been added. Children enjoy the fountains and meandering up the terraced path that goes between rows of flags from every state of the union. Also lining the path are large stones in the shape of each state made from materials indigenous to that particular state. At the top of this path is the **Museum** which houses various mementos worth seeing. Be sure to see the short 12-minute movie, a documentary about FDR which most children will enjoy.

Another path leads to the guard house, servant's quarters and the garage. Inside the garage is the glass-enclosed **1938 Ford convertible** that FDR actually used to drive around the grounds. You can view how the automobile was modified with hand controls to accomodate FDR's paralyzed legs, and you may push a button to hear a voice describe some interesting details about FDR and his car.

Next is the **Little White House** itself, where there is tape-recorded tour information and staff available to answer your questions. Children as well as baby boomers will enjoy the history lesson of seeing how few amenities even the rich had not too many years ago. The kitchen and its utensils can be viewed and compared to the modern kitchen of the 1990s, but you will soon be jolted out of your contemporary complacency. Entering the livingroom, 1945 does not seem so long ago as you stand just a few feet from the desk FDR was sitting at when he died. From that point on, the brief tour takes on a poignancy and immediacy we had not anticipated. You see Roosevelt's wheelchair, his dog's chain, other personal effects, photographs and additional memorabilia.

- There is a small snack bar and gift shop at the entrance gate.

- The town of Warm Springs has over 70 stores and restaurants as well as the Warm Springs Hotel.

- The Warm Springs **National Fish Hatchery** (655-3620) is located one mile south of the town on GA 27A. It has outdoor ponds and an indoor aquarium. It is open daily from 7:30am-4:00pm. FREE.

Hours: Open daily from 9:00am-5:00pm.

Admission: $4.00/adults, $2.00/children 6-18 years, and children under 6 are FREE.

Directions: Take I-85 south to GA 27A through Warm Springs. Turn left on Highway 85 W South.

CARTERSVILLE & LAKE ALLATOONA

The following terrific recreational, educational and historic sites may be visited one at a time, or several may be combined into one visit. Each place has much to offer, and the time you spend at any one facility will depend upon the ages and interests of your family members. And since these attractions are less than an hour's drive north of Atlanta, there is no need to hurry through any of them; you know you can always return.

LAKE ALLATOONA AND RED TOP MOUNTAIN STATE PARK

Lake Allatoona and Red Top Mountain State Park, I-75 to Exit #123 (975-4200). Your best bet is to access Lake Allatoona at Red Top Mountain State Park which is located on a peninsula along the lake. Here you may use the lake and park facilities during the day for FREE. There is a Trading Post which stocks refreshments, snacks and ice cream, has bathroom facilities, and many useful free brochures.

Among the many activities you many engage in are, swimming at the beach where you have use of a bathhouse from Memorial Day to Labor Day, a small playground with four picnic tables and grills, a small miniature golf course, tennis courts and 7 miles of nature trails. For families who bring their own boats or rent one here, there are boating ramps and docks with waterskiing and fishing permitted. If you are interested in camping, there are 286 tent and trailer sites, and if you want a quick getaway, stay in one of their eighteen 2-bedroom, fully-equipped rental cottages. Call 975-4200 for reservations. Another option is the Red Top Mountain Lodge which allows children to stay free, with dining at the Mountain Cove Restaurant which overlooks Lake Allatoona.

- An interesting historical site is near the dam–Cooper's Iron Works, a 143-year-old building where ammunition for the Civil War was manufactured.

- If you intend to fish and do not have a fishing license as required by Georgia State Law, there is a gas station at Exit #123 where you can purchase one.

- Dogs are permitted on leashes.

Hours: The park is open daily from 8:30am-8:30pm The Park Office is open daily from 8:30am-5:00pm.

AIR ACRES MUSEUM

Air Acres Museum, I-75 to Exit #124. Follow airplane signs through Cartersville (404/382-7030). "The Home of the Georgia Boy's" houses many airplanes, from vintage World War II planes which are kept in mint condition, to a sleek glider and a modern ultralight. These planes are not only shiny clean and interesting museum pieces, but they are also operational. Kids can touch the airplanes, look in some of the cockpits, and on one bomber, see up inside the belly of the plane.

- The Museum is in an old hangar alongside a runway of the airport.

- The Museum will not take long to tour, and since it is about a 50-minute drive from Atlanta, we suggest you combine this with a trip to Etowah Mounds State Historic Site (see below) and/or berry picking at Glen Cove Nursery (404/386-0207), 1/4 mile before you get to the Historic Site.

Hours: Open Mondays-Saturdays from 9:00am-5:00pm.

Admission: FREE, but donations of $1.00/person are welcome.

ETOWAH MOUNDS STATE HISTORIC SITE

Etowah Mounds State Historic Site, I-75 to Exit #124. Follow the brown "Etowah Mounds" signs (404/387-3747). The **Etowah Archaeological Museum** is your introduction to the lives and culture of the Mississippian Indians who inhabited this beautiful, serene, fertile valley from about 1000-1500 A.D. Be sure to view the film which discusses the history and culture of the Etowah people and describes the significance of some of the artifacts on display in the Museum. Among the artifacts excavated from the area are items that suggest the Indians decorated themselves with paint, copper and shell jewelry, tattoos and feathers. You will see pottery and marble statues as well as the burial site of a priest-chief excavated from a mound.

Exit the Museum and begin the peaceful, almost mystical walk to the **Etowah Indian Mounds**. This is a self-guided tour, and the Museum staff provides you with a very informative map and explanatory essay. You look down into a Borrow Pit, and have a difficult time comprehending how this enormous pit was dug by people carrying out hundreds of thousands of basketfulls of dirt in order to build the mounds. The task appears overwhelming. Your imagination comes alive picturing homes scattered around the clean swept central plaza and the bustling activity of people fishing, preparing food, and crafting pots and jewelry, and you can almost hear the laughter of children playing.

The steps of the mounds are not steep (there are just a lot of them, about 100 to the top of the tallest), so little legs can easily make it to the top. Two of the mounds were ceremonial and the third was a burial mound. From this mound scientists have gathered invaluable information about burial practices, diet, diseases, trading practices and class structure. It is from this third mound that the world famous marble figures displayed in the Museum were excavated.

The conclusion of the tour takes you alongside the river where the Indians fished, and by trees that provided fruit, and river cane that was the raw material for baskets, roofs, mats and arrow shafts. This **River Walk** has benches shaded by trees that are labeled with their names. When it was time to leave, my kids ran through the lush meadow –a timeless act–since meadows must have always beckoned children.

•   There are several special programs offered here thoughout the year such as Indian Skills Day in the spring and Artifacts Identification Day in April and November, plus astronomy programs. Call for information about the current offerings.

Hours: Open Tuesdays-Saturdays, 9:00am-5:00pm; Sundays, 2:00pm-5:30pm. Closed Mondays.

Admission: Museum admission is FREE. The Mound Tour costs $1.50/adults, 95¢ for kids 6-18 years, and FREE for those 5 years and under.

THE WILLIAM WEINMAN MINERAL MUSEUM

The William Weinman Mineral Museum, I-75 to Exit #126, on the left next to Denny's restaurant (404/386-0576). As you approach the Museum, your children will probably spot the outside portion of this Museum: old rusty mining equipment, a truck and a train used to carry iron ore, and a rock garden to touch and talk about. Inside, the Museum is divided into several rooms, each with a theme. In the Main Hall you may walk through a simulated limestone cave with stalactites and a fluorescent rock display, and see specimens from the state of Georgia, including fossils (which are always fascinating to kids). The Mayo Wing houses an international collection of specimens, petrified wood and an incredible array of geodes, some as high as three feet, that beg to be touched. The Paleontology Hall has numerous cases of fossils and Indian artifacts, some over 10,000 years old!

•   There is a gift shop with lots of rocks, books and jewelry.

•   The Museum is accessible to the handicapped.

•   There are educational and research facilities and specimen identification services for serious geologists.

Hours: Open Tuesdays-Saturdays from 10:00am-4:30pm and
               Sundays from 2:00pm-4:30pm.

Admission: $3.00/adult, $2.50/senior, $2.00/kids 6-11 years, and
               children under 6 are FREE.

DAHLONEGA

The cry of "We've found gold!" in Dahlonega in 1828 marked the start of
the first major gold rush in North America. By 1833, Dahlonega was a
bustling, vibrant town built to accommodate the numbers of pioneer gold-
miners who came to strike it rich. Between 1838 and 1861, over $6-million
in gold was coined by the U.S. Branch Mint in Dahlonega! The peaceful
mining town in the foothills of Georgia's Blue Ridge Mountains is now a
nice place to visit to view historic sites and scenic drives; to visit the
beautiful and historic campus of North Georgia College; to buy Appalachian crafts; and to enjoy canoeing, fishing, hiking, horseback riding and
many other outdoor activities.

Start your visit to Dahlonega with a walk around the historic town square
area. The **Chamber of Commerce** (404/864-3711) is located right on the
square and can provide you with handfulls of pamphlets and brochures,
including "A Small Town Sampler" which contains self-guided walking
tours of the town. You can also visit the many retail stores on the Square
which are filled with historical books and maps, Native American pottery
and jewelry, antiques, quilts, crafts and other treasures.

In the middle of the town Square lies the Old Courthouse Building, now
the site of the **Dahlonega Gold Museum** (404/864-2257). The exhibits,
films and slides shown at the historic Museum tell the story of the town's
gold rush. You will learn about the mining techniques of the prospectors,
see samples of the gold coins which were minted here and get a glimpse
of the lifestyles of the town's mining families. The Museum is open

Mondays through Saturdays from 9:00am-5:00pm, and Sundays from 10:00am-6:00pm. Closed Thanksgiving and Christmas Days. Admission is $1.50/adults, 75¢/children ages 6-12, and children under 6 are free.

After your tour, you can have a huge lunch at the **Smith House** (404/864-3566), Dahlonega's most famous dining facility. Meals are served family-style; you will be seated at a long table with other visitors, and huge platters of Southern-style meats, vegetables and biscuits will be brought to your table. As long as you can keep eating, more food will be served! (Closed on Mondays). Don't miss their buffet breakfast served during Gold Rush Week in October.

After your meal, there are more activities that await you. On the front lawn of the Smith House and at other locations throughout the town, children can, for a small fee, learn how to **Pan Gold** and other gemstones. Rocks, fossils and semi-precious gemstones are all available for purchase at local stops.

Behind the Smith House is Dahlonega's **Fire Station**, which is staffed with friendly volunteers. Our children had a wonderful time with firefighter "Mike" who let them sit in the trucks and showed them the tanker truck and other kinds of fire-fighting equipment city children usually don't get to see.

As you head out of town, you will pass lots and lots of signs leading you to camping facilities, horseback riding, stables, canoeing adventures, and scenic sites such as Amicalola Falls State Park and Unicoi State Park discussed in "North Georgia Mountains" later on in this chapter.

- A great time to visit is during one of Dahlonega's special festivals, such as the Wildflower Festival of the Arts (in May), Gold Rush Days (in October), and Old-Fashioned Christmas in Dahlonega (in December). These events are described further in our chapter "Festivals and Special Events."

Directions: Dahlonega is about 1 1/2-hours north of Atlanta. Take GA 400 to Hwy. 60 and head north. You will "dead-end" into Dahlonega.

HELEN

Back in the late 1960s, a few of Helen's business owners got together to figure out what to do about the dying lumber mill town. A local artist, John Kollock, envisioned the entire village in Alpine design, and a few water-color sketches later, the business community fell in love with the idea. Without much more fanfare, the entire village began its renovation and now, over 20 years later, the small village is a "Bit of Bavaria" in the North Georgia Mountains.

There are over 150 retail stores selling Alpine, Scandinavian and country gift items, such as music boxes, trolls, Viking hats, crystal, dinnerware, sweaters, quilts, and so forth. And, not to worry, for those shoppers who prefer modern retail stores, there is also Alpine Village Outlets which has two small shopping malls filled with factory outlet stores, including the Van Heusen Factory Store, Corning/Revere Factory Store and Bass Shoes Outlet Store. Stores are open for the most part Mondays through Saturdays from 10:00am-9:00pm, and Sundays from 12:00noon-6:00pm (earlier closing hours during winter months).

Helen is the site of year-round festivals, parades and special events such as Fasching Karnival and Parade (German Mardi Gras), Mayfest in the Mountains, Helen to Atlantic Balloon Race and the Hot Air Balloon Festival, Float the Fourth Tube Parade and Fireworks, Oktoberfest and Christmas in Helen. These special events are described in our chapter "Festivals and Special Events," or you may call the Chamber of Commerce for more information (404/878-2521). And for those who like water, contact Alpine Tubing (800/782-8823) or Garden Tubing (800/438-7742) for information about tubing down the Chattahoochee.

- **Alpine Amusement Park**, Main Street, Helen (404/878-2306). Bumper boats, antique cars, go-carts and lots of other rides and games are available at this small amusement park. *Hours:* 4:00pm-

11:00pm, Friday, 10:30am-11:00pm, Saturday, 12noon-9:00pm, Sunday.

• **The Museum of the Hills**, Main Street, Helen (404/878-3140). This is a self-guided tour through displays of the lifestyles of the hill country people in the South during turn-of-the-century America. There is also a Fantasy Kingdom containing castles and cottages of characters from nursery rhymes and fairy tales. *Hours:* 10:00am-9:00pm, daily. *Cost:* $4.00/adults; children 13 years and older $3.00; children 5-12 years, $2.00; and children under 5 are FREE.

• **Nora Mill Granary and Store**, Helen (404/878-2927). Located on GA 75 just a few miles south of Helen. This is a real working mill where you can see grain being ground on stones over 100 years old, powered by the Chattahoochee River. It is an awesome sight. Wholesome, natural grains, such as grits, cornmeal, whole wheat flour, rye and buckwheat flours, and even pancake mix, can be purchased at the store. *Hours:* 9:00am-5:00pm, daily.

• **Sautee-Nacoochee Indian Mound**, a Native American burial site on the National Register of Historic Places, is located at the junction of Georgia Highways 17 and 75. About 75 Native American skeletons have been unearthed here as well as numerous Indian artifacts dating as far back as 10,000 B.C.

• **Storyland Petting Zoo and Castle of the Dolls**, Highway 75 (4 miles south of Helen) (404/865-2939). Castle of the Dolls has miniature villages filled with over 150 Naber Kids, McGuffy Porcelain Dolls, Sweetheart Dolls and Raikes Bears. Storyland Petting Zoo has over 100 animals at the "zoo." *Hours:* 10:00am-6:00pm, daily. *Admission:* The zoo is FREE. Castle of the Dolls costs $2.00/person; children under 2 years are FREE.

Directions to Helen: Helen is located about 1 1/2-hours north of Atlanta off GA 75. See our section below called "North Georgia Mountains" for a description of attractions only about a mile or two north of Helen.

BABYLAND GENERAL HOSPITAL

Babyland General Hospital, 19 Underwood Street, Cleveland (404/865-5505 or 404/865-2171). Imagine a full-sized community hospital complete with a delivery room, nurseries, intensive-care units and play areas. Picture hundreds upon hundreds of Cabbage Patch Kids of all ages, sizes and color, standing in cribs, sitting on rocking chairs, playing in classrooms and going on various outings throughout the hospital complex. Next, visualize a large gift shop filled from top to bottom with Cabbage Patch Kids that are just waiting to be "adopted" by your children. And finally, listen for the announcement, "There's a Cabbage in labor!" and run to the delivery room to witness the delivery of a Cabbage Patch Kid (from a Mother Cabbage, of course). Are you interested? If so, visit Babyland General Hospital.

- For those of you who have children who do not like Cabbage Patch Kids, not to worry. Babyland also houses Moody Hollow General Store which is filled with Furskins Bears and other country craft gift items.

Hours: Open year-round on Mondays-Saturdays from 9:00am-5:00pm, and on Sundays from 1:00pm-5:00pm. (Later closing hours during the summer months.)

Admission: FREE. (However, it is difficult to leave without buying something!)

Directions: Babyland is about one hour north of Atlanta off US 129.

GOURDCRAFT ORIGINALS

Gourdcraft Originals, Foot of Mt. Yonah on GA 255, Cleveland (404/865-4048). Gourdcraft Originals began as a lark in 1976, but is now a serious museum displaying unusual gourds from around the world as well as early American exhibits. Besides the museum area, there is a retail store where you can buy decorative gourds for use as containers, utensils, planters, toys, puzzles, mobiles and more. As they say at Gourdcraft, "Have a Gourd Day!"

Hours: Open 10:00am-5:00pm, Monday-Saturday; and 1:00pm-5:00pm, Sunday, May-December. Open weekends and by appointment January-April.

Admission: FREE.

Directions: The Museum is about one hour north of Atlanta. Take GA 129 to GA 115 to GA 255.

LAKE LANIER ISLANDS

Lake Lanier Islands, 6950 Holiday Road, Lake Lanier Islands, Georgia 30518, Metro-Atlanta (932-7200). About 45 minutes from downtown Atlanta lies one of Atlanta's most precious resources. Lake Lanier provides us with beauty to nourish our souls, drinking water to nourish our bodies, and a recreational beach and lake to rejuvenate our spirits.

There is something for everyone at "Atlanta's Classic Resort," from horseback riding and camping to boating, golfing, bicycle riding and, of course, the **Beach and Water Park**. At the white sandy beach you may avail yourselves of lounge chairs, locker facilities, life preservers inner tubes and shade umbrellas. The Water Park has a wave pool and lots of splashing, twisting slides and tube rides as well as water attractions: a dark, tunnel-like slide aptly called The Typhoon, a waterslide called The Twister that has six 180-degree turns, the new "TripleThreat," "Intimidator," and a Kiddie Lagoon for young children that has slides, waterfalls, stationary water guns and more. Admission includes the use of sailboats, paddleboats and canoes.

The Water Park also has an 18-hole miniature golf course, a gift shop, a cafe that serves kids' favorite foods, a restaurant with barbequed chicken and hamburgers, and a refreshment stand for cold, unique drinks and ice cream.

Horseback Riding is available on miles of trails and for young children, there are pony rides. Rental rates are $12.00 for a one-hour trail ride and $5.00 for a 30-minute pony ride. **Bicycle Riding** is wonderful here. You may bring your own bikes or rent them at a cost of $2.50/hour or $10.00/day. Horse and bike rental facility operating hours are limited so call in advance.

Boat Rentals are available for houseboats, group boats, pontoons, fishing, run-abouts and skimmer boats. Canoes, paddleboats and sail-boats may also be rented. Call for detailed information including rates and hours of operation.

Campground facilities include lakeside tent and RV sites complete with amenities such as water and electricity, a convenience store and laundry facilities. Call for rates and reservations.

If a high class vacation is what you are after, Lake Lanier can accommodate you at its new **Hotel**, or the **Golf Club**, or one of two elegant **Resorts**. There are two-bedroom modern **Cottages** also available.

- **Lanier Museum of Natural History**, 2601 Buford Dam Road, Buford (945-3543) has exhibits that trace the history of the people and land of northern Georgia. There is an observation tower to view the Lake, a log cabin built by Cherokee Indians, an 1818 Homestead and a nature trail. It is open Tuesdays-Fridays from 12:00pm-5:00pm and Saturdays from 10:00am-5:00pm. FREE. Call for directions.

Hours: Generally, the Water Park is open weekends in May and September and daily between Memorial Day and Labor Day. For hours of other amenities call ahead.

Admission: Entrance fee: $3.00 for daily parking (annual pass $15.00). Beach and Water Park: FREE for those age 2 and under and age 60 and over, $3.50 for 3-year-olds or those under 42" (season pass $12.00), and $9.95 for adults (season pass $34.95). Season pass for a family of four, $130.00. There is a fee for locker, tube and umbrella rental.

Directions: Take I-85 north to I-985 and get off at Exit #1 or #2 and follow signs to the lake. Or take GA 400 to GA 20 and follow the signs.

MACON

Millions of years ago, ocean waters reached the edge of what is today Macon, Georgia. As the ocean receded, it left behind enormous deposits of kaolin, white clay used today to give paint, china and stationery a stark white color. In these kaolin deposits, people have found sea shells and fossils from prehistoric times. The first inhabitants of this fertile area were Native Americans, who settled here almost 10,000 years ago. In more recent history, the kaolin industry, the Ocumulgee River and the railroad combined to make Macon an important and thriving antebellum town economically. Today, Macon is dwarfed by Atlanta, but the lives of Native Americans, white settlers and aristocrats, and of African-Americans in these parts are chronicled in the many historical tours available, as well as through visits to the Ocmulgee National Monument and the Harriet Tubman Historical and Cultural Museum.

Stop by the County Convention and Visitor's Bureau at I-16 and Coliseum Drive for a free slide show which will orient you to the area, maps and brochures. There is a Welcome Center at I-75 South (912/745-2668) and one at 200 Cherry Street, Terminal Station (912/743-3401) for brochures and information. Both are open Monday-Friday from 9:00am-5:30pm.

OCMULGEE NATIONAL MONUMENT AND MUSEUM

Ocmulgee National Monument and Museum, 1207 Emery Highway, Macon (912/752-8257). Mississippi Indians settled here as well as in other locations throughout Georgia and built enormous mounds for ceremonial and burial purposes. (We discuss the Etowah Indian Mounds in our section on Cartersville in this chapter.) The highest in this particular region is a ceremonial 45-foot-high plateau built around 1,000 A.D. which you may climb. There is a reconstructed ceremonial "earthlodge" and nature trails on the grounds.

In the **Visitor's Center** you will see a short film "People of the Macon Plateau," dioramas, artifacts, and exhibits that describe what is known about these people's culture and the Creek Indians who succeeded them and occupied this site until their forced expulsion in the 1830s. There is also a gift shop. Handicapped access is limited. Open daily from 9:00am-5:00pm. Closed on Christmas Day and New Year's Day. Admission is $1.00/adults, and FREE for children 12 years and under.

HISTORICAL WALKING TOURS

Three different walking tours are available for the energetic family and we suggest that you acquire detailed brochures at the Convention and Visitors Bureau to assist you in planning your walk. These brochures will also be helpful if you prefer to drive around Macon to get a sense of its history.

HARRIET TUBMAN HISTORICAL AND CULTURAL MUSEUM

Harriet Tubman Historical and Cultural Museum, 340 Walnut Street, Macon (912/743-8544). This Museum displays the history, culture, art, and achievements of Black Americans of African and Caribbean descent. There is a Resource Room and a shop that sells books, art and crafts, posters and more. Open Mondays-Fridays from 10:00am-5:00pm and on Saturdays and Sundays from 2:00pm-6:00pm. Donations are appreciated.

MUSEUM OF ARTS AND SCIENCES/ MARK SMITH PLANETARIUM

Museum of Arts and Sciences/Mark Smith Planetarium, 4182 Forsyth Road, Macon (912/477-3232). This Museum houses fine arts exhibits, a gem and mineral collection, displays some artifacts unearthed in the area including one 40-million year old whale skeleton, and sometimes offers hands-on experiences for children, such as the recent "Muddy Hands" exhibit which permitted children to watch a real potter at work and then work with clay themselves. There is a gift shop. Open Mondays-Thursdays and Saturdays from 9:00am-5:00pm, Friday 9:00am-9:00pm, and Sundays from 1:00pm-5:00pm. Call for current prices. There are certain days and hours that the Museum is FREE.

The **Planetarium** is the second largest in Georgia (second to Atlanta's Fernbank Planetarium). Shows are offered on Fridays at 7:30pm and 9:00pm, Saturdays at 2:00pm and 3:00pm and Sundays at 3:00pm. The Observatory itself is open on Fridays at 8:30pm. The **Live Animal Shows** are held indoors. Be sure to pick up your tickets (FREE with Museum admission) when you arrive.

• Outside you will find a petting zoo and nature trails.

• The building that houses these two attractions has limited handicapped access. Call for specific access information.

FESTIVALS

You might try to arrange a trip to Macon to coincide with one of its fun festivals. The most spectacular is, of course, the 10-day annual Cherry Blossom Festival which boasts 130,000 pink and white blossomed Yoshino Cherry Trees. Macon calls itself the "Cherry Blosom Capital of the World," and indeed it has many more trees and flowers than Washington, D.C. This festival has a parade, a street party with music, dancing and food, hot air balloons, sports, tours and exhibits, cooking contests, storytellers, and in all, over 150 events. There is an Indian Festival each fall, a Southern Jubilee in September, and Georgia Music Week in December just to name a few more.

• The New Georgia Railroad has a special excursion to Macon. Read a description of this Museum and find steam-up schedule information in our chapter "Places To Go."

Directions: Take I-75 South from Atlanta directly to Macon.

NORTH GEORGIA MOUNTAINS

If you need an unhurried, relaxed day in your life, head to the north Georgia mountains! There are many places to go where you can picnic, hike, raft, bicycle, horseback ride, or enjoy the numerous waterfalls and scenic areas. Below are descriptions of some of our favorite places for a day trip that are not more than a 90 minute drive from Atlanta.

UNICOI STATE PARK

Unicoi State Park, 2 miles NE of Helen via GA 356 (404/878-2201). Just a few minutes north of Nora Mill Granary is Unicoi State Park, an area which is terrific for hiking, water play at the lake and beach, and camping (day or overnight). If you want to stay overnight but do not want to camp, Unicoi has a Lodge and cottages. They book up at the beginning of the season, so call well in advance. Unicoi also features special monthly programs, a Fireside Craft/Art Show in February and an Appalachian Music Festival in July. See our chapters "Festivals and Special Events" and "Performances" for more information about these events.

ANNA RUBY FALLS

From the northern boundary of Unicoi, drive on Anna Ruby Falls Road, park at the Visitor's Center ($2.00) and take a short, scenic 0.5-mile hike to the spectacular twin Anna Ruby Falls. These falls feed into Unicoi Lake, join the Chattahoochee River, flow across Florida and empty into the Gulf of Mexico. The path is smooth and wide enough for a stroller. There are picnic sites in the Anna Ruby Falls Scenic Area with tables, grills and drinking water. Sanitation facilities are not available in the winter. Call 404/878-1448 for more information.

DUKE'S CREEK RECREATION AREA

Duke's Creek Recreation Area, near Helen on GA 348, 1.5 miles west of its junction with GA 356. This is a great place for a family to spend a Sunday afternoon. You can take a brief 15-minute walk down to **Duke's Creek Falls**, hike back up (about 30 minutes), then have a well-deserved picnic. This is a fairly popular place, so if you find there are too many other families for your liking, head off on one of the side trails to find a quieter spot.

RAVEN CLIFFS

Raven Cliffs, just north of Helen on Richard Russell Scenic Highway (GA 348) about 1.3 miles from the Duke's Creek Recreation Area sign. Park in the gravel parking lot and begin your trek to Raven Cliffs along a 2.5 mile trail that is the most diverse of any hike we have taken in Georgia. There are a series of waterfalls, streams, a beautiful forest, and of course magnificent cliffs. This hike is wonderful for families with young children, even if you can make it only part way. A word of caution: Stay on the main path and avoid the side paths that head directly to the water, as they are often very slippery.

AMICALOLA STATE FALLS PARK

Amicalola State Falls Park, on Highway 52 west of Dahlonega (404/265-2885) is pushing our 90-minute driving limit for family day trips. Amicalola is a Cherokee Indian word that means "tumbling waters." These falls at 729 feet are the highest and most magnificent in the state. There are 3 1/2 miles of hiking trails around the mountains and falls, 3 playgrounds, fishing and camping. If you do not wish to hike and picnic, you can drive your car to the falls and eat nearby at a new restaurant with a panoramic view of the area.

DILLARD HOUSE

Dillard House, Highway 441 in Dillard (800/541-0671 or 404/746-5348). If you live on the northern outskirts of metropolitan Atlanta (North Fulton,

North DeKalb, Gwinnett or Cobb), you should definitely take a 90-minute day trip to the Dillard House, where you can eat your fill of a delicious meal served in a family style restaurant, visit their small petting zoo, and take the kids horseback riding. Even the youngest can ride, while you walk the horse around a grassy area. They also have more extensive facilities for day-long family horseback riding. The gift shop sells handicrafts, gift items, and their own jams, jellies, hams, peanut brittle and local honey. Dillard House also has overnight accommodations.

REVEREND HOWARD FINSTER

Reverend Howard Finster, Route 2, Box 106-A, Summerville, Georgia 30747. Reverend Finster is a folk artist of world renown whose work is increasingly popular. He did the cover artwork for David Byrne's Talking Heads album "Little Creatures," and his work has appeared in many galleries including a show at the Georgia State Capitol. A special trip to Summerville is worth your time: wander around the unique, interesting and playful yard of sculptures made from everyday items put together in provocative ways. We guarantee your conversations on the ride back to Atlanta will not be boring, as everyone, young and old, will have had their imaginations titillated.

8. Resources

SPECIAL ASSISTANCE TELEPHONE NUMBERS

Ambulance, Fire, Police 911
AL-ANON and ALATEEN Family Groups...................................843-0311
Alcoholics Anonymous 525-3178
Atlanta Area Services for the Blind 875-9011
Atlanta Teen Help Line 995-9332
Auditory Education Center........................... 352-4145 or351-4327

Child Abuse Hotlines
Clayton County 473-2337
Cobb County ....528-5015 or 499-3978
DeKalb County..370-5066 or 294-2574
Fulton County 756-4200
Gwinnett County..995-2122
Child Care Solutions–Save the Children 885-1578
Coke/Crack Help Line 800/COCAINE

Drug Abuse Hotlines
Clayton County 473-5400
Cobb County 422-0202
DeKalb County 894-5771
Fulton County 730-1600
Gwinnett County..963-8141

Georgia Council for International Visitors 873-6170

Georgia Council on Child Abuse
24-Hour Help Line 870-6555

Georgia Easter Seals 633-9609
Henrietta Egleston Hospital 325-6103
March of Dimes 350-9800
Missing Children Hotline 800/843-5678

Pediatric Dentists–North District
Dental Society Referral Service 270-1635

Pediatrician Referrals
Medical Association of Atlanta 881-1714

Poison Control Center 589-4400
Runaway Hotline 800/231-6946
Scottish Rite Children's Hospital 250-2065
Toy Safety Hotline...800/638-CPSC
United Way First Call for Help Hotline...527-7370

CONVENTION AND VISITOR'S BUREAUS

**Atlanta Convention and Visitor's
Bureau–Main Office**
233 Peachtree Street, N.E.
Atlanta, Georgia 30303
521-6600

**Atlanta Convention and Visitor's
Bureau Information Centers:
Peachtree Center Mall**
233 Peachtree Street
Atlanta, Georgia 30303
222-6688

Lenox Square Shopping Center
3393 Peachtree Road
Atlanta, Georgia 30326
266-1398

Underground Atlanta
Pryor and Alabama Streets
Atlanta, Georgia 30334
577-2148

Clayton County Local Welcome Center
Box 774
8712 Tara Boulevard
Jonesboro, Georgia 30237
478-6549

Cobb-Marietta Convention and Visitor's Bureau
P.O. Box COBB
Marietta, Georgia 30067-0033
980-2000 or 984-0161
800/451-3480

The DeKalb Convention and Visitor's Bureau
750 Commerce Drive
Suite 201
Decatur, Georgia 30030
378-2525

The Gwinnett Convention and Visitor's Bureau
1230 Atkinson Road
P.O. Box 1245
Lawrenceville, Georgia 30246
963-5128

Marietta Welcome Center
4 Depot Street
Marietta, Georgia 30060
429-1115

North Fulton County Chamber of Commerce
Tourist Division
1025 Old Roswell Road
Suite 101
Roswell, Georgia 30076
993-8806

Georgia Department of Industry Trade & Tourism
285 Peachtree Center Avenue
Atlanta, Georgia 30303
656-3545

Georgia Department of Natural Resources
Division of Parks, Recreation and Historical Sites
205 Butler Street, S.E.
Atlanta, Georgia 30334
656-3530
1-800-3GA-PARK (within Georgia)
1-800-5GA-PARK (outside Georgia)

PUBLICATIONS

The Atlanta Guidebook, Candace Springer, Longstreet Press, Inc., Atlanta, Georgia, 1991. General tourist guidebook.

Atlanta Jewish Times. Published weekly. News about Jewish events and performances. Cost is 75¢/issue; Subscription Rate is $29/year. (352-2400).

The Atlanta Journal and the Atlanta Constitution.–Saturday "Weekend" Section. Excellent summary of the week's events as well as feature articles on attractions, festivals and special events.

Atlanta Magazine. Published monthly. General overview of the month's major events. Cost is $2.50/issue; Subscription Rate is $15.00/year. (872-3100).

Atlanta Parent. Published monthly. Parenting newspaper with articles, calendars and advertisements geared to children. Available at libraries, schools, stores and other locations. Free. Subscription rate is $12.00/year. (325-1763).

The Atlanta Tribune. Published monthly. Available at libraries, stores and other locations. Cost is 75¢/issue. Newspaper with articles, calendars and advertisements catering to Black Atlanta. (587-0501).

Bed and Breakfast Directory. The Georgia Department of Industry, Trade and Tourism. An annual guide to Georgia bed and breakfast inns. Free. To obtain a directory call 651-9461.

Brown's Guide to the Georgia Outdoors. Edited by John W. English and assisted by Katie Baer, Cherokee Publishing Company, Atlanta, Georgia, 1986.

Community Newspapers. The Atlanta Daily World, Clayton News/Daily, The Clayton Sun, Decatur DeKalb News Era, DeKalb News Sun, Gwinnett Daily News, Marietta Daily Journal and lots more.

Creative Loafing. Published weekly. Available at stores, newstands, restaurants and other locations. Newspaper with detailed calendars of performances and special events, including many unusual and exotic listings (688-5623). Free.

Entertainment Atlanta (formerly *The Main Events Guide*). Published monthly. "Your Hour-By-Hour Guide to Entertainment Atlanta." Cost is $1.50/issue; Subscription Rate is $15.00/year. (263-8368).

Georgia Byways. Published quarterly. Available at bookstores and newstands. New publication about Georgia attractions. Cost is $3.50/issue; Subscription Rate is $14.00/year. (664-6432).

Georgia On My Mind. Georgia Hospitality and Travel Association, Atlanta, Georgia. Published annually. Travel Guide to Georgia. Distributed by the Georgia Deparatment of Industry Trade and Tourism. (800/VISIT GA). Free.

Great Science Outings in Georgia. Apple Corps, Inc., 1989. An excellent overview of all science and nature attractions in Georgia geared specifically to school groups, but also useful for families.

A Marmac Guide to Atlanta.. William Schemmel & Marge McDonald, Pelican Publishing Co., Gretna, 1987. A travel guide that is a bit outdated, but still useful to have around.

Youth View. Published monthly. Parenting newspaper with articles, calendars and advertisements geared to children. Available at libraries, schools, stores and other locations. Free. Subscription rate is $6.00/year. (350-9355).

TOP 20 PLACES TO GO AND THINGS TO DO

Airport Visits
American Adventures
Atlanta Botanical Garden
Big Shanty Museum
Book Stores and Libraries
Center for Puppetry Arts
Chattahoochee Nature Center
Farmers Markets and Pick Your Own
Fernbank Science Center
Georgia State Capitol Building/Georgia State Museum of Science
        and Industry
High Museum of Art–Woodruff Arts Center
The New Georgia Railroad
SciTrek
Six Flags Over Georgia
Southeastern Railway Museum
Stone Mountain Park
White Water Park
The Wren's Nest
Yellow River Game Ranch
Zoo Atlanta

FREE ACTIVITIES FOR FAMILIES

Airport Visits
Amnesty International–Human Rights Gallery
Animal Shelters and Humane Societies
Art Galleries
*Atlanta Botanical Garden
Atlanta Celebrity Walk
*Atlanta History Center
Atlanta International Museum/Atlanta Museum of Art & Design
Atlanta Journal and Constitution Lobby Exhibit
Atlanta State Farmer's Market
Book Stores
Bradley Observatory & Planetarium
Buford Fish Hatchery
Bush Mountain Outdoor Activity Center
Chattahoochee River National Recreational Area
Clayton County Plantation Driving Tour
Cobb County Petting Farm
Cobb County Youth Museum
DeKalb Historical Driving Tour
DeKalb Historical Society Museum
Delta Airlines Airport Tour
Emory University Museum of Art & Archaeology
Federal Reserve Monetary Museum
Fernbank Science Center (except the Planetarium Show)
Fort Peachtree
Georgia Department of Archives and History
Georgia Governor's Mansion
Georgia Historical Aviation Museum
Georgia State Capitol Building/Georgia State Museum of Science and
        Industry
Gwinnett County Museum
Gwinnett Plantation Tour of Homes
Hammonds House
Hapeville Depot Museum

Hard Labor Creek Obsrvatory
Harry's Farmers Market
Herndon Home
*High Museum at Woodruff Arts Center
High Museum at Georgia-Pacific Center
Hotel Hopping
Kennesaw Mountain National Battlefield Park
Martin Luther King, Jr. Historic Site (Birth Home; Center for Non-
        Violent Social Change; and, Ebenezer Baptist Church)
Libraries
Marietta Historical Walking Tours
Marietta National Cemetery
Medical Museum of Crawford Long Hospital
Johnny Mercer Exhibit
Monastery of the Holy Spirit
Nurseries
Oakland Cemetery
Panola Mountain
Pet Stores
W.H. Reynolds Nature Preserve
Roswell Fire Museum
Roswell Historical Tours
Shopping Malls
Southeastern Railway Museum
Southface Energy Institute
Sweet Auburn Curb Market (Atlanta Municipal Market)
Sweetwater Creek State Park
Telephone Museum
Tours of the Working World
Toy Stores
TULA
Underground Atlanta
Cator Woolford Memorial Garden
Your DeKalb Farmer's Market
Zachor Holocaust Center

*   During limited hours these attractions are free to the public.

BIRTHDAY PARTY IDEAS

American Adventures
Atlanta Attack
Atlanta Braves/Colonial Baking Company–Birthday Party Program
Birthday Party sections of *Youth View* newspaper provides names of
    clowns, magicians, musicians and other peformers available to
    entertain at parties.
Bowling
Center for the Puppetry Arts
Cobb County Petting Farm
Fernbank Science Center
Fire Departments
Gymnastic Centers
Ice Skating
Miniature Golf
The New Georgia Railroad
Peachtree-DeKalb Airport Observation Area
Pony Rides
The Red Barn
Roller Skating
SciTrek
Southern Order of Storytellers–Call the Wren's Nest for available performers
Stone Mountain Park–Play Structure
Swimming–Atlanta Marriott Northwest, Private Pools and some YWCAs
Tours of the Working World
Toy Stores–Party Rooms such as the DinoStore and Toy School
Yellow River Game Ranch

RAINY WEATHER IDEAS

African-American Panoramic Experience (APEX Museum)
American Adventures
Amnesty International–Human Rights Gallery

Animal Shelters and Humane Societies
Art Galleries
Atlanta Journal and Constitution Lobby Exhibit
Atlanta Museum
Big Shanty Museum
Book Stores
Bowling
Bulloch Hall
Carter Presidential Center–Museum of the Jimmy Carter Library
Center for the Puppetry Arts
CNN Studio Tour
Cobb County Youth Museum
Cyclorama
DeKalb Historical Society Museum
Doll Gallery
Emory Museum of Art & Archaeology
Federal Reserve Monetary Museum
Fernbank Science Center
Georgia Department of Archives and History
Georgia State Capitol Building/Georgia State Museum of Science
    and Industry
Gwinnett County Museum
Hammonds House
Hapeville Depot Museum
Hardware Stores
Harry's Farmers Market
Hartsfield Airport
Herndon Home
High Museum of Art–Woodruff Arts Center
High Museum at Georgia-Pacific Center
Hobby Shows and Collector Fairs
Hotel Hopping
Ice Skating
Libraries
Mauldin Doll Museum
McElreath Hall–Atlanta History Center
Medical Museum–Crawford Long Hospital
Miniature Golf–Indoors

The Nature Company
Pet Stores and Pet Shows
Roller Skating
Roswell Fire Museum
SciTrek
Shopping Malls
Sweet Auburn Curb Market (Atlanta Municipal Market)
Swimming–Indoor and Atlanta Marriott Northwest
Telephone Museum
Tours of the Working World
Toy Stores
TULA
Underground Atlanta
The World of Coca-Cola Pavilion
The Wren's Nest
Your DeKalb Farmers Market
Zachor Holocaust Center

SCHOOL AND SCOUT GROUP ACTIVITIES

<u>Note:</u>
- Be aware that some places are booked well ahead of time
- Verify group age and size
- Ask for special group rates
- Ask if a tour guide is available

Airports and Air Museums
Animal Shelters, Animal Societies and Pet Stores
Art Museums and Galleries
Atlanta Botanical Garden
Atlanta History Center–Center Tour, Tullie Smith Farm, Swan Woods Trail
Bowling
Bulloch Hall
Bush Mountain Outdoor Activity Center
Camping
Carter Presidential Center

Center for Puppetry Arts
Chattahoochee Nature Center
CNN Studio Tour
Cobb County Petting Farm
Cobb County Youth Museum
Cyclorama
Day Trips
Emory Museum of Art and Archaeology
Farmers Markets
Fernbank Science Center–Exhibition Hall, Planetarium, Forest and
    Trails
Georgia State Capitol
High Museum of Art–Spectacles, Docent tours for K-8
Hiking and Nature Trails
Martin Luther King, Jr. Historic Site
Monastery of the Holy Spirit
Nurseries
Panola Mountain
Performing Arts
The Red Barn
Roswell Fire Museum
SciTrek Museum–Overnight fun
Skating
Southface Energy Institute
Stone Mountain–Wildlife Trail and Petting Farm, Hike to the Top,
    Train Ride, Riverboat Ride, Overnight Camping
Sweetwater Creek State Conservation Park
Telephone Museum
Tours of the Working World–Fire Stations, Police Stations and Television
    Studios
World of Coca-Cola Pavilion
The Wren's Nest
Yellow River Game Ranch–Trails, Evening Wilderness Hayrides
Zoo Atlanta

CLASSES AND WORKSHOPS
SUMMER PROGRAMS AND CAMPS

There are extensive classes, workshops and summer programs for children of all ages offered by profit and non-profit facilities throughout the metropolitan Atlanta area, including courses in the visual arts, performing arts, literary arts, foreign languages, sciences, nature, computer, cooking and other fields. Our list could not be all inclusive, so we limited it to the classes and programs offered by museums, art centers, nature centers, those schools and colleges which offer varied or unique classes and a handful of other organizations of which you may not be aware.

COMPUTER AND ACADEMICS

Georgia State University
Kennesaw College

FOLK ARTS AND HISTORY

Atlanta History Center
Atlanta Preservation Center Tours
Bulloch Hall
Chattahoochee Nature Center
DeKalb Historic Complex
Emory Museum of Art and Archaeology
Georgia Department of Natural Resources
Georgia State University
Sweetwater Creek State Conservation Park

FOREIGN LANGUAGES

Arts Exchange
Georgia State University

LITERARY ARTS

Arts Exchange

Georgia State University
Pinckneyville Arts Center

MUSIC

A.R.T. Station
Arts Exchange
Georgia Department of Natural Resources
Georgia State University
North Arts Center
Soapstone Center for the Arts

NATURE AND SCIENCES

Atlanta Botanical Garden
Atlanta Humane Society
Bush Mountain Outdoor Activity Center
Chattahoochee Nature Center
Fernbank Science Center
Georgia Department of Natural Resources
Georgia State University
Panola Mountain
W.H. Reynolds Nature Preserve
SciTrek
Sweetwater Creek State Conservation Park
U.S. Space Camp

PERFORMING ARTS

Alliance Theater School
A.R.T. Station
Arts Exchange
Atlanta Jewish Community Center
Atlanta Workshop Players
Bulloch Hall
Callanwolde Arts Center
Center for Puppetry Arts
Children's Television Workshop
Doraville Arts Theatre
Emory Museum of Art and Archaeology
Georgia State University

North Arts Center
Pinckneyville Arts Center
Soapstone Center for the Arts
Stage Door Players
Steeplehouse Arts Center

VISUAL ARTS

Abernathy Arts and Crafts Center
A.R.T. Station
The Arts Connection (Oxford Book Store at Pharr Road)
Arts Exchange
Atlanta College of Art
Atlanta History Center
Bulloch Hall
Callanwolde Arts Center
Chastain Arts Center
Emory Museum of Art and Archaeology
Georgia State University
Gilbert House
Gwinnett Council for the Arts
High Museum of Art
Kennesaw College
Marietta/Cobb Museum of Art
Nexus Contemporary Arts Center
North Arts Center
Pinckneyville Arts Center
Soapstone Center for the Arts
South Cobb Arts Alliance (Mable House)
Steeplehouse Arts Center

SUMMER PROGRAMS AND CAMPS

Abernathy Arts and Crafts Center
Agnes Scott College
Alliance Theatre School
A.R.T. Station
Artsbusters/CREATE
Arts Exchange
Atlanta Attack
Atlanta Botanical Garden
Atlanta College of Art

Atlanta Hawks
Atlanta Jewish Community Center
Atlanta Workshop Players
Bulloch Hall
Bush Mountain Outdoor Activity Center
Callanwolde Fine Arts Center
Center for Puppetry Arts
Challengers Club Space Camp
Chastain Arts Center
Chattahooche Nature Center
Clark Atlanta University–African Summer Camp
DeKalb College
Emory Museum of Art and Archaeology
Emory University Sports Camps
Emory University Tennis and Computer Camp
Fernbank Science Center
Georgia Department of Natural Resources
Georgia Institute of Technology
Georgia State University
Gwinnett Council for the Arts
High Museum of Art
Kennesaw College
Kennesaw Mountain National Battlefield Park
Marietta/Cobb Museum of Art
Neighborhood Playhouse
North Arts Center
Oglethorpe University
Outdoor Survival Camp
Panola Mountain
Pinckneyville Arts Center
Recreation Centers and Youth Organizations
SciTrek
Soapstone Center for the Arts
South Cobb Arts Alliance (Mable House)
Spelman College
Steeplehouse Arts Center
Stone Mountain Park
Sweetwater Creek State Conservation Park
TellTale Theater Camp
Zoo Atlanta

9. Index

A

B

300